THE MOVEMENT:

16,942

w Left,

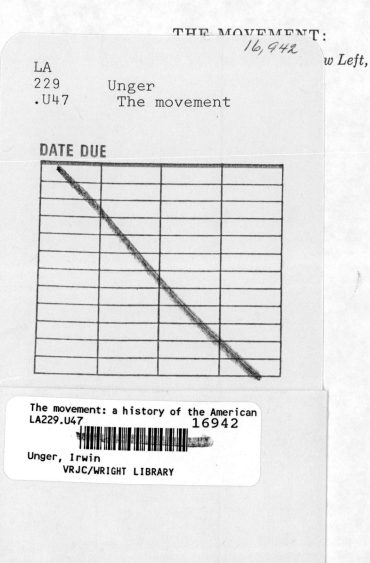

THE MOVEMENT:

A History of the American New Left 1959-1972

by IRWIN UNGER

NEW YORK UNIVERSITY

with the assistance of
Debi Unger

DODD, MEAD & COMPANY
New York 1975

To Mary and Sam
with affection and gratitude

Second Printing

COPYRIGHT © 1974 BY DODD, MEAD & COMPANY, INC.
ALL RIGHTS RESERVED

LIBRARY OF CONGRESS CATALOG CARD NUMBER: 73-21168
COLLEGE EDITION ISBN: 0-396-06939-8
TRADE EDITION ISBN: 0-396-06940-1

PRINTED IN THE UNITED STATES OF AMERICA

DESIGNED BY JEFFREY M. BARRIE

Introduction

THE PHENOMENON we called the New Left is over. For something over a decade it flourished and made the Western world livelier and more exciting. Now that it has passed, Western Europe and America will be less interesting though quieter places.

Obviously the political left has not ceased to exist entirely. There will always be a left—and a right—so long as we continue to live by the political terms of the modern world. These terms were established by the French Revolution, that complex upheaval that also marked the emergence of the modern West as we know it. Until the influence of that great Age of Revolution has dissipated, we shall use "radical" and "radicalism," "left" and "right" as key terms to measure and define the political environments of modern nations and political systems.

Yet, as a distinct phase of the radical assault on Western Establishments, the New Left has dwindled away and in the United States, at least, has ended. In what way is this true? Until Watergate and galloping inflation blanketed the public consciousness, ordinary Americans were still concerned about radicals and their deeds and misdeeds. The more important radical publications—*Ramparts, Liberation, The Realist, The Guardian*, even *New Left Notes* [1]—continue to be issued in the 1970s. Many of the under-

[1] Though not the original *New Left Notes*. See Chapter 6.

ground papers published in large cities and university towns survive. In 1972 we had the McGovern presidential campaign. If not strictly New Left, it represented about as much as the New Left could realistically expect of standard electoral politics. Certainly to most of us who watched the Democratic Convention at Miami on our television sets, the people who supported George McGovern appeared to epitomize many of the radical political and cultural currents that had marked the nation since the early 1960s. The 1972 convention in Miami seemed almost to be a replay of 1968, only this time the people on the street were in the convention hall wearing delegates' badges.

Nor is the death of the New Left seemingly borne out by a superficial survey of the college campuses. Sproul Plaza, at Berkeley, where much of it began, seems to be as lively as ever. The tables with signs proclaiming "Stop the War!" "End Racism!" "Big Rally Tonight!" "Support SDS Against the Administration" are still in front of the student union. On Telegraph Avenue, the street people still sell their leatherwork and their pottery, and still collect money for the Free Clinic from the squares and the students. And if Berkeley, the radical "mother church," is still as lively as ever, so too, it would seem, are the daughter establishments. I have not been to Boston University, or the University of Pennsylvania, or SUNY at Buffalo, or San Francisco State for a while, but the recent copies of *New Left Notes* and Progressive Labor's *Challenge* that I have seen assure me that the student left is also alive and well in these places.

And yet these appearances are deceiving. Something has ended, and most people who were a part of it will agree that it has. The New Left that emerged during the period from 1959 to 1962 was a well-defined phenomenon. Socially it was distinguished by its middle-class personnel, most of its members being university students or young professionals. The youthfulness of the New Left set it apart from the radical movements of America's past. Europe, perhaps, had had its radical youth movements during the nineteenth century, but the United States had not. Previous American radical movements had been led by adults with youth affiliates or auxiliaries trailing behind. Now, for the first time, young American men and women led an autonomous movement for social change without the supervision and control of middle-aged veterans.

The New Left was also distinguished from immediately preceding radical movements in this country, and in the West generally, by its rejection of the dogmatic "scientific socialism" of the Second and Third Internationals. As a distinct phenomenon, the New Left found the Marxist–Leninist emphasis on the working class, a disciplined "vanguard" party, and society's economic relations dated and irrelevant. As we shall see, the humanistic socialism of the early Marx, as embellished by such men as Herbert Marcuse, Paul Goodman, C. Wright Mills, Serge Mallet, and André Gorz, along with the teachings and practices of the philosophical anarchists, seemed to the New Left far better suited to the circumstances of modern, "post-industrial" America and far more relevant to the sort of society that had created disenchanted youth as a class. The New Left ended sometime between 1969 and 1972 with the conquest of the Students for a Democratic Society (SDS) by hard-line, orthodox Leninism. Perhaps a generation from now we will say that only phase one of the New Left ended in these years, but it seems clear to me that with this philosophical overthrow something distinctive came to an end and can now be treated as a completed whole.

I must make one important point clear at the outset. I define the New Left as a movement of *white* middle-class youth. The civil rights movement and black liberation helped shape the New Left and were important in their own right, of course, but I maintain that they did not supply its central thrust. Rather, I think, racial injustice in America, though especially acute, was—along with philistinism, cultural conformity, sexual puritanism, social hypocrisy, economic inequality, and international opportunism—one of those social deficiencies that always exist in varying degrees and can always be used to indict existing society. Black activists and militants, particularly the younger members of the Student Nonviolent Coordinating Committee (SNCC), the Congress of Racial Equality (CORE), and the Black Panthers, goaded the consciences of young white radicals. Often they helped push the New Left in one direction or another. At times, too, blacks, the Black Panthers in particular, even participated in New Left deliberations and decisions. By and large, however, blacks were fighting for their own goals and in their own way, and they often regarded the radical students with amused contempt. I think the fact that the New Left was a phenomenon common to all the affluent industrial countries and yet in none of them, except the United States, was there a serious racial problem is conclusive evidence of this point.

Like all scholars, I have received cheerful and generous help from many people. My greatest debt is to my wife and collaborator, Debi. It is not necessary or appropriate to talk about the personal side of my gratitude to her, but I would like to express my deepest thanks for her valuable professional help as researcher, editor, amanuensis, and aide-de-camp. Her name on the title page is far more than a courtesy.

I should next like to thank my own university, New York University, which granted me a sabbatical leave, part of which I used for completing this work, and the John Simon Guggenheim Foundation for the grant which helped to support me and my family during its gestation period. I also owe a very large debt to my editor, Charles Woodford, whose suggestion initiated this book and whose encouraging words helped to sustain it.

Some of the work, as the pages that follow will make clear, I wrote at Berkeley, and I am indebted to the University of California at Berkeley for its help. The people at the university library, especially the periodical room, the newspaper reading room, and the Bancroft Library, were extremely kind in giving me access to material, some of which was unique. I would especially like to thank Bill Gottleib and Frances Finn of the newspaper room for their cheerful help. Finally I wish to thank Professor Delmer Brown, Chairman of the Berkeley History Department, who accorded me research associate status at the university, Professor Richard Abrams who sponsored me with the department, and Professor Paul Goodman of the University of California at Davis whose enthusiastic hospitality made my stay in the Bay Area comfortable.

Doris Craven typed the manuscript with intelligence and dispatch. Genia Graves of Dodd, Mead gave the manuscript careful and perceptive editorial attention.

IRWIN UNGER

Contents

1

Origins
1945-1960

T HE DECADE following V-J Day was a difficult period for the American left. Yet at the time of Japan's surrender, few people could have foreseen what trying times lay ahead for radicalism in the United States. In 1945 the world as a whole seemed bright for the left. The Western democracies had just won a great war against fascism in alliance with socialist Russia. The end of the war seemed certain to unleash great pent-up forces of social discontent, and the years to come promised a socialist rebirth. The startling victory of the British Labour party in the general elections of June, 1945, and the advent of socialist governments in many of the former Nazi-occupied European countries appeared to signal the start of a major world shift leftward.

The chief beneficiary of this trend in the United States was the Communist party of America, the most important group within the American left in 1945. The old Socialist party survived, as did the Trotskyite Socialist Workers, and a few other tiny fragments of the socialist past, but the great party of Eugene V. Debs was a pitiful remnant of what it had formerly been. As the nation turned its attention to peacetime pursuits, the Communist party came close to being *the* American left.

Yet all was not well with American communism. The Communist party worked under immense handicaps. Forged in 1919

from the left wing of the Socialist party, it never became acclimated
to America. Generally it operated as an extension of Soviet foreign
policy rather than as an indigenous radical movement attentive to
the domestic needs and problems of the United States. With every
change in Soviet fortunes or Russian national interests, the American Communist party tail was whipped about frantically. To
some extent, Moscow's control depended on direct lines of com-
mand between officials of the Comintern, with headquarters in the
Soviet capital, and American party officials. Orders passed between
Moscow and the Communist party headquarters at Union Square
in New York; so did what professional anti-Communists came to
call Soviet gold. Undoubtedly more important in linking Union
Square with the Kremlin, however, was the profound conviction of
American Communists that the Soviet Union, "the Socialist
Fatherland," was the vanguard of the world revolution and the
last, best hope of oppressed mankind.

But whether gold or faith ruled the American Communist
party, its members were heavily burdened by the task of making
Party positions fit the needs of two nations separated by enormous differences in interests, traditions, experience, and social structure. To the Party's true believers the difficulty was not insurmountable. Whenever Russian and American interests diverged,
they believed the Russians were right. To most Americans, however, it was hard to understand how the United States could always
be wrong. During World War II, when American and Russian
policies and interests overlapped, there was little apparent conflict
between Communist party membership and patriotism. Following
1945, however, only those Americans who were profoundly alienated from their own country could comfortably accept the Party's
political leadership and guidance.

And there was still another burden: the need to square the
Party's Marxist–Leninist ideology with the realities of American life
and American history. By the 1920s world communism adhered to
a firm set of principles that had taken on the qualities of a secular
religion. The Communist canon had grown over the years and like
any evolving world view contained inconsistencies and anomalies.
Yet if the house that Marx and Lenin built had some curious pas-
sageways and awkward-looking towers, the plan of the main structure was clear.

At the heart of Communist dogma was a theory of history

called dialectical materialism. According to Marx and his followers, human history moved by stages that could be identified with specific systems of production. The ancient world was based on slave labor, and slavery defined the essential nature of the Greco-Roman world. Ancient slavery eventually gave way to feudalism, a system in which the relationship between feudal lord and unfree serf, or peasant, was the predominant social institution. Feudalism in turn was superseded by capitalism. In feudalism the nobility and the peasants were tied together by immemorial customs and traditions of mutual obligations and duties. In capitalism the capitalist and his worker were linked only by money. The working man (proletarian) under capitalism, unlike the feudal peasant, was legally a free man who could leave his work and move anywhere he wished. But he was also a man stripped of the protection of customary law and deprived of traditional rights. In capitalist society, then, the working class was formally free, but actually enslaved because the means of production were entirely in the hands of the new ruling group, the capitalists or bourgeoisie, while the working man had only his physical strength to offer in the marketplace.

Though Marx and the Marxists were the foremost critics of capitalism, they were also, in some ways, its staunchest defenders. In its early phases, they held, capitalism was a progressive historical force. Feudalism was tied to primitive technology and distribution methods and was incapable of creating the abundance necessary for the good life for mankind. The feudal nobility were not interested in increasing the output of their lands, and the masses within feudal society were doomed by its economic backwardness to perpetual poverty, want, and misery.

The capitalist class, arising as a middle element between the nobility and the peasants, was, on the other hand, driven by the desire for ever greater efficiency, output, and profits. In its determined and aggressive quest for gain, it created new production techniques that culminated in the industrial revolution and furnished the means to attain material abundance. It also created new institutions and social relationships compatible with its needs as a class. It was the new bourgeoisie therefore that had destroyed the old feudal system, helped establish the modern nation-state, and finally overturned the Old Régime in Western Europe and replaced it with liberal democracy.

All of these changes were progressive and necessary, the Marxists held, but they did not produce utopia. Capitalism was, in some ways, even more brutal and exploitative than feudalism. The working class suffered immensely from the crushing burdens of the new industrial system. Long hours, low wages, child labor, frequent unemployment, industrial disease and accidents, and early death were concomitants of the new factory system. Though capitalism created abundance, it reserved the benefits of this new wealth for the capitalists alone. Equally deplorable was the growing alienation of men from their work as the industrial process became more and more complex and the laborer lost contact with the meaning and importance of his efforts. Under capitalism men were dissociated from their work. They did not own their own tools, and they had little to do with the final product of their labors. Generally they were small cogs in the great productive machines and received little or no satisfaction from the monotonous, repetitive drudgery they performed. Pride of workmanship, or even a simple understanding of where one stood in the productive process, had no place in this regime, and modern workers in capitalist society were inevitably alienated from their labor.

As time passed, things got worse, not better. Contradictions began to appear within capitalism, as they had within feudalism. Desiring ever greater profits, the capitalists continually forced down the wages of the working classes. Simultaneously, the smaller capitalists—the petite bourgeoisie—were increasingly forced out of business by growing giant monopolies and demoted to the ranks of the proletariat. With little beyond a subsistence wage, the workers were less and less able to buy the output of the factories where they labored. As a consequence capitalism encountered successive crises of underconsumption and depression.

To solve these problems, the capitalist nations sought out markets abroad, often in less developed countries, which they soon reduced to exploited colonies. This imperialist thrust of late capitalism did stave off the day of reckoning, but only for a while. Eventually, according to Marx, the great mass of the proletariat, made class conscious by its increasing immiserization under the capitalist system, would rise up in bloody revolution and seize the machinery of government. The revolution would establish the "dictatorship of the proletariat" under which the worker-controlled state would manage and direct the means of production and gradually eliminate the last vestiges of private property and of the former ruling capitalist class. Eventually the state itself would "wither away" and be replaced by a voluntary society freed of the grim goad of material necessity and freed of class conflict. Man's long historical bondage to necessity and his entrapment in conflict would be replaced by a regime of peace, freedom, and brotherly love.

However insistently sophisticated Marxist intellectuals later sought to befuddle the fact, Marxism was clearly materialist. All institutions—marriage, the family, the church, the state—were outgrowths of the existing production system and reflected the needs of the class that controlled it. Ideas, art, and even science were also part of the superstructure of the existing production relationships. The prevailing social ills of capitalism were also by-products of class control. The exploitation of women and non-whites, for example, was a direct outgrowth of the capitalists' need both to weaken the proletariat and to ensure a cheap pool of docile labor. Marx was not a crude economic determinist, perhaps, but for him and for most of his disciples, productive relationships were primary, all others derivative.

The Marxist doctrine was also dialectical. Change took place not in a linear way but by a series of sharp zigzags. Within any system of production—whether ancient slavery, feudalism, or capitalism—contradictions would occur eventually. These were inherent in the very nature of the existing system and could not be alleviated for very long. Thus although imperialism might delay the contradictions of capitalism, it could not solve them. Nor could liberal or social-democratic reform. Capitalism could not *avoid* creating a discontented and impoverished working class, and this working class, aroused to its own misery, would inevitably and cataclysmically pull down the system in its entirety. In the jargon of the Hegelian dialectic that Marx borrowed, "thesis" would produce its "antithesis," followed by a new "synthesis."

This complex theory of history, society, and revolution was bequeathed virtually whole to American communism in the 1920s. It proved a heavy cross to carry. By then the United States had become the most advanced capitalist country in the world. Here, in the heartland of world capitalism, if anywhere, the process of working class immiserization and growing proletarian class consciousness should have proceeded the furthest. Yet compared to Western Europe, the American working class seemed prosperous and indifferent, or even hostile, to socialist and Marxist ideas. To make the problem more difficult, American imperialism seemed feeble compared with that of England, France, and the other capitalist nations of Western Europe. In short the Marxist–Leninist scheme seemed to bear little relation to the situation of the United States during the prosperous 1920s.

During the Communist party's first decade, a number of American Marxists attempted to modify the dogmas of the standard canon to reflect American circumstances. In 1927 and 1928 Jay Lovestone and Bertram Wolfe developed the notion of American exceptionalism that professed to demonstrate that the absence of a feudal past and the extraordinary natural endowment of the United States had modified the dialectical process in this country. This idea was soon branded a heresy by Moscow, and the American comrades who had compromised with the true dogma were expelled from the Communist party.

The 1930s were better years for American communism. The collapse of 1929 and the Great Depression that followed seemed to confirm the direst predictions of Marxism. Never before had the American capitalist system been in such deep trouble. National income plunged; factories stopped; millions were thrown out of work. The cities were full of hungry men and women, while farmers burned unsalable crops. Class struggle seemed finally to have become an undeniable reality in the United States. Riots, farmers' strikes, sit-downs in the great automobile plants of Detroit marked the grim slide of the economy ever downward.

The Communist party of the United States, and to a lesser degree the older Marxist party, the Socialists, benefited from the growing misery and resentment of American labor. Membership in the Communist party grew, and for the first time the Party's influence in the labor movement became significant. Equally important, the Party became intellectually respectable. Sensitive and humane artists, writers, professors, students, and professional men could now see with their own eyes the prescience and wisdom of the Marxist analysis of capitalist failure. It was only necessary to compare the plight of the capitalist West with the growing economic might and power of the Soviet Union under its various Five Year Plans to see which system was superior.

The international upheaval of the 1930s reinforced the growing prestige of communism in America. The rise of fascism was deplored by liberals and Marxists alike, but at least until 1939, it was the Soviet Union and, by extension, its system, rather than the Western democracies and theirs, that seemed honestly dedicated to stopping the dictators. England and France retreated in the face of Hitler, Mussolini, the Japanese militarists, and Franco, the Spanish dictator, while the Soviet Union made frantic, though unsuccessful, efforts to organize an international coalition, a United Front, of liberals and leftists, to stop them.

Briefly, in the period 1939–1941, the Soviet Union reversed this growing tide of approval by its sudden and shocking détente with Hitler. The Hitler–Stalin Pact of August, 1939, followed by the absorption of the Baltic Republics and the Russian invasion of Finland, alienated many Party members and fellow travelers. But then Hitler attacked Russia in 1941 and turned her into an ally of the European capitalist democracies. After America's own entrance into the war, the Soviet Union became our ally as well. During the period from 1941 to 1945, the media abruptly adopted the attitudes long associated with the Soviet propaganda apparatus. Even Hollywood, in a series of saccharine movies, glorified the victimized Soviet Union and its heroic citizens.

Following 1945 the prestige and goodwill of both the Soviet Union and the American left were quickly dissipated. The Cold War, already anticipated by strains within the wartime Grand Alliance, soon came to overshadow Soviet–American relations. The growing crisis between East and West brought out the worst in both Russia and America. In the Soviet Union it fed Joseph Stalin's paranoia and led to mass purges, jailings, and executions of suspected dissidents and traitors. In the United States it also led to an obsession with loyalty and to fears of subversion and treason. No one in the United States, with the exception of Julius and Ethel Rosenberg, directly lost his life to the Cold War, but thousands lost their jobs, their reputations, and their peace of mind.

During these years liberals did not always acquit themselves heroically. Early twentieth-century liberalism was a composite of social generosity, cultural elitism, and intellectual tolerance that was particularly strong among intellectuals, people in the media, and certain ethnic groups, especially Jews and middle-class Negroes. Liberals believed in equality of condition, and by the 1930s they were willing to use the state to help correct social and eco-

nomic inequities. They were skeptical of the American conservative reliance on a "fair field and no favor" to take care of social
inequalities; yet while fearing "bigness," they did not disparage
private property when held in small amounts or employed in socially useful ways. Although liberals sympathized with the underdog,
in the cultural realm they often deplored the "degraded" cultural
characteristics that ordinary Americans had acquired. These, of
course, were no fault of the man-in-the-street, but in a just
society these characteristics would disappear as all men acquired
the means to lead fuller, more comfortable, more abundant lives.
Finally liberals professed to be fierce defenders of ideological and
intellectual dissent. No group took more seriously First Amendment
guarantees of free speech and a free press, or denounced more
vehemently totalitarianism or vigilante intimidation of the free,
inquiring spirit.

Liberals, unhappily, sometimes disgracefully betrayed their
libertarian principles in the years following the war. The first
sweeping investigations of loyalty in government departments began in 1947 under the liberal Truman administration. In later years
many avowed liberals abandoned their principles and either con-
doned loyalty oaths and witch-hunting or betrayed radical associates from the days when they themselves had flirted with the left.
It was the liberal Senator from Minnesota, Hubert Humphrey,
who sponsored the amendment to the Communist Control Act of
1954 that made the Communist party of the United States an
illegal body.

Still, the main impetus to the great postwar Red scare was
supplied by conservatives, and its victims were often liberals. Conservatives—of the American variety—were really old-fashioned
laissez-faire liberals. They believed in individualism and self-help
and despised the welfare state that the liberals had created during
the New Deal era. This seemed to them indistinguishable from
socialism, a political system they considered godless and anarchistic,
although at the same time they attacked it as dogmatic and authoritarian. Creeping socialism at home and galloping socialism abroad
seemed to conservatives the two greatest dangers of the age, and
they felt compelled to make war on both in the name of humanity
and civilization. On the domestic scene Senator Joseph McCarthy
was supported by the traditional right in his home state of Wisconsin, and much of the financing for such groups as the John

Birch Society and the Christian Anti-Communist Crusade was supplied by rightist Texas and California "new money."

Whether inspired by liberals or conservatives, fear and distrust polluted the nation's political and intellectual atmosphere during the late 1940s and early 1950s. Hunting for "subversives" who wished to undermine the American way and substitute socialism seemed to become a major national occupation. Almost every cranny of American life was affected. Teachers and professors were required to take oaths of loyalty and to reveal their past political associations on pain of dismissal. Actors and performers were placed on blacklists for casual left political activities during the 1930s. Scientists working for private concerns were denied "clearance" to examine and use classified government documents and reports and were effectively blocked from practicing their professions. In 1949 eleven top leaders of the Communist party were indicted and convicted under the 1940 Smith Act, which had made it unlawful to advocate or teach the violent overthrow of the government.

The effect of all this on the American left was devastating, but repression and Red baiting were not solely responsible for the left's troubles. Soviet policy was also crippling. Premier Nikita Khrushchev's revelations in 1956 of Stalin's mass purges shocked and dismayed many sensitive, if naïve, members of the left. What could be said for a system that permitted such a man to control the lives of millions of people? Still more damaging was the brutal Soviet suppression of the Hungarian uprising of the same year.

Finally the vigorous good health of the postwar capitalist economy conspired to frustrate American socialists. Instead of the massive recession predicted for the American economy after the Axis defeat, a great boom marked the postwar years. The gross national product burgeoned far beyond all expectations. Unemployment remained low, while real wages leaped ahead. Increasingly, skilled labor and the rapidly growing white-collar class were converted into suburbanized home owners with a stake in an expanding, consumer-oriented economy.

Prosperity, repression, and Soviet truculence together almost destroyed the American left. Formal membership in radical organizations, especially the Communist party, decreased sharply. The seventy-five to eighty thousand Communist party members of 1945 had declined to fewer than three thousand by 1958. In that year publication of the *Daily Worker*, the Communist party paper for thirty-four years, ceased because its readership had dwindled away. By the end of the 1950s the Communist party consisted of only a few narrow-minded professionals and a sad collection of older folk, who had made the Party their whole existence and could not find another anchor for their lives.

As the left fell, the right rose. The decade and a half following 1945 was the era of a revived right, ranging all the way from Taft Republicanism to Lincoln Rockwell's Nazi Party of America. Organizations such as the John Birch Society and the American Nazi party scarcely won the approval of the nation's intellectuals. Yet the intellectual community was affected by the shift to the right. The tarnished reputation of many liberal former fellow travelers damaged liberalism generally. Though McCarthy and the House Un-American Activities Committee frequently besmirched honest men and were often more interested in publicity than in uncovering serious conspirators against the United States, nevertheless it was hard to deny that too many intelligent liberals had been taken in by communism in the 1930s. As the liberal orthodoxy of the prewar decade came to seem naïve and vulnerable, it became possible, almost for the first time in the century, for the conservative voice to get a respectful hearing. In the 1950s thinkers such as Russell Kirk, Leo Strauss, Clinton Rossiter, and Reinhold Niebuhr were listened to when they spoke of natural aristocracy, social deference, the tragic human condition, the need for faith, and the reality of original sin. Even intellectuals such as Dwight MacDonald, who remained left in sentiment, sometimes became elitist in sympathies. MacDonald's mordant attacks on mass taste expressed total contempt for the degraded cultural and intellectual level of ordinary Americans, seemingly unrelieved by any understanding of its causes. On the popular level there was the phenomenon of Ayn Rand, whose books began appearing in the 1940s. Her gargantuan 1943 novel, *The Fountainhead*, glorifying the culture hero who refused to bow to the vulgar tastes of the masses, became a best seller and established Mrs. Rand in the postwar years as the pop artist of the new conservatism.

This new conservatism enjoyed only a brief vogue, however. Most Americans were not turned right so much as turned off politically. For every ardent rightest in these years there were twenty organization men, who were reluctant to exhibit any strong political views. Legions of young conformists in gray flannel uniforms emerged from the colleges by the thousands, seemingly intent on nothing more than keeping their noses clean and getting ahead. Even outstanding material success was usually beyond their ambition. All they appeared to want was leisure, moderate comfort, and, above all, security to live the private life of home, family, and friends. If they had any politics at all, it was the mild corporate conservatism of the large organizations they worked for. This was not a matter of conviction, moreover, but of expediency. If I may mix the labels of two prominent sociologists of the day, the organization men were other-directed men and expressed the predominant views of those around them rather than any firmly held convictions of their own.[1]

The academic equivalent of this retreat from politics might best be called neoliberalism. In later years the revived left would claim that this retreat was inherently conservative. Perhaps it was, but it deserves to be distinguished from the new conservatism.

Neoliberalism rejected the "tragic vision" of the human condition that the new conservatives so pretentiously proclaimed. Instead it was frankly optimistic. Social problems had been solved in the past and could be solved in the future. Indeed, America was living proof of the ability of men to alleviate human misery and avoid bloody conflict. What was needed was a spirit of reasonableness and compromise and the proper application of expert knowledge to the difficulties society faced. Unlike the new conservatism, neoliberalism also rejected intellectual systems and dogmas, its implication being that one should forget about ideology. Ideology only obscured solutions and generated irreconcilable differences. Give every political and social voice a hearing and let people reach conclusions by balancing one interest against another.

Neoliberalism was also democratic. Generally neoliberals respected the tastes and aspirations of the masses and believed that people were the best judges of their own needs and goals. America was a success because it was what most Americans wanted it to be. However much intellectuals and creative men might deplore mass

[1] The term "organization man" was coined by William Whyte. "Other-directed" is the expression David Reisman popularized in his influential book *The Lonely Crowd*.

taste or the lack of rigor in popular thought, American society had worked because mass taste and mass thought had been heeded.

Distinct from the new conservatives in many ways, the neo-liberals also differed from the Old Left. The left's vision of society, both past and present, emphasized dualistic conflict. Two parties, two groups, two classes, two ideas struggled for supremacy within every social system. One of these represented the exploiters, the other the exploited. Whether the struggle was between capitalists and workers, the classes and the masses, or the interests and the people, it was two-sided. Though most readily identifiable with Marxism, the dualistic critique of society was also inherent in such native American dissenting traditions as Populism and Progressivism.

The new social thinkers and theorists of the 1950s denied this dualistic picture of social action. Conflict no doubt had existed in the past and survived into the present, but in America, at least, the conflict had only been over secondary matters. All Americans accepted private property and political democracy; they merely disagreed over details. Moreover, whatever conflict had taken place had not been dualistic, but pluralistic. Not two great antagonists, but many smaller ones had occupied the stage of history. Many interest groups, classes, and factions had pushed, shoved, shouted, and groaned. Within the confused crowd scene, it was difficult to identify heroes and villains, saints and sinners, victims and oppressors. As for the American present, it represented an object lesson in the virtues of pluralistic, democratic capitalism as suitably modified by the New Deal. The United States had achieved economic and social stability through high productivity and relatively equal distribution of goods and benefits.

What I call neoliberalism was never given a single label in its day. Yet it permeated the whole academic world and strongly influenced the country's intellectuals. In the discipline of history it was called consensus, and its chief exemplars were held to be Richard Hofstadter, Oscar Handlin, Daniel Boorstin, and Forrest Macdonald. In political science it was referred to as pluralism, and its chief practitioners were said to be Robert Dahl, Seymour Lipset, Louis Hartz, and the scholars connected with the University of Michigan Survey Research Center. In sociology it went by the label end of ideology and was practiced by Daniel Bell and, in a less explicit way, by the group associated with Paul Lazarsfeld at Columbia's

Bureau of Applied Social Research. Whatever the descriptive term, in each of the social sciences neoliberalism emphasized the positive and functional side of existing institutions and seemed at times to be saying that modern America was the best of all possible worlds.

The defection of the intellectual and academic communities from the left's vision of society and history, as well as the direct attack of the witch-hunters and professional anti-Communists, reduced the Old Left to near impotence. Yet here and there a spark continued to glow. One point of light was the peace movement. Many Americans in these Cold War years were oppressed by the fear of atomic warfare. Regardless of who represented the gravest danger to world peace, Russia or America, intelligent men and women understood that no one would win a third world war. Even the testing of atomic weapons represented a serious threat to mankind. Each test explosion produced radioactive fallout that passed inexorably into the environment and promised to damage irrevocably mankind's biological heritage.

Most of the peace movement was moderate politically. SANE (Committee for a Sane Nuclear Policy), founded in 1957, was composed predominantly of old liberals such as Mrs. Roosevelt, Elmo Roper, Paul Tillich, Roger Baldwin, and Norman Cousins. It eschewed politics beyond demonstrating and lobbying for disarmament or a nuclear test ban treaty among the great powers. In 1960, when Senator Thomas Dodd of Connecticut charged that several SANE chapters had been infiltrated by Communists, Norman Cousins, SANE's current head, promptly ordered an investigation of the accused chapters and in effect purged the organization of its Communist members.

One small group within the peace movement, however, was uncompromisingly political and radical. This was composed, initially, of pacifists and World War II conscientious objectors, often members of the Fellowship of Reconciliation or the War Resisters' League, who opposed war and at the same time rejected capitalism. Many of these men had met during World War II at Civilian Public Service Camps or federal prisons, where they were under sentence for refusing to serve in the armed forces. Unlike many conscientious objectors, they were prison activists who would not abide by the rules laid down by prison or camp authorities, and were frequently in trouble for refusing to work or for organizing resistance to racial discrimination and other common prison practices they considered unjust.

After their release in 1945 a number of these pacifist–activists, led by Dave Dellinger, established the journal *Direct Action* to help disseminate radical-pacifist views. The attitudes expressed in the early issues of *Direct Action* are a remarkable anticipation of some major themes of the New Left. In the journal's first issue the editors called for "strikes, sabotage, and seizure of public property now being held by private owners." One writer for the publication suggested a scheme of "radical banditry," where "we take rather than buy what we want." Another advocated "a mass invasion of A & P supermarkets by housewives with hungry families, for the express purpose of emptying the shelves . . . [and] keeping down the profits of the masters." [2]

In the winter of 1945–1946 the radical pacifists organized the Committee for Non-Violent Revolution (CNVR), composed of "radical elements from the groups devoted to wartime resistance, socialism, militant labor, consumer cooperation and racial equality . . . ." These were to "come together in a common program of revolutionary action." The CNVR's founding statement, among other things, advocated "democratic representation of workers on planning agencies." [3]

In 1948 a portion of CNVR's membership merged with an organization called Peacemakers, which A. J. Muste, Dwight MacDonald, and Milton Mayer had put together from various radical pacifist groups. Unlike the Marxist-oriented CNVR, Peacemakers was Gandhian and emphasized nonviolent resistance to exploitative institutions and war. Specifically, it advised young men to refuse to register for the draft and established a Tax Refusal Committee to promote nonpayment of federal taxes that were being used for armaments or warfare. If CNVR's violent rhetoric and participatory democracy foreshadowed the Students for a Democratic Society (SDS), Peacemakers' moral witness and civil disobedience anticipated the Resistance and the Mobe of the mid- and late 1960s.

Still another contribution of early radical pacifism to the later New Left was the concept that to be free, men and women must

[2] Quoted in Lawrence Wittner, *Rebels Against War: The American Peace Movement, 1941–1960* (New York: Columbia University Press, 1969), p. 154.

[3] *Ibid.*, pp. 154–155.

start to live freely themselves. This could not be done easily in the larger society, and in the late 1940s a number of pacifists, including Dave Dellinger, went off to live in cooperative communities in Georgia and New Jersey. If the United States, then just experiencing the first chilling effects of the Cold War, could not be changed, perhaps a few dissenters might escape its blight by withdrawing from it. It was a tactic that despairing American radicals had turned to before and would eventually turn to again.

One interesting offshoot of the early postwar peace movement was the Pacifica Foundation, established in the San Francisco Bay Area in 1946. "Pacifica" in the title of this organization meant "peaceful," not "on the Pacific Coast." The idea of listener-supported, noncommercial radio was conceived by a group of Bay Area conscientious objectors, many of them affiliated with the radical wing of pacifism. Pacifica eventually opened stations in Los Angeles and New York in addition to its original transmitter in Berkeley. In varying degrees all three stations became active agencies for spreading both antiwar and radical ideas. Indeed, in the Bay Area KPFA was to be an important catalyst in that special combination of radicalism and cultural dissent that characterized Berkeley and San Francisco in the 1960s.

Though I am concerned here mostly with white radicals, the white New Left cannot be separated completely from the black revolution of the post-World War II era. Throughout the radical decade of the 1960s, there was a dialogue between the civil rights movement and the New Left. Even when SNCC and the other militant black organizations banished the young white activists from their ranks, black militants and white activists continued to talk to each other, if only angrily and contemptuously, and to learn from each other, if only what *not* to do.

In the 1950s the ambivalence, the guilt, and the hostility had not yet emerged, and white radicals came to draw sustenance from the civil rights movement. In the immediate postwar years, however, the influence and energy flowed from white to black. As we have noticed, wartime radical pacifists had attacked the racist practices of the federal prison system. After 1945 the pacifists continued to work for the Negro's rights. Early in its existence, the Fellowship of Reconciliation underwrote the Committee of Racial Equality (CORE), which was led by black pacifists James Farmer and

Bayard Rustin. CORE and the Fellowship were technically separate organizations, but for years A. J. Muste, the Fellowship's elderly but dynamic leader, was a principal fund raiser for CORE, and George Houser of the Fellowship staff served as CORE's executive secretary. Martin Luther King, as a young theology student, listened to Muste lecture and was deeply moved by his words. Though, as King later explained, he was more intensely affected by Gandhi and the practical advantages of nonviolence to Southern blacks, his obligation to Muste and the Fellowship was real. In the latter 1950s King joined the Fellowship.

By this time the inspiration had begun to flow from the civil rights movement to the white radicals. In 1954 the Supreme Court declared segregation contrary to the Fourteenth Amendment in its monumental *Brown* v. *the Board of Education of Topeka* decision. The decision electrified the left everywhere. In the next half dozen years the black revolution, especially in its civil disobedience phase, inspired the white left. These were the years of Little Rock and the courageous efforts of black parents to force the Arkansas authorities to abide by the court's decision. They were the years, also, of the Montgomery bus boycott, which Martin Luther King called after Mrs. Rosa Parks' famous refusal to move to the back of a segregated bus at the end of her hard day's work as a seamstress.

At a time when there was little else to encourage the American left, these events in the South seemed immensely hopeful. *Liberation*, founded in 1956 by Dave Dellinger, A. J. Muste, Bayard Rustin, Sidney Lens, Mulford Sibley, and other radical pacifists, was quick to endorse black nonviolent protest and resistance, and to inform its readers of civil rights developments in the South. *Dissent*, another journal of the left, founded in 1954 by Irving Howe, a former Trotskyite,[4] with Muste, Eric Fromm, and Lens as early contributing editors, also opened its pages to news of the emerging black revolution. The Montgomery bus boycott, Howe wrote in 1956, was

[4] The Trotskyites were followers of Leon Trotsky, one of Lenin's chief lieutenants in making the Bolshevik Revolution. After Lenin's death in 1924, Trotsky and Stalin engaged in a fierce struggle for control. Stalin won, forced Trotsky into exile, and concentrating on "socialism in one country," brutally bent the Soviet people to his will. To Trotskyites throughout the world, Stalin and Soviet Russia seemed to have diverted Leninism from its true goal of world revolution and to have made the Third International into a tool of Russian foreign policy.

"one of the most encouraging events in 20th-century American life."
It was "what all of us . . . have been waiting for. . . . That the
mute should find their voices. . . ." [5]

The advent of *Liberation* and *Dissent* portended important
changes in the political climate of the mid-1950s. There were also
important intimations of the cultural insurgency and dissent of the
following decade. Here and there by the middle of the 1950s—in
North Beach in San Francisco, Greenwich Village in New York, and
the Venice district of Los Angeles—groups of young bohemians
began to create the new sensibility that would eventually be called
the counter culture.

The new phenomenon was eclectic. The beats, as these young
bohemians were called, borrowed much from traditional bohemia.
They detested the rat race of nine-to-five jobs, material accumula-
tion, and the new suburbia. They despised the sexual repression,
cultural timidity, and emotional obtuseness of middle-class life.
They defied square bourgeois standards in their dress, their cultural
tastes, and even their syntax. They deplored what Allen Ginsberg
called "Moloch the loveless!," "Moloch the crossbone soulless jail-
house and Congress of sorrows!" in his raw, orgasmic poem "Howl,"
which set the mood for the whole beat literary flowering.

The beats borrowed from the urban Negro cultural underground. Though they generally rejected the "cool" style of the black
hipsters—as the tough, semidelinquent black street youths were
then called—they admired the black jazz musicians and were attracted to the pot and hard drugs that permeated the world of progressive jazz.

The beats also borrowed from Hindu mysticism and Zen Bud-
dhism, filtered through Ginsberg and Alan Watts, a former Episco-
pal priest turned Zen philosopher. Inner space rather than outer
space was what was important. The "real world" seemed scarcely
as real as what went on within one's own head.

The beats were apolitical. Although many of them probably
came from radical families, they themselves were "alienated," and
in the climate of the 1950s, politics seemed irrelevant in any case. As
Lawrence Lipton explained it in *The Holy Barbarians*, "the dis-

[5] Irving Howe, "Reverberations in the North," *Dissent*, Spring, 1956, p.
121.

affiliate has no blueprint for the future. He joins no political
parties . . . ." He has social sympathies, but no sense of outrage.

> If the disaffiliate is on the side of the accused instead of on the side
> of the accusers, it is because the accuser *has* his spokesmen, a host
> of them well paid, with all the mass media at their command and all
> the laws and the police on their side.
>
> Where the choice is between two rival tyrannies, however pious
> their pretensions, the disaffiliate says, not a plague but a pity on both
> your houses.[6]

This disaffiliation, this dropping out of society and of political
life, would be bequeathed to the later counter culture, and it would
give rise to a disquieting ambiguity in the relationship between the
cultural and political radicals of the following decade.

As the 1950s wore on, McCarthyite repression receded, and the
shibboleths of the Cold War increasingly lost their power. With
growing momentum, the left began to move once again.

The label "New Left" first appeared, surprisingly, in stodgy
Great Britain, where a group of younger socialists came together
during the 1950s to reinvigorate the tired program of the Labour
party and to restore a radical voice to British political life. The
British New Left group, composed of young intellectuals at the
major universities, began to publish the *New Left Review* early
in 1960, and this journal soon attracted attention in American college communities. By this time, however, radical intellectuals on
this side of the Atlantic, had already begun to criticize America,
industrial society, and the Cold War, making comments that
seemed new and fresh.

One of these new thinkers was Paul Goodman, a Gestalt psy-
chologist and social philosopher, whose dissent in an era of conformity was possibly related to his homosexuality. Writing for
Liberation in the mid-1950s, Goodman began to discuss the failing
work ethic in America. In 1959 his article "Growing Up Absurd"
appeared in the liberal journal *Commentary*. Further articles followed and were combined into a book (*Growing Up Absurd*) that
touched a responsive nerve among the literate public. In this critical look at youth and labor, Goodman pointed out how ineffective the new, affluent society had been in providing meaningful work

[6] Lawrence Lipton, *The Holy Barbarians* (New York: Julian Messner,
1959), pp. 149–150.

for its young people. Americans had little reason for the pompous self-congratulation that was so universal. If American society produced material abundance, it also produced alienation, especially among its youth.

Goodman was not alone in denouncing American complacency and self-satisfaction. Simultaneously a young diplomatic historian, William A. Williams, trained, incongruously, at Annapolis and Wisconsin, began to attack the consensus historians' celebration of the United States. Williams' thesis was that America had been able to evade the serious social problems of industrial society only because of its open frontier and abundant resources. Now that these escape hatches were closed, we were attempting to continue evasion by "embarking on crusades to save somebody else." Under the auspices of "corporate state radicalism," an apparently liberal regime actually dominated by the larger corporations, the United States was becoming an overcentralized and outwardly aggressive state. We must, Williams insisted, abandon both our aggressive internationalism and our growing economic centralization. This would mean returning power in the economic sphere to the people and a neo-isolationist response in foreign relations.[7]

In 1957 Williams moved from the University of Oregon to the more congenial environs of the University of Wisconsin, where he reestablished contact with an already venerable tradition of native left dissent. Soon there gathered around him a group of bright young history graduate students, who eagerly adopted his concept of corporate radicalism (or, later, "corporate liberalism") and made it a tool for analyzing the failings of modern America. In 1959 a number of these students, including Lloyd Gardner, Lee Baxendall, Saul Landau, James Weinstein,[8] and others founded *Studies on the Left* as a forum for critical appraisals of American society and history.

Williams and Goodman both became spiritual guides of the New Left, but the thinker who did the most to define an emerging new radicalism was the sociologist C. Wright Mills of Columbia University. Mills was a social and intellectual maverick, who seemed out of place at Columbia in the 1950s. A Texan who did his grad-

---

[7] See William Appleman Williams, "Go Left or Go Under," *Liberation*, April, 1957, pp. 14–17.

[8] Though a Columbia, rather than a Wisconsin, graduate student, Weinstein was *Studies on the Left*'s man in New York and was strongly influenced by Williams.

uate training at the University of Wisconsin when that school still retained its Farmer–Labor radicalism from the earlier part of the century, Mills refused to accept what Columbia represented. At the time when the Ivy League was dominated by the natural-shoulder tweed jacket and the foreign sports car, Mills wore old army clothes and rode to his office on a motorcycle. More to the point, he refused to conform to the intellectual mood that prevailed at Columbia. His first book, *The New Men of Power* (1948), attacked American labor leadership for betraying the working class. His *White Collar*, published in 1951, was a critique of the new middle class of teachers, clerks, technicians, secretaries, and bookkeepers, whose numbers were growing rapidly at mid-century. Mills saw these people as powerless and exploited. Unlike the small businessmen, farmers, and independent professionals of the older middle class, their true condition was little above the level of industrial wage earners. Though they clung to shreds of middle-class status, they falsely perceived their situation and scarcely realized how impotent and insecure they actually were.

White Collar expressed Mills' refusal to go along with the emerging complacency about American life in the postwar era. A still more direct demurrer from the prevailing intellectual mood of the 1950s was *The Power Elite* (1956). In this work Mills insisted that a small group of men, joined by family, background, education, and class interest, ruled America. Mills denied the neoliberal orthodoxies of pluralism and consensus. America was a class society, composed of rulers and the ruled, though the reality was disguised by an egalitarian ideology and formal democracy.

Mills kept in touch with the new British left and in 1960, in a letter addressed to the *New Left Review,* composed a manifesto that was to be an intellectual foundation stone of the New Left movement in the United States. The "Letter to the New Left" was both personal and paternal. Mills noted at the outset that since the end of World War II "smug conservatives, tired liberals and disillusioned radicals" had "carried on a weary discourse in which issues are blurred, and potential debate muted. . . ." In this atmosphere "the sickness of complacency has prevailed, [and] . . . bi-partisan banality has flourished."

Mills objected to the conservatives, of course, but he was particularly critical of the neoliberals and especially those in political science and sociology who identified with Daniel Bell and his end of ideology concepts. These men made a fetish of facts in the name of freeing themselves from enslavement to false ideas, but their supposed scientific empiricism, bereft of guiding theory, produced trivial results and answers. More important than the intellectual inadequacies of the neoliberal social thinkers, however, was their political inadequacy. Mills insisted that their presumed value-free social science actually masked a profoundly conservative, counter-revolutionary bias. The end of ideology was an implicit rejection of socialism and utopian thinking in favor of a pragmatic conservatism.

The time had now come to reverse this trend. But how? As Mills' own work indicated, the nation's labor leaders had been bought off by gifts of power, and the white-collar classes were be-mused by a false picture of social reality. If, contrary to Marx's expectations, the working class in the capitalist West was leaderless and content, and the lower middle class could not see where its true interests lay, how could any fundamental social change be brought about?

It would not be easy, Mills acknowledged, but there was no reason for despair. There was still "a possible, immediate, radical agency of change"—the young intellectuals. "[Who] is it that is getting fed up? Who is it that is getting disgusted with what Marx called 'all the old crap'? Who is it that is thinking and acting in radical ways? All over the world—in the [Soviet] bloc, outside the [Soviet] bloc and in between—the answer's the same: it is the young intelligentsia." [9]

Mills' letter reflected the discomfort of a middle-aged radical from America's heartland with a conformist, self-celebrating intel-lectual climate that denied his principles and offended his sensi-bilities. It also demonstrated the disenchantment of a postwar radical intellectual with the industrial working class. Mills agreed with the neoliberals that industrial labor in the West had become fat and contented. Indeed, it was painfully clear in the 1950s that much of organized labor and many individual working men in America were zealous supporters of Joseph McCarthy and Cold War foreign policy.

Shifting the revolutionary center of gravity to the young in-

[9] C. Wright Mills, "Letter to the New Left," *New Left Review,* Septem-ber-October, 1960, pp. 18–23.

tellectuals was a brilliant response to both these dislikes, but Mills failed to consider a whole range of questions that he implicitly raised. Why were only the young intellectuals discontented? Were they perhaps exploited? Were they perhaps denied legitimate access to positions of wealth and power? Even assuming valid reasons for their discontent, how could they justify revolution? If most people in advanced capitalist countries were relatively content with their lives, what right did the young intellectuals have to tear these painfully constructed lives up by the roots and disrupt the society that made it possible for men and women to obtain a modicum of contentment and comfort?

Revolutions were not—yet—for the fun of it. They were bloody and destructive. They tore down the existing structures of society and only with difficulty replaced them with new ones. They had a way of devouring their own children, and they also had a way of slipping all the way back after the first advances. Why should the ordinary man replace the existing social system, which brought at least modest rewards, with an alternative that at best was problematical, at worst destructive?

And how was this revolution to come about if it was only the young intelligentsia that were disaffected? Nowhere were they more than a fraction of the total population. Nowhere were they a large enough group to make the revolution themselves. Besides, in the Western nations and particularly in the United States, the intelligentsia was distrusted by the ordinary man on the street. Vice-President Agnew had not yet popularized the epithet "effete snob," but "egghead" was already used to describe the ordinary American's contemptuous attitude toward those whom Mills saw as the hope of the future. Finally could a small group of thinkers, no matter how great their resolve or their finesse, be turned into a revolutionary class in advanced capitalist societies, where literacy was widespread and the middle class was numerous? America in the 1960s was not czarist Russia in 1917. No coup d'état by a small group of leaders could become a revolution.

At least part of the answer to these questions was provided by the neo-Marxist philosopher Herbert Marcuse. Marcuse was a Marxist with a difference. His Marx was not the mature economic theoretician of *Das Kapital*, but the "humanistic" philosopher of the youthful essays of 1844. In these, supposedly, the young Marx detected the true iniquity of capitalist society. Not economic exploitation, but alienation—of man from man, man from woman, man from art, man from work, man from nature, and man from his true self—was the essence of the crime capitalism committed against humanity.

Marcuse was also a Freudian and joined Marx's notion of alienation with Freud's concept of repression. Like Freud, Marcuse argued that society had to subordinate instinctual drives in order to survive. This basic repression was tolerable. It did not produce the alienation that made life in industrial society an empty misery. What did distort and damage capitalism was "surplus repression," or the *excessive* denial of instinctual gratification that was necessary, not for society's survival, but for the dominant class to impose its will on the masses.

Thus the crime of capitalism—and also of the system of state capitalism that existed in the Soviet Union—was not primarily economic; it was cultural, aesthetic, and psychosexual. Men suffered deeply under the capitalist system, but they often did not know it. Borrowing a term coined by Marx's devoted disciple Friedrich Engels, Marcuse emphasized the power of "false consciousness" to obscure the true consciousness of the masses of people. Bemused by the bread and circuses supplied by advanced industrial society, the exploited citizens of such societies had come to love their prison, or rather, had come not even to notice that it was a prison at all. The advanced technological society created a multitude of false wants through advertising and other types of conditioning and then allowed society to satisfy these wants, at least up to a point. It even offered some erotic release in the form of commercialized sex and pornography, but this was false coin that did not buy true instinctual gratification. In the end the masses remained in leaden bondage to an evil, if evasive, system.

Here in essence was a theory that both explained the apparent indifference of the masses to their plight and justified revolution in their name. Not crude economic deprivation, but alienation from love and work produced the quiet desperation that afflicted most men in industrial society. Yet all of this was hidden from the victims by a system of propaganda, miseducation, and manipulation so powerful that it could obscure man's basic needs and basic nature.

Though Marcuse provided a rationale for revolution, there were many unanswered questions in this analysis too. Why were some men able to see the misery of others, while the victims themselves could not? Wasn't there a danger that the prophets were mistaken? How could one man take it on himself to tell another that he was really unhappy? Who was unhappy, after all—the accused sufferer or the accuser? Moreover, wasn't the whole thesis elitist at heart? Placing the humanistic values of the perceptive few before the materialistic values of the deluded mass implied a hierarchy of taste that was hard to distinguish from conventional elitist attacks on mass culture. Finally the concept of false consciousness was evasive. Wasn't it, fundamentally, the argument of the sore loser? Having lost the battle for men's minds, the defeated party cries fraud.

For a decade or more the New Left would wrestle with these difficulties. At times New Left thinkers would propound ingenious solutions, but at the end the problems would remain as puzzling and intractable as at the beginning. Still, as the 1960s commenced, the inherent intellectual and practical difficulties of reconstructing a left position that would fit the circumstances of the modern industrial world did not seem insurmountable. Something was happening. Men of feeling and intellect were no longer using their energies to defend the status quo. Western intellectuals, the enemies of bourgeois culture and materialistic values ever since the late eighteenth century, were once again returning to their old jobs as adversaries of the society that nurtured and rewarded them. The long eclipse was over, and one could now begin to see a thin rim of sunlight emerging at the left edge of the moon.

CHAPTER

2

A New Beginning
1960-1963

B Y THE END of the 1950s, then, the political and intellectual climate that had marked the early Cold War had begun to alter. Clearly something was happening that deserved attention. As one stumbled on Paul Goodman in the pages of *Commentary,* one knew that here was a refreshing new voice; the advent of *Studies on the Left* was an exciting event. Many young academics and graduate students, depressed at the dull uniformity of the decade, must have felt a lift and exhilaration as they encountered the first signs of a bold new attack on the status quo.

No doubt the simple release of pressure contributed to the change that was taking place. The repressions and the disillusionments of the Cold War era had aborted what might have been a promising postwar American shift to the left. As Irving Howe later remarked, a whole left generation was denied existence by the events of the 1950s. Clearly this was an abnormal situation and could not, under any circumstances, have lasted indefinitely.

Yet there was more to the rise of the New Left than the simple release of a compressed spring. And there was also more than the intellectual impact of some clever and trenchant thinkers. Marcuse, Mills, Goodman, and the others did not create the New Left. The writings of the neo-radicals were eagerly read and talked about by the post-1950s young, but more was necessary to create a movement with the mass, the longevity, and the influence of the New Left than some interesting and pointedly expressed ideas. Obviously there was something about the circumstances of this new generation that made it receptive to the ideas beginning to circulate in the Western countries. What characterized this generation? Why was it receptive to the new intellectual trends? Why did it differ from the generation that preceded it?

No one, except for the most "vulgar" of "vulgar Marxists," would suggest that the young men and women reaching college age in 1960 and thereafter constituted a deprived and exploited class, newly awakened to its oppression. In fact no group in America had ever been so free from the trammels of economic necessity or insecurity, or had had such encouraging prospects of power and influence, as those who favored revolutionizing American society between 1960 and 1972. This was no mob of beaten-down peasants, starving handloom weavers, or brutalized and exploited factory operatives.

Was the emerging New Left then responding to intolerable conditions for others? It is true that as the 1950s gave way to the 1960s the dazzling achievements of postwar America began to tarnish. Though national income had risen far beyond the levels of even 1929, as it rose an ever smaller proportion was spent on public needs. As John K. Galbraith noted, we lived in a nation where private affluence existed side by side with public squalor.

Soon after the publication in 1958 of Galbraith's *The Affluent Society,* many people began to doubt the generalization implied by the title. In 1963 Michael Harrington rediscovered American poverty, and he, Gabriel Kolko, and others soon convinced many people that blacks, Spanish-Americans, old people, widows, divorcees, and a long list of other groups had not shared in the abundance of America.

And public and private poverty scarcely exhausted the list of ills and injustices that came to the surface in the late 1950s and early 1960s. Racism permeated every aspect of American life; and blacks, American Indians, and Chicanos had lower incomes, shorter lives, and poorer housing and education than whites. Women were discriminated against in jobs and education, and the American family was male-dominated. An overblown federal bureaucracy was becoming increasingly remote from the people it was supposed to serve and more arbitrary in its actions. Private institutions—universities, foundations, churches—were becoming hidebound, authoritarian, and indifferent to their constituents and clientele. Cultural intolerance reigned in the nation, and those who diverged from the great middle in dress, attitudes, or sexual preferences were ostracized or ridiculed.

Finally there was the problem of America's international behavior. To many Americans it seemed that the country was turning into the world's bully. Having saved Europe from Hitler, the United States had now apparently taken over Europe's former role of world oppressor. Few events anywhere on the globe failed to concern this country, and almost every change—especially changes directed against the traditional, conservative ruling classes of Third World nations—was treated as a threat to the United States. Not only were we a defender of conservative regimes in our own hemisphere, but we had become the great bastion of counterrevolution everywhere else in the world. To make matters worse, our international role was not the result of some temporary aberration. It seemed to be imposed by a powerful institutional arrangement built into the system of corporate liberalism—an arrangement that was beginning to be called the military–industrial complex.

There is no need to catalog further the apparent failings and imperfections of the United States in the 1950s and early 1960s. The work of the new muckrakers like Galbraith and Harrington vividly portrayed them, and many liberal Americans admitted and regretted their existence. The New Left would loudly denounce them for over a decade.

No committed radical needs to look beyond these flaws for an explanation of the New Left. The New Left, he would say, was composed of those young people who as yet had no stake in the corporation-dominated "warfare state." Such young men and women could see its terrible flaws as no other group could and were free to express their anger.

But is this explanation enough? If it was possible to view America at the end of the 1950s as an authoritarian, exploitative, bellicose, corporation-dominated society, it was also possible to see it in other, more favorable, ways. Was the nation's social health worse in 1960, say, than in the past? No, it was better. There were fewer poor in the United States than ever before, and these poor were less deprived in an absolute sense than their counterparts in past periods. The racism that had afflicted America from its beginning was weakening and receding in the 1950s. The black middle class was growing proportionately, and the income of black families was increasing more quickly than that of whites. Black longevity was catching up with that of the white majority. There were also many more black students in colleges and universities than ever before.

Women too were better off than in the past. More were working, and many had achieved a degree of economic independence. Divorce and property laws now often favored them over men. Women lived far longer than men, and the longevity gap between the two sexes was widening.

War? Yes. Interventionism? Yes. In Iran, the Dominican Republic, Cuba, and other places, too, the United States had intervened to shore up conservative regimes. The Vietnam War, already sucking the United States into its vortex by 1961, would be a miserable misadventure, eventually execrated by almost all decent Americans. But was this so different from the past? For a century we had considered the Caribbean and Latin America our special preserve and had seldom hesitated to throw our weight there on the side of friendly conservative regimes. In 1950–1953 we had fought another war in East Asia—in Korea. It too had dragged on for a long time, and to supply the manpower needed thousands of young men had been drafted. Yet few Americans had opposed the Korean involvement. Though scarcely popular, it was accepted as an unavoidable necessity.

In a word, although much was clearly wrong with America in 1960, the record was scarcely all bad. In fact many things were getting better, and in any case much that now seemed wrong had aroused little indignation in the past.

Even the New Left would admit that in the material realm it was not easy to fault the United States. Although as time passed young radicals became more and more insistent on the survival of economic injustice, at the beginning few denied that American capitalism had achieved some sort of material breakthrough after 1945. As Robert Scheer, writing for an early New Left publication, *Root and Branch,* noted, "American capitalism has solved many of the problems which fired the spirit of an older generation of radicals. The problems of income distribution, full employment and the rights of labor unions are not the major crises faced by modern America."[1]

What *were* the "major crises," then, that presumably activated the New Left? Scheer, in the remainder of his article, did note the continued Cold War and our relations with other nations as an important issue, but it seems to be an afterthought. What bothered Scheer, and many of the other early New Leftists, was something less precise and indeed something difficult even for them to grasp. It concerned, Scheer wrote, "the style and quality of our lives." It had to do "with the reality of life in Los Angeles, Syracuse, and Sacramento, with their bowling alleys and shopping centers, and those vast stretches of America which are a blight upon the idea that man is sensitive, searching, poetic, and capable of love."[2]

Here, then, in capsule form, is an alternative explanation of the origins of the New Left: it was composed of young men and women who felt more intensely than most the subtle existential oppression imposed by modern America. These young people believed that they had penetrated the false consciousness generated by our society and perceived the disguised slavery and degradation that defined men's lives. They felt that they had learned to see through the shiny surface of life in an advanced industrial society to the ugly gray underbelly.

The New Left was not created by a coterie of clever intellectuals with novel, catchy ideas, although these men provided the terms of the argument at many points and influenced its direction. It was not brought into being by the sudden surfacing of new problems that had never before afflicted the country, although some new problems came to the fore. It was created by the new perception of their society that young people in the Western capitalist world and in America in particular had developed, and by a new attitude concerning the proper way of responding to that society. Something in the experience of many young men and women at the end of the 1950s had produced an altered consciousness that made for a critical, disapproving, and hostile view of American—and Western European—life and created a desire to change it in drastic ways.

At no time were the dissenters more than a small minority of

[1] Robert Scheer, "Notes on the New Left," *Root and Branch*, No. 2, p. 21. (Issue No. 1 of this quarterly, which only lasted for two numbers, is dated Winter, 1962. The second number, accordingly, was probably issued early in 1963.)

[2] *Ibid.,* pp. 24, 27.

the American people. Most Americans, through the grimmest period of race riots and Vietnam defeats, remained boosters and conventional patriots. Obviously the radicals were drastically different. What set them apart from their fellow Americans?

To answer this we must consider especially the social background of the New Left. Admittedly a social profile is not enough to tell us why the New Left radicals were radical. We must also keep in mind that American society was scarcely perfect when we consider why some people marched and protested and sat-in and braved the wrath of public opinion and the authorities. We must also recognize that individual, personal life experiences profoundly affect what people believe and do. Human beings are more than bits of data for a statistical distribution table. Perhaps in the end the only way truly to "explain" a political movement is by psychoanalyzing each individual within it. But aside from the practical difficulties of such an effort, it would still leave overall group social patterns unexplained. These clearly emerge as we consider the social characteristics of those who became members of the New Left in the 1960s.

The outstanding feature of the New Left was its youth. Aside from the group of radical pacifists connected with *Liberation* and middle-aged or elderly gurus like Goodman and Marcuse, few New Left radicals were born before the late 1930s. The cry "Don't trust anyone over thirty," coined by a Berkeley Free Speech Movement leader in 1964, expressed the New Left's own perception of this fact.

On the face of it, this youthfulness does not seem to require elaborate explanation. Over two thousand years ago Aristotle noted that young people "do everything to excess, love, hate and everything else," and Aristotle's observation, of course, merely expresses the folk wisdom of a hundred generations of parents and adults since the fourth century B.C.

Mere passionate, headstrong youthfulness, however, is not enough to account for the New Left. Not every generation of American young people has been radical. The young of the 1950s, in fact, seemed more conservative than their parents. At no time in America's past have more than a handful of young men and women taken strong left activist positions. Even during the 1930s most radicals were adults; the radicalized young of the Young Communist League, American Youth for Democracy, or the Young People's Socialist League (YPSL) were tiny groups, confined largely to a very few of the country's more cosmopolitan campuses.

More important, never in the American past has a major political movement been run by young people themselves. Other countries have had politically active youth movements, but as Lewis Feuer has noted, the United States did not until the 1960s.[3] Young America's enthusiasms and rebelliousness had generally taken the form of sexual experimentation, defiance of parents, adolescent high jinks, or delinquency, rather than politics.

Still another qualification is needed here. Not all the youth in the radical generation of the 1960s were radical. In fact even when the New Left was at its apogee, the proportion of radicals among the young people of the United States was only a small fraction of the total. A 1969 survey by the Yankelovich survey organization and CBS showed that among non-college youth some 50 percent were moderate politically and another 21 percent conservative. Even among college youth, moreover, only 3 percent considered themselves revolutionaries, and only another 10 percent could be called radical dissidents. Other polls by Harris, Roper, and Rossi all point to similar conclusions: the radical perspective was largely confined to the campuses, and even there it was a minority position.[4]

What the survey results point to is that the New Left was composed predominantly of well-educated, middle-class youth. Let us consider each half of this formula. The sociological data frequently emphasize the impressive intellectual caliber of radical youth. Not that all American college students were widely read and broadly educated. The mass higher education of the United States following 1945 was heavily weighted on the side of practical vocational training or technology. Most American college students read little besides texts while in school, and read little if anything afterward. Within the leadership of the New Left itself, there were occasional complaints about the ignorance of the rank and file. An analysis of the Students for a Democratic Society in 1967 by Carl Davidson, an SDS national vice-president, distinguished between the "shock troops," who constituted 80 percent of SDS, and the

[3] See Lewis Feuer, *The Conflict of Generations: The Character and Significance of Student Movements* (New York: Basic Books, 1969), especially Chapter 7. In citing Feuer on this point, I am not endorsing his entire view of the American New Left.

[4] See Seymour M. Lipset and Gerald M. Schaflander, *Passion and Politics: Student Activism in America* (Boston: Little, Brown, 1971), Chapter 2, pp. 39 ff., for a convenient summary of the opinion survey material.

remaining 20 percent, divided between "organizers" and "super-intellectuals." The shock troops, generally the younger members, Davidson noted, "[are] staunchly anti-intellectual and rarely read anything unless it comes from the underground press syndicate. They have never heard of C. Wright Mills, or even Bob Moses [an early SNCC leader], nor do they care to find out . . . ."[5]

Through the entire radical decade a constant battle went on between the activists, who were uninterested in ideas or openly contemptuous of theory, and the intellectuals, who felt that without theory and ideas the Movement was lost. Still, the weight of evidence is on the side of those who emphasize how bright and well-informed the radical students were. Generally the left students were to be found in the humanities and the social sciences, where the reading lists were longer and the exposure to humane learning and social ideas was more intense. The left students were also located disproportionately in the better, more cosmopolitan universities and the superior liberal arts colleges. This fact would eventually be recognized as a problem by student radicals, though by that time it would be too late. As for Davidson's description of SDS, no doubt it represented some measure of the truth about that organization at a time when hundreds were beginning to join for the excitement of campus disruptions. Even when it was most popular, however, SDS was led by a group of highly articulate young people. Certainly at the beginning the New Left dissenters were disproportionately drawn from the American student intelligentsia. Indeed, to a remarkable degree, they fit C. Wright Mills' prophetic description of the new "historical agencies of change" of his 1960 "Letter to the New Left."

The other significant dimension of the American New Left that the surveys spotlight is its middle-class base. To the end, the New Left remained incapable of winning a following among young, white, working people. White, working-class youths were moderately susceptible to the counter culture that paralleled the left, a fact often considered promising by New Left leaders, but they proved to be almost impervious to the political radicalism of the period.

This middle-class base is of course implied by the student status of so much of the New Left. Even in America a smaller proportion

    [5] See Carl Davidson, "National Vice-President's Report: Has SDS Gone to Pot?" New Left Notes, February 3, 1967.

of the sons and daughters of blue-collar workers than of white-collar workers, business, and professional people go to college, and those who do generally go to the institutions and choose the fields that are most vocationally geared and the least susceptible to a radical appeal. And even within the "soft majors," like literature, history, sociology, and political science, and within the elite schools, the radical students tended to be from the more prosperous families. The sociologist Richard Flacks, himself an early New Left leader, has noted that most left activists on campuses came from upper middle-class families of professional background in which both parents frequently had had four years of college education themselves. These young people were less upwardly mobile than many American college students—not because they were stuck at the bottom, but because the social breakthrough for their families took place before they had arrived on the scene.[6]

Here is a situation that virtually no social theorist had prepared us for. C. Wright Mills, of course, did notice the growing significance of the young intellectuals in 1960, but Mills, I think, failed to see the ironies and ambiguities of his conclusion. It almost seems as if the fundamental "contradiction" in capitalist society may not be that it gives birth to an impoverished and revolutionary proletariat, but that it creates an angry and radical intelligentsia. From Marx himself onward, it has been the intellectual sons and daughters of the middle class who have been the chief antagonists of the bourgeois culture out of which they have sprung and the major thrust behind the attempt to supersede that culture.

A word of caution is in order here. It has become the dullest of clichés to attribute the New Left to a generation gap, and yet the analysis thus far is consistent with this interpretation. There was indeed a gap between the young political activists and their elders, but it was not a simple chronological phenomenon. Generally, the young radicals were not merely turning their parents' world and values upside down. The typical student activist's family was left of center. An unusually large proportion of the activists' parents, in fact, had themselves been members of the left in an earlier period, though in many cases they later abandoned their formal affiliations

[6] See Richard Flacks, "Who Protests: The Social Bases of the Student Movement," in Julian Foster and Durwood Long (eds.), *Protest! Student Activism in America* (New York: William Morrow, 1970), *passim*.

and accepted the rewards of bourgeois society. In many cases the young left activists of the 1960s were fulfilling their parents' political dreams and yearnings rather than repudiating them. The old folks now usually stood on the sidelines, but they often cheered on their offspring like suburban mothers at a little league game.

However, even the parents of the "Red diaper babies" were often aghast when their sons and daughters went beyond the limits of propriety, endangering careers and futures, disregarding physical safety, and expecting too much too soon.[7] The sons and daughters for their part often went to the barricades with one eye cocked to see if mom and dad were watching the performance. Sometimes, no doubt, they felt they were redeeming their parents' pledge, but it is hard to escape the feeling that at times the message being sent back to the suburbs from the college campuses was the taunt "You sold out; I won't!"

To locate the young radicals sociologically is not to explain why they were radical. We still have not established the connection between upper middle-class, elite college student status and radical politics. Why were so many of the 1960s' middle-class young drawn to left causes?

To begin with, only middle-class college students could afford radicalism. As we have seen, the liberal parents and the radical children shared similar social values and sympathies—but only the children were free, materially and emotionally, to do something about their convictions.

No two generations in America have ever had such widely different formative experiences as the radical children and the liberal parents. The parents had a strong sense that they had narrowly escaped disaster. Born in the 1910s or the early 1920s, they had grown up in the 1930s. Their childhoods had been clouded by the fear and insecurity of the depression and the rise of the dictators. As young people they had struggled for an education and had fought to stay off the breadlines. Later they watched while the democratic

[7] A particularly poignant expression of this dismay is Joseph Starobin's remarks about the suicide of his son, Professor Robert S. Starobin of SUNY at Binghamton, a young radical leader from the time of the Berkeley Free Speech Movement in 1964 to his death in 1971. See Joseph Starobin, *American Communism in Crisis, 1943–1947* (Cambridge, Mass.: Harvard University Press, 1972), pp. xiv–xv.

world threatened to collapse. Soon many of the men found themselves wearing uniforms in strange lands, facing death or dismem-
berment.

Through all of this upheaval and danger, America and its government seemed ultimately virtuous. Even those who were Communist party members, and most skeptical of capitalism generally,
upheld the system in the name of the antifascist United Front, and
by 1939 or 1940 they came to support the official institutions of their
nation. Figuratively, if not literally, they voted time and again for
Roosevelt, the New Deal, and America. Though saved from international and domestic disaster in the end, they grew to believe that
peace and prosperity were precarious and rather rare commodities
and that the social fabric, though admittedly imperfect, was fragile.
Victory over the dictators in 1945 and postwar prosperity had been
a joyous surprise, and they never fully lost the feeling that they
and their generation had cheated the devil.

How different the experiences of the children! Those who
reached their eighteenth year in 1960 were born during the wartime
boom. Few could remember the war itself. Their early consciousness
corresponded with the exuberant days of postwar affluence and the
family's move to suburbia after father came back from overseas.
When they were children, the lives of their parents were not without
struggles and pains; but each passing year dad moved up in his job
or his profession, and the family's horizons seemed to widen as a
matter of course. As children they went to good suburban schools,
summer camps, took music and art lessons. In high school they ran
for student government office, worked on the school newspaper, and
were elected to honor societies. According to Kenneth Kenniston,
though many of them experienced a period of anguish and withdrawal in early adolescence, "in senior high school, and usually
continuing into college, these young radicals describe a pattern of
outstanding success and leadership." [8]

The more thoughtful young radicals were aware of the historical gap that separated them from their parents and understood the
consequences of it. Mark Gerzon, a young Harvard activist, writing
at the height of the New Left, noted the crucial difference between

[8] Kenneth Kenniston, *Young Radicals: Notes on Committed Youth* (New
York: Harcourt Brace Jovanovich, 1968), p. 87. See Chapter 3.

the attitudes that flowed from prewar poverty and those that flowed from postwar affluence:

> To the postwar generation . . . prosperity was the normal state of affairs. These young people had never experienced anything else. The economic conditions which their parents—the young people of the Depression—had to fight and work for were given to the next generation in childhood. Looking through the picture windows of their suburban homes, with Father's big car (and perhaps even Mother's compact car) sitting in the driveway, many members of this generation are clearly experiencing a world radically different from that of their parents. The traditional bond of material scarcity which formerly united generations has been severed. These young people not only do not have to concern themselves with their families' welfare, but really do not have to worry about eventually making a living themselves.

Moreover, Gerzon noted, the difference between the generations' experiences extended to international and domestic politics. "Whatever really happened," he emphatically observed of the searing years of Hitler and Joe McCarthy, *"half of America's citizens would have to read a history book to know about it."* [9]

No doubt there were other reasons why the young and their parents felt differently about the postwar world. The eclipse of the printed word caused by the visual image, the change that Marshall McLuhan described in his popular books about the media, separated the two generations. The stylishness of this explanation should make us a little wary of it perhaps. Yet it is probably true that television, particularly, encouraged a tendency among the young to expect wishes to be converted into immediate action, without consideration of means and consequences. More important, I think, television affected and molded the quality of youth protest, when protest became the daily fare on college campuses. It has even been claimed that without television there would have been no New Left. Marches and building occupations were staged for the six o'clock network news, and New Left leaders were defined as those who gave interesting interviews to David Susskind or Mike Wallace. This is a great exaggeration, of course, but toward the end of the radical decade,

[9] Mark Gerzon, *The Whole World Is Watching: A Young Man Looks at Youth's Dissent* (New York: Paperback Library, 1969), pp. 29, 31.

a thoughtful man of the left would claim that the ability of the young rebels to manipulate television imagery both made and broke the Movement.[10]

Even when these differences in experience and perception were acknowledged by both sides, it did not promote understanding between the generations. To the parents, life was chancy and uncertain, and success was neither easy nor contemptible. Life did not need elaborate justification or some transcendent meaning. Life was pushing, always pushing—for stability, comfort, and security—and it was a hard and challenging enterprise well worth the effort. Even the erstwhile radicals among the parents, while retaining sensitive social consciences, were pleased with their own accomplishments and derived satisfaction from their lives.

To the children, material success and conventional achievement seemed deadening and contemptible. Ronald Aronson, a young New Left college professor, a student of Marcuse, has told us of his own feelings as he passed through the crisis of choosing a life course for himself.

> Somehow I had gotten on this machine in motion, had become the machine, acting on behalf of some enormous power I couldn't even begin to fathom. To follow out its and my momentum led to the "good life" whose every detail I already knew in some instructive way: professional work, marrying, the struggling young couple getting set up, vacation trips, a wonderful child, a small house at first, then living better, making more money. My own steps led naturally into the full-fledged American way of life, a life in which I could look good for other people and smile Hello and buy and "live better and better." Phyllis and I called it "the whole bit." Somewhere inside I knew what attitudes and feelings were required for entry into this good life: despair, boredom, the relentless drive to keep moving, being "realistic" by putting society's demands first and my own second, giving up on happiness, lying about pain.[11]

After reading Aronson's apologia one is puzzled by his activism. Why not simply drop out? Actually, as Aronson further explains,

[10] See Norman Fruchter, "Games in the Arena: Movement Propaganda and the Culture of the Spectacle," *Liberation,* May, 1971, pp. 4–13; and also Todd Gitlin's critique, *ibid.,* pp. 18–19.

[11] Ronald Aronson, "Dear Herbert," in George Fischer (ed.), *The Revival of American Socialism: Selected Papers of the Socialist Scholars' Conference* (New York: Oxford University Press, 1971), pp. 267–268.

he did try dropping out by leaving the academy and going off to teach in a country school. It did not bring the satisfaction he had hoped for. He soon came to realize "that breaking free to live humanely meant attacking the America which had made me fit only to live inhumanely." [12]

Aronson's experience was a common one among the young college-trained generation of the late 1950s. Affluent America with its promise of comfort and security produced despair, not joy, among its apparent beneficiaries. They wanted something better for themselves and, by extension, for others. That something was the sort of self-fulfillment, or self-realization, that did not come from successful, conventional careers, but did seem to be possible in political activism. Aronson, Greg Calvert, and other articulate New Left activists noted that the fundamentally important difference between the New Left and the liberals was that people of the left were trying to free *themselves*, that they wished to change themselves before changing others. Liberals, on the other hand, they insisted, were by and large contented with their lives and wished only to raise to their own level those who remained below it. [13]

This quest for meaning, of course, was not unique to young Americans growing up between 1950 and 1970. It is a universal human trait that recurs with each generation and will no doubt repeat itself until the last echo of recorded time. Yet it is not always the same quest. Like everything else, it is modified by culture and historical circumstances. It is one thing in the East, where it traditionally becomes a submergence of self and a putting aside of all desire. It is another thing in the West, where it is generally related to some sort of personal fulfillment. It varies over time. In the Western world at least it has often been defined as including wealth, adventure, creativity, fame, and "success." This definition is characteristic of young, still-untested societies in a phase of rapid growth and expansion. Meaning has also been defined in the West as safety, comfort, security, and peace. This tends to be characteristic, as we saw, of societies that have just had a close brush with disaster.

[12] *Ibid.*, p. 270.
[13] See Aronson, *ibid.*, p. 278; Greg Calvert, "In White America: Radical Consciousness and Social Change," printed pamphlet version of a speech originally given at an SDS conference in Princeton in February, 1967. In Radical Education File, Social Protest Project, Bancroft Library, University of California, Berkeley.

Finally, the search for meaning sometimes takes the form of an attempt to reestablish human relationships on a basis of love and spontaneous, "authentic" emotion. This is the distinctive mode of a society—or a segment of that society—that has achieved its other goals and either has not been exposed to disaster or has survived such exposure.

Frequently those who seek the meaning of life in this third way will insist that only their meaning is meaningful, and perhaps they are right. No matter how hard we try, it is impossible to ignore a persistent strain of Western thought that rejects material advantage, whether in the confident version or the timid one, and insists that the striving for material gain can be justified only as a necessary preliminary to the more important search for love and human freedom. Among those lucky enough, or perhaps, miserable enough, to mature in a society enabling them to believe that the traditional battles for survival have been won, there always seems to be an attempt to find a "deeper" meaning in personal relationships, or in self-exploration. Prosperous and sensitive young men and women living in affluent times always seem to insist that life must offer more than mere personal glory and physical comfort. Who will say they are wrong? Even liberals in the 1950s asserted that the quality of life demanded attention now that the material issues had been virtually settled.

There can be little question that for many who entered the Movement the hope for a better and more purposeful life was at least for a while fulfilled. Many young people, who had been leading lives that seemed useless and barren, found in the Movement the warm approval, the camaraderie, the sense of high purpose that they missed in the conventional world. The accounts young radicals give of the dramatic "confrontations" that marked their careers in the Movement invariably convey the sense of community that the shared excitement and danger created among the participants. At times, in fact, the subjective experience of those who took part in radical actions, rather than any specific objective goals, seems to be the force that drove them.

This yearning for a more interesting and meaningful life was a link between the New Left and the hippie counterculture that was emerging at about the same time. Ronald Aronson's experience of withdrawing from society to find a new personal life-style was to be repeated by others. Though the questing young men and women usually did not go off to teach in rural schools, they often passed back and forth between a life of activism and a life of withdrawal into personal experience. Many political activists of the 1960s spent time experimenting with drugs, communal living, and doing their own thing. Bona fide hippies generally were radicals in a diffuse way, and many eventually moved over to the political life. The free movement back and forth between the two groups did not preclude a good deal of mutual skepticism and even disdain, but it resulted in a coloring of the attitudes of both types of dissenters.[14]

Even before they appeared on the college campuses these social and psychological factors often predisposed young men and women to radicalism. Then, as freshmen, they found much to feed their inclinations. The students who descended on American colleges in the late 1950s and early 1960s were often disappointed with what they encountered. Classes were large and impersonal, the result in part of the enormous bulge in the birth rate after 1945. Professors were inaccessible. In fact they were almost as inaccessible as dad was back home, and apparently for the same reason: they were wrapped up in furthering their careers. The fraternities and sororities, the student government and intercollegiate athletics, which used to provide students with close friends and substitute families, had become delegitimatized for many students. The "Greeks" were often arrogant and anachronistic snobs; athletics had become almost pure commercial enterprise; student government was powerless and controlled by the fraternities.

By the end of the 1950s a subculture of independents had developed on some campuses, providing many students, who could no longer comfortably follow the traditional paths, with a sense of belonging. This subculture was a kind of bohemia, often composed of the more cosmopolitan students from the big cities. It had its characteristic dress—the girls wore peasant blouses, wide skirts, and long hair tied in a pony tail or worn loose; the boys wore army clothes or corduroys and had begun to grow beards. Both sexes

---

[14] This mixture of radicalism and bohemia was not unique to the 1960s New Left. In New York's Greenwich Village during the 1920s and 1930s, the same combination existed, though it was relatively rare in the Communist party itself. One writer has called the 1930s Village experience a fusion of Washington Square and Union Square. See Bernard Wolfe, *Memoirs of a Not Altogether Shy Pornographer* (New York: Doubleday, 1972), chapter entitled "Village Nights."

favored sandals. It had its characteristic art: folk and Baroque in music, the impressionists and postimpressionists in painting, and the beat poets and novelists—Allen Ginsberg, Lawrence Ferlinghetti, Jack Kerouac—in literature.

It did not yet have its characteristic politics, however. The campus independents were liberals; very few were radical, except perhaps in a casual and highly theoretical way. Student radicalism in the 1950s was moribund except at a very few campuses. When André Schiffrin, the New York publisher, joined the Student League for Industrial Democracy (SLID) in 1954 at Yale, his behavior was considered rather peculiar. The SLID was virtually dead. Founded as the Intercollegiate Socialist Society in 1905, it had only a few dozen members in the entire country in the mid-fifties.[15] Small groups of students belonged to the Young People's Socialist League, and the liberal group, Students for a Democratic America (SDA)— the student affiliate of Americans for Democratic Action (ADA)— had a few chapters at the larger universities. In 1960 a group of young Trotskyites organized the Young Socialist Alliance. But as yet, few students, even among the independents, were politically minded. The National Student Association (NSA), an organization representing student governments at a large number of the country's colleges, was an anti-Communist student body, secretly financed by the Central Intelligence Agency to combat the Communist appeal to students both internationally and at home. Despite this, NSA was liberal in its politics, but it was closer to college administrators and student government leaders than to the ordinary student.

When we consider the social environment out of which the New Left emerged, we should also remember the matter of numbers. The number of young people in the 1960s represented an unusually large proportion of the total population. Beginning in the 1950s the average age of Americans began to decrease sharply as more and more children were added to the population. By 1963 there were over 27 million young people between 15 and 24 years of age. By 1967 about half the population of the country was under 27.

A large proportion of these young people, moreover, now went to college, where they represented a potent concentration of the age group most prone to rebellion against established forms and values.

---

[15] See André Schiffrin, "The Student Movement in the 1950's: A Reminiscence," *Radical America*, May–June, 1968, *passim*.

As far back as the nineteenth century, young men in particular were found in the forefront of riots and civil disturbances in the United States. The adventurousness and impulsiveness of males in their late teens and early twenties is well-known to the insurance actuaries and is reflected in such things as the higher automobile insurance rates for young male drivers. Even if the *proportion* of adventure-prone students on college campuses had been no greater in the 1960s than formerly, their total number was far larger, and this made a difference. Any call for campus action in 1968 inevitably appealed to more students than previously, if only because there were more students *in toto*. A demonstration by a thousand angry and exuberant young people had a far greater impact and visibility than one by, say, a hundred, even if the thousand represented the same proportion of the student body as the hundred did earlier.

Still, when all this is said about postwar American college-age youth, at only one campus—the University of California at Berkeley —was there a promising student radical movement by the end of the 1950s. A certain caution is in order here. At no time, even at Berkeley, was more than a minority of the college community thoroughly radicalized. But nowhere in the country, whether at the beginning of the New Left or at its end, was any community so willing to support dissent against the established political and cultural institutions of the nation, as Berkeley, both the college and the city.

The Berkeley scene was a special case of the Bay Area climate in general. San Francisco and its environs had a long history of liberal and left activities. The city had a strong and militant labor union tradition. It had sheltered one of the most colorful of the nation's bohemias for many years. In the 1950s the beats had made North Beach and the City Lights Bookstore their headquarters. Between San Francisco and the university campus across the Bay there was quick and frequent communication.

By 1957 students at Berkeley who were disenchanted with the usual "sand box" politics of the Associated Students of the University of California (ASUC) had formed a campus political organization called SLATE. SLATE candidates, unlike the usual student politicians, were willing to tackle campus issues that challenged the local commercial interests of Berkeley and the East Bay. SLATE was also oriented toward a dissenting view on national and international issues, particularly as they affected students.

SLATE soon began to attract attention at other campuses. In the summer of 1960 SLATE sponsored a conference at Mount Madonna Park near San Jose to discuss the general question of student political organizing. The meeting attracted 140 participants from Berkeley and other campuses and served a useful educational purpose for some of the young dissenters. One of the visitors was Tom Hayden, the editor of the University of Michigan *Daily*. Hayden had come to the Bay Area as an agent for VOICE—a recently formed student political party at Michigan, modeled after the Berkeley group—to learn about the new kind of student politics. He would leave with a better idea of how to politicize a university student body, and the knowledge would have important consequences.

Two major events in the Bay Area soon ignited the dry political tinder that lay about so abundantly. One was the execution in the San Quentin gas chamber of Caryl Chessman, a convicted rapist, in early May, 1960. Chessman's crime was a capital offense only because the state had been able to convict him of the technical charge of kidnapping. While he waited on death row at San Quentin, Chessman and his lawyers carried out a successful series of moves to have his execution stayed pending further investigation of the case. Chessman himself helped prepare the appeal briefs and wrote a number of articles and books ably defending himself. To many people, it seemed that he had thoroughly rehabilitated himself and had paid his debt to society, and that if ever a case of capital punishment seemed outrageous, it was this one. Chessman's plight was widely advertised on Pacifica radio, both in Los Angeles and in San Francisco, and the broadcasts stirred the consciences of many Californians, particularly in the Bay Area.

Pressured by thousands of concerned citizens and personally hostile to capital punishment, Governor Pat Brown postponed Chessman's scheduled execution in February, pending consideration by the California state legislature of a law abolishing the death penalty. But when the legislature failed to act, Brown refused to intervene further. As May 2, the day of execution, approached, a group of Quaker pacifists held vigils outside the walls of San Quentin, where they were joined by students from Berkeley, Stanford, and other Bay Area colleges. At first the gatherings were quiet, as befitted meetings called by pacifists. On the morning of May 2, however, the watchers' patience wore through, and they attempted to

stop a press car entering the prison gates by sitting down in front
of it. The prison guards tried to remove the protesters and then
kicked them and roughed them up. In the end the vigil was to no
avail. At the last minute the State Supreme Court refused to grant
Chessman a stay, and at 10 A.M. he went to the gas chamber.

The Chessman case is a prototype of the radicalizing experience that so often in the next decade would mark the odyssey of
young people to the left. The vigil had a remarkable effect on those
people who participated in it, even if only vicariously. Michael Rossman, who was at the May 2 vigil, later wrote:

> . . . I think we were feeling more than simple distaste for society's
> murder rituals when we stood outside San Quentin's gates and lis-
> tened to the wind. Our eyes were opening, a mystification was break-
> ing, we were beginning to see the acts of Official America as ugly,
> wherever we looked.[16]

Many of the participants shared Rossman's feeling that Chessman's
execution had provided a brief, searing glimpse of the inherent
cruelty of American society.

An early instance of the radicalizing experience, the Chessman
execution also anticipates the important element of "personal witness" within the New Left. The feeling that each man must demonstrate by some personal act of protest or defiance that he will not
accept injustice was bequeathed to the young leftists of the 1960s by
the radical pacifists. Touching as it does a deep Christian chord in
Western culture, personal witness would become an appealing part
of the Movement. Yet another side of radical pacifism, which was
also absorbed by the young leftists (and is more ambiguous morally),
also surfaces in the Chessman affair. Participants in the May vigil,
besides being politically radicalized by the experience, also learned
something of the personal catharsis that bearing witness could provide. As one thoughtful student told Rossman while they waited
outside the San Quentin walls, "I keep feeling that what we're doing
is helping each of us more than it can possibly help Chessman." [17]
As this remark suggests, the personal need to bear witness, while
understandable in psychological terms, held some grave dangers.
Surely decent men had to speak out, had to act out their convictions.

---

[16] Michael Rossman, "The Vigil at Chessman's Execution," in *The Wedding Within the War* (New York: Doubleday, 1971), p. 34.
[17] *Ibid.*, p. 41.

But it was obviously possible for the need to bear witness to become more important than rectifying the injustice itself and for it to degenerate into mere personal self-indulgence. Rossman's fellow vigil keeper for one, though seemingly guilty about his reaction, appears less impressed with Chessman's fate than with his own subjective response.

But such problems remained for the future. Meanwhile another event soon served to radicalize Bay Area students further. In May, 1959, the House Un-American Activities Committee (HUAC) announced that it intended to come to California to investigate Communist influence in the public schools. The committee promptly subpoenaed some forty individuals in northern California and then leaked their names to the press. Soon after, it dropped its plans to come West; but it had already damaged personal reputations, and a number of the subpoenaed schoolteachers were fired.

Such tactics were typical of HUAC. Established in 1938 to investigate Nazi, Fascist, Communist and other un-American groups, the committee had generally reserved its attacks for the left. Under Martin Dies, and then a succession of other conservative chairmen, it had chosen to investigate left dissent by methods that disregarded the rights and reputations of the accused and ignored the usual sort of judicial processes that protect the innocent. At times during the McCarthy era, the committee outdid the Wisconsin Senator's witch-hunting tactics and not only disgusted and outraged liberals but also disturbed many sensitive conservatives.

Shortly after Chessman's execution in 1960 the committee finally arrived in San Francisco to conduct its postponed hearings. Liberals and radicals in the Bay Area were ready for it, and HUAC was greeted by a massive protest demonstration. Many of the demonstrators came from Berkeley, where SLATE and the *Daily Californian*, the campus newspaper, had urged students to turn out en masse and picket the committee. The students were particularly enraged because most of those subpoenaed in this second round were civil rights activists and people who had opposed HUAC rather than known Communists.

Under the leadership of a group called Students for Civil Liberties, hundreds of university students crossed the Bay to San Francisco and marched around City Hall, where the hearings were being held. Many protesters tried to enter the hearing room, and a number succeeded. The pickets outside the building were noisy, but they did not interrupt the hearings. Those inside hammered on the doors and may have disturbed the proceedings in the hearing room. In any event, on the second day of the demonstrations, Inspector Michael Maguire of the San Francisco police suddenly lost his patience and ordered his men to play the City Hall fire hoses on those in the corridors. Soon the high-pressure hoses had pushed the protesters out of the building. Many were arrested, while others were dragged roughly down the long flight of outside steps.

This was the first time that *white* students had been so harshly treated by the police and the experience provided a second radicalizing lesson for northern California students. As Michael Rossman, once more in the thick of things, saw the HUAC hearings, they portended a new left movement in America that would "be non-partisan, indiscriminate in its condemnation of reactionaries and old style radicals, not inclined to organization . . . and uncapturable by either the splintered old left or by progressive elements in present major parties." [18]

At Berkeley the HUAC "riot" set off a round of resolutions, meetings, and efforts to raise bail for the arrested demonstrators, but the students' most effective reaction came after the committee produced a film, "Operation Abolition," made up of the television footage taken during the incident. This film grossly distorted the events of mid-May and made them appear to be part of a Communist conspiracy to undermine the effectiveness of HUAC.

Millions of people saw the film, and many of them apparently accepted the committee's version of the event without question. On the many campuses where the film was shown, however, the response was predominantly hostile. At Berkeley, SLATE produced a record, "Sounds of Protest," as a retort to the movie. During the summer a group of those who had been arrested established a committee to abolish HUAC and put together a pamphlet to refute the film that was distributed widely as an antidote to HUAC propaganda. On many other liberal campuses—Harvard, Chicago, Minnesota, Michigan, Wisconsin, Columbia, and CCNY—"Operation Abolition" aroused contempt and derision. Even on more conservative campuses, the committee's propaganda effort was often self-defeating. Although students were frequently puzzled about what to

[18] Michael Rossman, "The Protest Against HUAC," in *The Wedding Within the War, op. cit.,* pp. 68–69.

believe, the film disclosed that a white student movement now existed in America. Protest against the political status quo, it was
becoming clear, was not confined to young blacks alone.

The incidents in San Francisco and Berkeley were, of course,
most important for the growth of the Bay Area's own radicalism.
By 1960 the region around the Bay had already become a left enclave where radicals felt at home and could congregate for mutual
support and encouragement. Eventually Berkeley would become a
pilgrim's shrine for students from all over the country seeking inspiration and enlightenment in the ways of radical action and consciousness.

At first, however, the Bay Area seemed almost unique. A few
campuses besides Berkeley, Michigan, and Wisconsin had active
circles of student radicals, and at others the ingredients of student
radicalism were rapidly accumulating. But most of the country's
student body still remained inert. This began to change rapidly in
1960–1961. The year that witnessed the Chessman and HUAC affairs in northern California also saw the beginnings of mass support for opposition politics at many of the nation's more cosmopolitan universities.

An important element in the thaw was the inspiration of civil
rights activism in the South and particularly the black student sit-
ins that began in February, 1960. The sit-in movement erupted spontaneously when four black freshmen at North Carolina Agricultural
and Technical College at Greensboro decided to demand service at
a downtown lunch counter. When no one would serve them, they
stayed in their seats, refusing to leave until closing time. They returned the next day with several more students and repeated the
performance, with the same result. Back they came the day after,
and for many days after that. Though often jeered at and reviled
by store patrons, the well-groomed students behaved with exem-
plary patience and dignity. The Greensboro tactics quickly caught
on throughout the South. Within a few weeks hundreds of other
black students were emulating the Greensboro pioneers in more
than fifty cities throughout the region.

The black student sit-ins were like an electric shock to the still
sluggish mass of Northern students. Young white students found it
easy to identify with the black students in the South. They admired
the blacks' courage and felt ashamed that they were not doing

more themselves to help stamp out the curse of racism. Fortunately
the opportunity to help was close by. The Kress and Woolworth
companies, which segregated their stores in the South, also had
branches in the North. In the spring of 1960, as the Chessman and
HUAC affairs came to a climax, thousands of Northern college students turned out to picket the local five-and-dime chains, demanding that they end segregation at their Southern outlets.

The sympathy for the Southern sit-ins did not seem particularly radical. Southern black students, after all, were only demanding what they could expect in the North as a matter of course. Even
the National Student Association drafted a resolution supporting
the black students, though it refused to go so far as to endorse picketing of the five-and-dime chains in Northern cities. Yet for many
Northern students the experience was a radicalizing one. Besides
meeting many Old Leftists on the picket lines and listening to them
praise the radical vision, the act of carrying signs and chanting
slogans somehow broke the political ice. When James O'Brien—
now a radical scholar, then a freshman at Minnesota's Carleton
College—recalled how the picketing awakened his dormant political
sympathies, he was describing the experience of many white supporters of the sit-ins.

For the next two or three years white students in increasing
numbers participated in the Southern civil rights movement. SNCC,
the Student Nonviolent Coordinating Committee, formed in 1960 to
coordinate the sit-ins, included among its charter members a number of white students, mostly from the North. The year following,
1961, saw the beginning of the freedom rides. Organized by CORE
and the radical pacifist Fellowship of Reconciliation, the rides were
intended to dramatize the continuing segregation on Southern bus
lines and at bus terminals. Freedom riders boarded the buses in
Northern cities and refused to accept segregated accommodations
at terminals, lunch counters, and rest rooms along their route
through the South. Both black and white students joined the rides,
and a number of students, of both races, were attacked and badly
beaten by angry white segregationists.

The climax of white student participation in the Southern civil
rights movement came in Mississippi in the summer of 1964. Early
in 1964 CORE and SNCC announced their plans to organize the
blacks of this most backward and racist of Southern states and register them to vote. The two organizations, along with the National

Council of Churches, set about early in the year recruiting students for the Mississippi drive. About five hundred white students went South from many colleges in the North and West, with particularly large contingents coming from Stanford, Yale, Berkeley, Harvard, and Reed. Before they began their assignments, the students were given a two-week orientation at the Western College for Women in Ohio, where, among other things, they were told how to protect themselves against beatings. Then, under the auspices of the Council of Federated Organizations (COFO), the students moved South and were soon registering Mississippi blacks to vote, organizing Freedom Schools, and establishing black community centers. One significant aspect of the Summer Freedom Project involved the Mississippi Freedom Democratic party, which was founded just before the summer as an alternative to the segregationist regular state Democrats. Although the party had no legal standing under Mississippi law, it ran a slate of candidates for state and national offices in the fall and received some sixty-nine thousand votes.

The white students were deeply affected by what they encountered in Mississippi. The poverty and illiteracy of rural Southern blacks appalled them, as did the cruelty and brutality toward blacks of many of the native whites. They had never seen anything like it in their own rich suburban communities. Though few of them were committed radicals when they went to Mississippi at the beginning of the summer, many of them were when they returned in the fall. As one white girl wrote to her parents from Gulfport in August:

> I have learned more about politics here from running my own precinct meetings than I could from any Government professor . . . . For the first time in my life, I am seeing what it is like to be poor, oppressed, and hated. And what I see here does not apply only to Gulfport or Mississippi or even to the South . . . . The people we're killing in Vietnam are the same people whom we've been killing for years in Mississippi. True we didn't tie the knot in Mississippi and we didn't pull the trigger in Vietnam—that is personally—but we've been standing behind the knot-tiers and the trigger-pullers too long.[19]

The students not only learned about racism and injustice, they also learned about fear and courage. Most white Mississippians regarded the Northern students as an invading hostile army. Through-

---

[19] Quoted in Massimo Teodori (ed.), *The New Left: A Documentary History* (Indianapolis: Bobbs-Merrill, 1969), p. 108.

out the summer the students lived in a climate of fear and danger. Things might have been still worse for most of them if it hadn't been for the tragedy that took place at the very beginning, when, in June, three civil rights workers—Michael Schwerner, a Cornell graduate student, James Cheney, a black CORE worker, and Andrew Goodman, a Queens College freshman—disappeared under mysterious circumstances. Scores of federal agents swarmed into the state to look for them, a quest that finally ended six weeks later when their bodies were discovered buried in an earthen dam in Nashoba County. The presence of the agents gave many of the bigots pause and undoubtedly held down the violence of the rest of the summer. Still, the many threats and small incidents, and the hostility of the white community, not to speak of the three murders, taught the Freedom Summer students much about the uses of courage. Many of them would return to their campuses in September with a new sense of what was wrong with the country and a new sense of their own ability to bear up to intimidation and coercion.

CHAPTER

3

The Student Left Emerges
1960-1964

F REEDOM SUMMER was in 1964. By this time an organization that eventually provided the framework for the white student New Left had been in existence for five years.

Students for a Democratic Society had actually been formed in 1930 as the Student League for Industrial Democracy. The parent organization of SLID was the League for Industrial Democracy (LID), a socialist group founded before World War I by Jack London and Upton Sinclair and composed of intellectuals and left-leaning trade unionists. In 1935 SLID merged with another student group, and the two became the American Student Union. In 1945 SLID reassumed its earlier name, and during the 1950s, as André Schiffrin has noted (see p. 41), it was one of the few radical groups that continued to limp along on American campuses. Among its prominent members in the 1950s were James Farmer and Gabriel Kolko, both of whom served as executive secretaries of SLID.

In 1959 the parent League, detecting new signs of left activism among the country's college students, reorganized SLID and gave it a new name—Students for a Democratic Society. At this point SDS, like its adult counterpart, was a coalition of socialists, liberals, and unclassifiable radicals, who were pledged to "raise issues" about social questions so long as the solutions did not jeopardize the "values of maximum freedom for the individual." [1]

SDS might have remained a polite, ineffectual student auxiliary of the League if not for one of those memorable accidents where the right man got the right job at the right time. In 1960 Robert Alan ("Al") Haber, VOICE activist at Michigan and son of a University of Michigan professor, became president of SDS. More than most student politicians Haber saw that the time was ripe for launching a new left-oriented political organization with a campus base. "If any really radical liberal force is going to develop in America," he wrote LID officials soon after he moved into SDS's New York office, "it is going to come from the colleges and the young." [2]

Haber soon began to charge SDS with his own superabundant enthusiasm and energy. Essential to his plans for SDS was a much larger membership, and in the summer of 1961 he made a determined effort to recruit students for SDS from among members of the National Student Association (NSA) gathered for its annual convention at the University of Wisconsin. He was moderately successful. Haber and Tom Hayden, who had become Haber's close associate, managed to interest a number of NSA members in SDS. They failed to get Hayden elected as NSA's national affairs vice-president, but they did succeed in getting Paul Potter, one of the new converts from NSA, elected to that office.

As yet, as Haber's unusual term "radical liberal force" suggests, SDS was still as much a liberal as a radical organization. An SDS pamphlet of early 1962, "What is the S.D.S.?," defined the organization as an association of young people "bringing together liberals and radicals, activists and scholars, students and faculty." The liberal aspects of the organization included its unwillingness as yet to give up on the liberal wing of the Democratic party, its continuing faith in the universities and the welfare state, its anticommunism, and its concern about the dangers of the far right. [3] At this point it would have been hard to distinguish SDS from Students for Demo-

[1] Quoted by Edward J. Bacciocco, "The New Left from 1956–1969: A Study of Community, Reform, and Revolution," doctoral dissertation, Department of Political Science, University of Colorado, 1971, p. 182.

[2] Robert Haber to Frank Trager, March 11, 1961, quoted in Kirkpatrick Sale, *SDS* (New York: Random House, 1973), p. 24.

[3] See "What is the S.D.S.?," SDS File, Social Protest Project, Bancroft Library, University of California, Berkeley.

cratic Action, the college affiliate of ADA, an organization representing primarily the left wing of the Democratic party.

But under Haber and Hayden these liberal characteristics soon began to be jettisoned. The beginning of the drift to the left came in mid-1962. In June SDS met for its annual convention at the United Auto Workers summer camp in Port Huron, Michigan, and adopted a lengthy declaration of principles that helped shape the New Left for the next five years. The group of fifty-nine that assembled at the FDR Labor Camp was a heterogeneous one. Besides SDS members it included representatives from SNCC, NSA, the Young People's Socialist League, the Student Christian Movement, and the Young Democrats. Virtually all were in college or were recent graduates. The adopted manifesto, which was written by Tom Hayden and polished by many hands, attempted to reconcile the wide range of views represented at the convention and within SDS. The document rambled on for over sixty pages and managed to touch virtually every reformist–liberal base. Yet the Port Huron Statement was a landmark that succeeded in setting apart the phenomenon of the emerging student left and distinguishing it from the left of the past.

At the outset the statement identified the signers as "people of this generation, bred in at least modest comfort, housed now in universities, looking uncomfortably on the world we inherit." In 1962 the world was not what it had been in their childhood, the students declared. Racism, the Cold War, the threat of nuclear holocaust, and poverty in the midst of plenty had tarnished their "image of American virtue."

Unfortunately, the delegates admitted, they were a minority. Most Americans regarded "the temporary equilibriums of our society and world as eternally functional parts," so that there seemed "no viable alternatives to the present." Indeed, Americans were afraid of change. Even though life was empty for many of them, they were "fearful of the thought that at any moment things might be thrust out of control." Material prosperity seemed enough without further tampering. The reason for this combination of fear and indifference was not, however, the objective virtues of existing society, but rather the fact that men were manipulated. Men did not control their fate any longer. It was controlled for them by powerful others while they remained impotent and apathetic.

This preamble spoke in the authentic tones of the emerging New Left. Hayden and his associates were literate young intellectu-

als, who had read Mills, Camus, William A. Williams, and the early
Marx. Hayden in fact had written a paper on Mills at Michigan.
But having established the dilemma of an advanced capitalist society by borrowing from the masters, these young intellectuals went
on to propose a theoretical solution of their own. "We would replace
power rooted in possession, privilege or circumstances," the statement continued, "by power . . . rooted in love, reflectiveness, reason
and creativity. As a social system we seek the establishment of a
democracy of individual participation . . . ." This participatory
democracy would allow people to join in making the political and
economic decisions that affected their lives. Men and women would
have access to knowledge and power enabling them to control their
environment both in the civic and the economic realms. Work in
particular would be made more satisfying by allowing those who
performed it to help determine its course and its characteristics.

This formulation—participatory democracy—was not an entirely original concept. Its anti-authoritarianism and individualistic
quality echoed both the American Jeffersonian tradition and classic
anarchism. One quality that the New Left would share with both
old-fashioned libertarians and adherents of the Anarchist Black International was its distaste for institutions and bureaucracies. This
distaste even extended to the structures of the New Left itself.
Throughout its brief but dramatic history, SDS would be plagued
by strong misgivings over delegating power within the organization
to any individual or secretariat and would reduce its efficiency and
effectiveness as a result. At the same time the emphasis on individualism would create an unusual alliance between the New Left and a
group of extreme individualistic conservatives whose intellectual
spokesman was the economic historian Murray Rothbart.

Whatever curious or unfortunate results participatory democracy might produce, it was a central defining characteristic of the
New Left, setting it apart from the bureaucratic Old Left both
theoretically and pragmatically. From the outset the student New
Left sought to avoid the idea of a "vanguard party" that would lead
and direct the revolution. The role that the young radicals would
actually play in the changes they wanted would be a matter of
extended and inconclusive debate, but it was clear that they did not
wish to repeat the mistakes of either Lenin or the American Communists. In the Soviet Union, student dissenters believed, faith in a
small disciplined party had led to an authoritarian regime marked

by brutal repression of dissent. In this country it had led to a sectarian, quasi-religious party line that was imposed by the party on its members. In both instances the end result had cut the revolutionary movement off from the people and resulted in a perversion of noble goals.

The remainder of the Port Huron Statement included a catalog of the failings of the United States and a program for change. Universities were isolated and their students were apathetic; the two major parties were too close on most issues, and the public was deprived of a real choice; foreign policy was determined by a militant and undiscriminating anticommunism, and the military–industrial complex was often the governing voice; poverty and inequality continued to exist, even though the means for ending them were becoming increasingly available, and millions suffered unnecessarily from their effects.

This indictment was neither novel nor extreme. The program proposed was even more conventional and moderate. To rectify these evils, the public sector should be greatly enlarged; the country should give social issues priority over private ones; Congress should approve public housing legislation and enlarge health insurance programs; the United States should agree to disarm unilaterally and disengage internationally; and the Dixiecrats, the Southern conservatives, should be expelled from the Democratic party.

If none of these suggestions were particularly radical, neither were the agencies that were to carry them out. Organized labor was attacked for its inertia, but its role in bringing about change was still judged as central. Student efforts to improve the quality of life in universities, were important but students could not effect major reforms themselves. They needed allies "in labor, civil rights, and other liberal forces outside the campus." Liberals and socialists, both, would be needed to help change the country, the first because they were relevant, the second because they possessed a "sense of thoroughgoing reform."

All told, the Port Huron Statement took the student dissenters only a short step beyond the New Deal–Fair Deal–New Frontier tradition of Roosevelt, Truman, and Kennedy.[4]

Despite the heterogeneity of the delegates who toiled at Port

[4] [Tom Hayden], *The Port Huron Statement* (New York: SDS, 1962), *passim.*

Huron, the only part of this manifesto that caused disagreements and trouble was the foreign policy section. Representatives of the old socialist groups, especially the delegates from the Young People's Socialist League (YPSL) and Michael Harrington of the parent League for Industrial Democracy, believed the document failed to condemn the Soviet Union explicitly enough for its mistakes and failings. The statement admittedly was anti-Stalinist in general purport, but both Harrington and the YPSL people still remembered the enthrallment of the Old Left with Soviet policy and feared that the young leftists had not learned sufficiently the lessons of the past. This political naïveté was underscored by the convention's vote, despite a specific Communist exclusion rule in the SDS constitution, to give visitor status to a representative of a youth auxiliary of the Communist party.

This underdeveloped sense of the Stalinist danger now got SDS in trouble with the parent League. Following the convention LID suspended both Haber and Hayden and attempted to reorganize SDS along more aggressively anti-Communist principles. However, under the strong urging of the socialist elder statesman Norman Thomas, and of Harold Taylor, president of Sarah Lawrence College, the League executive committee soon relented. In a few weeks SDS was reinstated as a subsidized affiliate of LID.

SDS intended the Port Huron Statement to define the emerging student left, and encouraged its wide circulation on college campuses and among student leaders. In the next two years SDS distributed some twenty thousand mimeographed copies, and in 1964 printed an additional twenty thousand bound as a pamphlet.

Yet despite the favorable publicity it brought, the statement did little to spur SDS growth. During the 1962–1963 school year the University of Michigan chapter remained the strongest one, though membership in the New York and Boston areas also expanded a bit. Whatever its ambitions, SDS had not yet become the focus of the burgeoning new student left.

In the year following the Port Huron convention, SDS leaders labored to make the organization the center of the Movement. They had to do so on a tiny budget, which reflected SDS's still modest membership list, and with a small, overworked staff consisting of Jim Monsonis, national secretary; Don McKelvey, assistant national secretary; and Steve Max, field secretary. Amid the clutter and noise of a small office on Manhattan's grubby East 19th Street, donated to SDS by the League, these young men worked long hours, answering letters and telephones, arranging meetings, and fitfully getting out the new *SDS Bulletin.*

During the 1962–1963 school year SDS was still too feeble to carry out any sort of vigorous program, and members had to be content with vague rhetoric about the need for radical change. One line of attack that seemed promising for a while was university reform, then just beginning to emerge as an issue among college students and faculty. At two conferences in the Boston area, SDS members heard Paul Potter, Tom Hayden, Paul Goodman, and Herbert Marcuse attack universities for complicity in the larger evils of American society and demand that they reform themselves. This interest in university reform might have become more than talk, but as yet SDS was neither intellectually nor psychologically ready to take on the educational establishment. The colleges still appeared to be benevolent havens in a harsh world and still seemed worthy of preservation and respect. The conferences accordingly led to no immediate results. Inaction, however, was not congenial to SDS leaders, nor was it likely to raise SDS from the status of a debating society. Faced with the prospect of coming to an obvious dead end, the members of SDS began to stir themselves in 1963 to implement SDS's professed goal of improving the lot of Americans.

Two groups seemed ripe for the attention of radical students: Northern working-class whites, and blacks, both Northern and Southern. SDS continued to be concerned with the civil rights struggle, but it was already apparent that blacks generally, and SNCC in particular, would carry most of the fight for racial equality. In this area whites could probably help most—or so SNCC leaders said —if they worked with their own people to alert them to the dangers and the penalties of racism.

There was a serious ambiguity in this scheme, however. The white working class clearly was not revolutionary. The Port Huron Statement recognized this fact, and according to the teachings of C. Wright Mills, it was doubtful that the working class could ever be made to initiate drastic change in industrial society. Yet they were oppressed, if only covertly. Besides, what other group was large enough, and potentially powerful enough, to move mass society? Surely it was worth trying to see if the students could stir the inert mass of the white poor to action against the oppressive system. Concerned that they would remain little more than a small discussion group, and anxious to emulate SNCC in an activist approach to problems, SDS leaders put aside their own professed theory and turned to organizing efforts in the white Northern slums. This program would be loosely coordinated with the work of SNCC as an "interracial movement of the poor."

Aside from strategic considerations, there was also, as was usual with SDS, an immediate intellectual rationale for this new approach. The dangers of recession and worsening economic climate were much in the air in 1963. Early in the year Michael Harrington's seminal book *The Other America*, with its revelation of continuing poverty in the United States, was published. Also much discussed in 1963 was the volume *The Triple Revolution*, written by a mixed group of younger and older radicals and liberals, including A. J. Muste, H. Stuart Hughes, Linus Pauling, Gunnar Myrdal, Tom Hayden, and Todd Gitlin. This book warned of the grave dangers to come if America failed to take into account the "triple revolution" of the day—Third World unrest, the Negro revolt, and the accelerating cybernetic, or automation, revolution. Without extensive social planning and massive government support, the writers declared, this last revolution would bring severe technological unemployment and depression as computers inevitably replaced men. At the 1963 SDS convention Richard Flacks' paper *America and the New Era* made the point that the new industrial technology, combined with the tremendous increase in the labor force, threatened to raise unemployment rates and worsen the plight of the poor in America.

The supposed dangers of recession strengthened SDS's decision to organize in the slums. The outcome was the formation of the Economic Research and Action Project (ERAP) in the summer of 1963, ostensibly to take advantage of a $7,500 grant that the United Automobile Workers gave to SDS for a campaign to educate students in economic matters. Other money soon came in from liberal academics such as David Reisman and Harold Taylor and from A. J. Muste and the radical journalist I. F. Stone.

In December Rennie Davis, a former Oberlin student, was placed in charge of ERAP, and the following summer ten ERAP projects were launched. These ranged from one in the Boston area to commission unemployed scientists and engineers to plan for demobilization and disarmament, to one in Hazard, Kentucky, to provide legal support to coal miners charged with industrial sabotage. More typical, however, were the operations in eight Northern and Border State cities to mobilize white wage earners around the issues of job security, better housing, and racial solidarity and to provide them with some means for expressing community grievances.

The ERAP personnel consisted of a small cadre of SDS leaders and a larger group of socially conscious college student volunteers. These, mostly white, were fired with the desire to do something constructive to improve society and in their mood resembled the Russian student *Narodniks*, who left the universities in the 1870s to bring enlightenment to the peasants in the countryside—or, perhaps, the middle-class young men and women who went to the slum settlement houses early in the century to uplift the immigrant poor. Though the purpose of ERAP was to work with white people primarily, a number of these projects, especially those in Philadelphia, Newark, and Baltimore, through inadvertence came to be located largely in black ghettos.

The actual work done by the volunteers varied from project to project. In Chicago the ERAP endeavor, called JOIN (Jobs and Income Now), focused on getting jobs for unemployed workers and convincing the employed that under the existing economic system their jobs were in jeopardy. ERAP volunteers set up local committees in North Side neighborhoods, established a storefront office, and handed out leaflets to workers lined up before unemployment insurance offices. In Cleveland ERAP workers took up residence in a decrepit frame house in a poor white neighborhood and mingled with the local people, gathering information about community problems. Armed with this data, they then encouraged various community groups to organize and put pressure for reform on the appropriate public agencies. In Baltimore ERAP students helped poor people fill out welfare forms. In Newark, ERAP volunteers worked mostly in the black ghetto helping the community in a variety of projects for local betterment, many of them concerned with improved housing.

A problem the students had in all of these activities was how to avoid dominating and manipulating the people they were trying to help. As the radical journalist Andrew Kopkind noted in his report on ERAP, "the temptation to direct the course of the movement [of the poor in ERAP projects] is strong, and the SDS workers have all they can do to stay in the background." [5] The ERAP workers tried to get the community people to take the initiative whenever possible, but it is obvious that much of what took place was decidedly affected by the students' own perceptions and preferences.

Another difficulty was the improving economy. The predictions of a serious business downturn proved false. Rather than a slump, the country was experiencing a full-blown boom by mid-1964, brought on by the conservative Keynesian fiscal policies of the Kennedy–Johnson administrations. Instead of a growing army of receptive, jobless men, the ERAP workers encountered the political indifference of the newly reemployed. As Lee Webb, a JOIN leader, later remarked, "just as we got to Chicago, lines at the unemployment compensation center started to get shorter." [6] It would not be the last time that the capitalist economy's surprising performance would catch SDS and the New Left unaware.

Though ERAP continued for about a year longer, a number of the 1964 projects were abandoned as the summer ended and the volunteers returned to the campuses. Here was one of the serious problems of the New Left as a whole: how could a movement that relied so heavily on student effort retain its continuity in the face of the uncertainties of student character and the pressures of student life? There was, of course, the natural impatience of youth. Students expected immediate answers and immediate results; disillusionment with people, institutions, or tactics followed hard on frustration. Also, the school year limited student commitment. Community projects could only last from June to September. So long as a young activist remained a student, he could only be a summer soldier in the slums and ghettos. When the campuses became the centers of student activism, the corollary was that revolutions could last only from September to June and, indeed, because of the interruption of the Christmas holidays in December, they tended to be concentrated in the spring.

[5] Andrew Kopkind, "Of, By and For the Poor," *New Republic*, June 19, 1965.

[6] Quoted in Sale, *op. cit.*, p. 134.

These difficulties were not obvious in 1964–1965, however, and despite the short life of most ERAP projects, some SDS leaders considered the experiment encouraging. Soon after the first summer, Todd Gitlin wrote that "in the stifling American context," it was "no mean achievement to have threatened the thesis . . . that the poor are too disorganized to come together in their own interests." [7]

Gitlin's positive reaction was not shared by all his colleagues, and as time passed, it became clearer that it was immensely difficult to mobilize the poor either to help themselves or, in the case of whites, to recognize the penalties of racism. Many student dissenters also learned what a great social and cultural gulf separated them from blue-collar workers. C. Wright Mills' warning notwithstanding, they had, they saw, sentimentalized the working class and exaggerated its self-awareness. As for making the Establishment more responsive to social needs, little had been accomplished. Neither organized labor nor the power structure had taken the students seriously, and many ERAP workers came away convinced that the system was "totally inflexible and unresponsive to demands from below . . . ." [8]

Yet the ERAP venture was undoubtedly important in the evolution of the New Left. It stimulated SDS's growth and influenced its future shape. Many of those who came from the campuses to the slums returned to school confirmed members of SDS. By mid-1965 there were seventy-five SDS chapters on college campuses with some two thousand members, a sharp increase over the year before. Even the failures of ERAP had useful consequences. The projects were an education for the participants. Naïve students, straight from their government and sociology classes, ran head on into the realities of life as led by the urban poor. If some of them came away discouraged, others became more resolute. For the optimists ERAP had the same awakening and radicalizing effect as Freedom Summer had for those who went to Mississippi in 1964. As Paul Potter, SDS president in 1965 and an ERAP worker in Cleveland, noted, the experience had "created for us all a greater sense of the reality of America . . . [and] provided a tool with which to cut through the

[7] Mimeographed speech by Todd Gitlin, "On Organizing the Poor in America," SDS File, Social Protest Project, Bancroft Library, University of California, Berkeley, p. 5.

[8] Richard Rothstein, "ERAP: Evolution of the Organizers," *Radical America*, March–April, 1968, p. 12.

shrouds of sophistry that allowed people to rationalize their dehumanization and that of others." [9]

It was an irony of ERAP that it served in many cases to redirect student attention to the academic environment. The students returning from America's urban plague spots no longer saw their campuses as safe and uncontaminated refuges. Rather, the universities now seemed to have increasingly become disguised and evasive versions of the larger world of powerlessness and oppression.

As the 1964–1965 academic year began, nowhere was this mood so apparent as at the University of California at Berkeley. As we have noted, by the early 1960s the Berkeley student body was the most radicalized and politicized in the country. The Chessman case, HUAC and "Operation Abolition," the Woolworth and Kress sit-ins were only the most recent events that had worked their effects on the Berkeley campus. Equally important, a surprisingly large number of Berkeley students had been in Mississippi during Freedom Summer and had participated in other ways in the Southern civil rights movement.

These off-campus experiences created a small nucleus of student radicals who, having braved the wrath of Southern racists, would not easily be fazed by college administrators. Meanwhile at the university itself campus conditions were creating an explosive situation. When the fall term of 1964 opened, Berkeley had twenty-seven thousand students. These were a rather select group. The University of California accepted only the top 12 percent of the state's high school graduates, and the best of these went to Berkeley. Many highly capable out-of-staters were attracted to Berkeley's world-famous graduate departments, and many older students, some only loosely tied to the university community, made the neighborhood adjacent to the campus their home, vaguely plugging away at dissertations or haphazardly picking up course credit for advanced degrees. None of the other six campuses of the state university system, and few campuses anywhere in America, had such a large proportion of highly trained, earnest, and demanding young adults attending its classes, relying on its services, or living in its environs.

[9] Quoted in James P. O'Brien, "The Development of a New Left in the United States," doctoral dissertation, Department of History, University of Wisconsin, 1971, p. 294.

Berkeley was generally acknowledged to be neck and neck with Harvard in the race for the nation's most distinguished university. But if Berkeley promised much, it did not always deliver the educational goods. The campus was tremendously overcrowded. Required courses were packed with hundreds of students, filling every seat and spilling over into the aisles of lecture halls. At times so many students were registered for the American history survey that they had to be divided between two different rooms, with one group watching the lecturer on closed-circuit television. Even at the graduate level, the congestion created a sense of impersonality and isolation. It was hard for students to see busy faculty and to get to know one another.

The numbers created complex administrative problems. The university administration was hard-pressed to keep track of its hordes by conventional means and turned to computers for help. Each student carried a personally numbered IBM punch card to class at the beginning of the semester, and at the end he received his grade on an IBM print-out sheet. Today, perhaps, we take such automation of clerical details for granted; in 1964 it seemed a chilling symbol of the dehumanization of the campus.

Still another unattractive characteristic of the university was its might. The size of the university seemed to be matched by its power. One of the great myths of the 1960s was that the American system of higher education was the hub around which the whole society revolved. Universities supposedly were dynamos, charging and enlivening every aspect of American life. In government they supplied the ideas and personnel for the increasingly technocratic regimes. In business and economics they were the "knowledge industries" that made much of modern, postwar technology possible and provided the essential information and expertise for the great postwar spurt of economic growth. In day-to-day life they seemed to dominate the cultural environment, serving as the new patrons of painters, writers, musicians, and sculptors. Finally, with the growing mania for academic credentials, universities appeared to be the gatekeepers into the world of professional and business success, in effect allowing only those they approved to enter the middle class.

The universities themselves were happy to cultivate this image of might and indispensability. Clark Kerr, president of the University of California system, noted in his book *The Uses of the University* that American higher education had "become a prime instrument of national purpose" and was "at the center of the knowledge process," that fueled the national economy. Writing from the perspective of an old-fashioned liberal academic, Kerr was proud of the ways in which the university "served" the larger society, but to others the universities' self-confidence smacked of hubris.[10]

Students inevitably accepted the universities' evaluation of themselves. These were no fragile ivory towers of earnest and impractical scholars wanting only to add to man's knowledge and understanding. These were tough, bureaucratic, rich, privileged, and highly successful institutions closely connected, by their own admission, to the power structure of both the states and the nation. In their relations with their constituents, moreover, they behaved like the coercive state itself. During these years parietal rules tightly hedged about the lives of undergraduates. The university seemed to peer into almost every aspect of student life. Rules in the dorms were strict. Students, especially women, had to be in the dorm by a certain hour, and dorm residents could not have visitors of the opposite sex. They could not have liquor in their rooms, nor could they gamble. Smoking marijuana or taking any other sort of drug on campus was generally treated with immediate dismissal from the university if detected. If students got into trouble with town authorities, they would often be punished by university authorities. The theory behind these rules was that students were minors and the university must act *in loco parentis*.

Surprisingly, the regime at Berkeley was less permissive in some ways than that at many universities of equal caliber. The so-called Kerr Directives of October, 1959, placed rather tough limitations on student political activity. Under them, the student government was responsible to the campus chancellor's office and was forbidden to take stands on off-campus issues. Student organizations in general had to have a faculty adviser and could not advocate positions on issues that did not concern the campus.

Much of this illiberality can be explained by events in the immediate past. When Kerr became chancellor at Berkeley in 1952, his appointment represented the end of a McCarthyite period for the university. In 1949 the Regents, the University of California's highest governing body, had required all university employees to take a

[10] See Clark Kerr, *The Uses of the University* (Cambridge, Mass.: Harvard University Press, 1963), pp. 87–88.

loyalty oath. The faculty fight against the oath, which seemed to single out university people for special distrust, had been bitter, and a number of distinguished professors had resigned rather than compromise their principles. As chancellor, and then, beginning in 1959, as president of the whole seven-campus system, Kerr opened up the university to dissenters. The loyalty oath was dropped and various political organizations and speakers whose words were judged to be of educational value were allowed to use campus facilities. For these liberalizing changes the Kerr administration was awarded the Alexander Meiklejohn Prize in 1964 by the American Association of University Professors. Still, the state and the Regents were sensitive to the issue of radicalism and subversion, and when SLATE, the left student political party, began to agitate against compulsory ROTC in the fall of 1959, Kerr responded with his directives. Various student groups were quick to protest against these rules, and the Associated Students of the University of California (ASUC), the official Berkeley student association, conducted a survey that proved the Kerr Directives restricted student expression more than the equivalent rules at twenty other comparable campuses.

But the real failings of universities in general and of Berkeley in particular were not the only factors in the background of the Berkeley student revolt of 1964–1965. On campus a handful, but a talented and articulate handful, of radical student activists was anxious to test the direct-action techniques that had been tried in the civil rights movement and in such back-to-the-people movements as ERAP. Many of these students had recently cooperated with CORE in picketing Berkeley and Oakland stores and businesses that followed discriminatory hiring practices. The demonstrations had resulted in a number of arrests and some violence.

Students beginning classes in the fall of 1964 were greeted by a SLATE manifesto composed by Bradford Cleaveland, a former political science graduate student, calling for an undergraduate uprising against the university. Cleaveland detailed Berkeley's failings, emphasizing its goal of turning out organization men unaware of the triple revolution of black liberation, automation, and Third World insurgency, and its close involvement with the Department of Defense and the warfare state. "I am no longer interested in cajoling you, arguing with you, or describing to you something you already know . . ." Cleaveland proclaimed.

I will entreat you to furiously throw your comforting feelings of duty
and responsibility for this institution to the winds and act on your
situation. This institution . . . does not deserve a response of loyalty
and allegiance from you. There is only one proper response to Berkeley from undergraduates: that you *organize and split this campus
wide open!*
FROM THIS POINT ON, DO NOT MISUNDERSTAND ME. MY INTENTION IS
TO CONVINCE YOU THAT YOU DO NOTHING LESS THAN BEGIN AN OPEN,
FIERCE, AND THOROUGHGOING REBELLION ON THIS CAMPUS.

These goals, soon to become familiar to Americans, were to be
implemented by equally familiar tactics. The rebellion was to begin
with the students presenting an impossible list of demands to the
administration. The list would include elimination of course grades
and an end to the rigid unit course system; the cancellation of parietal rules in the dorms; an independent student voice in university
governance; a new undergraduate faculty to concentrate on teaching; new, more open courses; the firing of Clark Kerr and other
administrators; a reshuffling of the powers of the state Board of
Regents; and a committee to negotiate the demands with the university officials.[11]

Given the time and place, these demands were totally unrealistic, and they do not represent serious, practical goals. Cleaveland's
intention was to provoke an uprising, not improve the immediate
educational climate at Berkeley. I think it would be a mistake to
detect in this manifesto the outlines of a sinister plot to disrupt
the campus. Much of what took place during the Berkeley Free
Speech Movement (FSM) was a spontaneous and sincere response
to what the students viewed as provoking and arbitrary moves by
the university administration. Yet the disruption of campus peace
at Berkeley also owed much to concerns not strictly academic, with
an important minority of FSM leaders viewing the disruption as a
means for achieving larger revolutionary ends. It is significant that
as the student uprising gathered momentum, demands such as
Cleaveland's began increasingly to become part of the rhetoric of
the insurgent leadership.

The actual spark that ignited the Berkeley campus was the
question of whether student political activities and recruiting for
off-campus issues should be permitted on a strip of university prop-

[11] *Daily Californian,* September 15, 1964.

erty along Bancroft Avenue where it meets Telegraph. This small area had been the marshaling yard for student activists for many months without serious protest from university authorities. Most recently the Ad Hoc Committee to End Discrimination had used it to conduct noon meetings where Michael Myerson announced plans to picket the *Oakland Tribune* for its racist labor practices. On September 15, 1964, in a memo dated two days before, Dean of Students Katherine Towle notified the heads of all student organizations that beginning the following week political tables for distributing political literature, or for holding rallies, could no longer be placed on the Bancroft-Telegraph strip if these activities involved off-campus issues.

The reason for the university's action seems relatively clear. The charge that former Senator William Knowland, the conservative editor of the *Tribune,* had placed pressure on university officials may not be literally true. The university admitted, however, that it was concerned with the great expansion of the students' political activities, an expansion that seemed likely to continue as the election year campaign gained momentum. The students' increasingly more aggressive activities had upset many groups in the community and promised to provoke them still more as the weeks passed. In all likelihood, university officials feared the political consequences of student actions that seemed extreme to them, and believed they were well within their rights to restrict the students' activities under the Kerr Directives. Here was an example of how men and women in their middle years, who were used to wielding authority over their "charges," had lost touch with the drastically altered feelings of many university students about political and racial issues. Clark Kerr and his subordinates believed themselves to be liberal men and women. Kerr himself had been a member of the League for Industrial Democracy. But their liberalism was the timid and beleaguered variety of the 1950s, and they could not understand the mood of student leaders raised on Mills and tempered by the experiences of Freedom Summer and the civil rights movement.

The reaction of student leaders was swift. Many of them were sincerely outraged by the new regulations, which they considered an authoritarian denial of the First Amendment right of free speech. Others, such as Michael Rossman, were primarily afraid the new ruling would seriously damage the civil rights movement in the Bay Area by preventing campus groups from helping SNCC and CORE.

Some student activists believed the new restrictions provided an issue that could be used to dramatize larger off-campus issues of racism, powerlessness, and revolution. Finally, some students were probably bent on nothing more than mischief or merely bored with school and looking for diversion.

On September 17 representatives of some eighteen student groups met with Dean Towle to ask her to modify the previous directives. The dean refused, and the following day the organizations submitted a petition once more asking for the right to place student-manned tables along Bancroft for distributing literature advocating various political causes. At a meeting on September 20 the groups decided to picket, conduct vigils, and employ civil disobedience if the university continued to sit tight. They agreed, however, to wait until after a meeting scheduled for the following morning with Dean Towle.

Dean Towle proved to be accommodating up to a point. Students could use the Bancroft-Telegraph strip to advocate causes, but they could not raise money for those causes; nor was it "permissible . . . to urge a specific vote, call for direct social or political action, or to seek to recruit individuals for such action." [12]

That night about a hundred students held a vigil on the steps of Sproul Hall, the administration building just within the campus gates near Bancroft Avenue. The next day the official student government at Berkeley, the Senate of the Associated Students of the University of California, voted to support a petition to the Regents to alter the rules so that soliciting, advocacy, and recruiting would be permitted on the free speech strip. A day later Edward Strong, chancellor of the Berkeley campus, reiterated Dean Towle's position, and he was soon seconded by President Kerr.

The student groups, including radical, liberal, and even conservative organizations, now threatened to picket and march to protest the administration's adamant refusal to permit free speech. Chancellor Strong responded by retreating—a bit. The university would not interfere in any way with the students' right to distribute political material either on the disputed strip or on the other "Hyde Park" areas designated on the campus. The students could continue

[12] Quoted in Seymour Martin Lipset and Sheldon S. Wolin (eds.), *The Berkeley Student Revolt: Facts and Interpretations* (New York: Doubleday, 1965), p. 104.

to use the tables to propagandize for any cause, but they could not use them to recruit for off-campus political actions or to raise money for these actions. Only organizations that pledged to abide by this rule would be authorized to set up such tables.

The students took this concession as a sign of their power and decided to press on. One student spokesman declared, "We won't stop now until we've made the entire campus a bastion of free speech." To many students, it now seemed that the administration's previous position—that its hands were tied by the Regents' regulations—had been proved patently false. Strong, Kerr, and the others could obviously interpret the Regents' regulations as they pleased, and there seemed no point in stopping at half a loaf.

The next few weeks saw the most profound and massive upheaval in the history of any American university campus. On September 29 students set up tables without authorization. The dean of men, Arleigh Williams, and campus police informed the students that they were engaging in unauthorized activities and that the university would remove the tables. The next day, when the tables remained where they were, university officials took down the names of five students and told them to appear before Dean Williams at Sproul Hall for disciplinary action that afternoon at 3:00.

Instead of five students, five hundred gathered and marched into Sproul Hall led by Mario Savio, Arthur Goldberg, and Sandor Fuchs. Savio presented a petition signed by more than five hundred students, declaring that they were equally guilty of manning unauthorized tables and demanding that they be punished along with the summoned five. At four o'clock the dean requested that the original accused five, plus the three leaders of the march, appear before him. No one appeared. At midnight, with the building still occupied by the protesters, Chancellor Strong announced that all eight students would be suspended.

Later that night the students voted to leave Sproul voluntarily, but not before agreeing to fight the disciplinary action against the eight students or against any student, and pledging to continue the free speech fight until it was won. On October 1 campus police arrested a former student, Jack Weinberg, for soliciting funds for CORE on campus. They removed him to a police car only to find themselves surrounded by a crowd of angry young men and women shouting for his release. For the next thirty hours, as the crowd swelled into the thousands, the police and Weinberg remained trapped in the car while excitement grew to a crescendo all over the campus, and all over the state. During this period statements and counterstatements flew back and forth from the Free Speech leaders, university officials, and Governor Edmund Brown, either supporting or condemning the demonstrators. By this time there had been some scuffling in Sproul Hall between campus police and student intruders.

Shortly before university officials prepared to authorize city, county, and state police to move in to free the trapped campus police car, a negotiated settlement was arranged. The university agreed not to press charges against Weinberg; it agreed to appoint a combined student–faculty–administration committee to look into the question of campus political activity; it agreed to submit the question of the eight student suspensions to a faculty committee; and it agreed to look into the possibility of deeding the Bancroft-Telegraph strip either to the City of Berkeley or to the ASUC. In return, the students agreed to stop the illegal protest against the university regulations. With this compromise the demonstrators disbanded, and the battered police car was released.

In the next few weeks the university attempted to implement the hastily written agreement, but nothing seemed to go right. Charges against Weinberg were indeed dropped, but the local district attorney hinted that he would prosecute him anyway. There was no standing faculty committee to handle student discipline; under university rules the only authorized faculty committee charged with student discipline was one appointed wholly by the administration. Finally, in making up the student–faculty–administration committee to consider the issue of campus political activities, the administration insisted on appointing ten out of the twelve members. A part of this anomalous result was accidental; but some of it was in fact an attempt by the administration to retain control of student activities, and the Free Speech Movement leaders were convinced that the impasse represented bad faith on the part of the administration.

On October 16 Kerr yielded several points. He agreed to expand the joint student–faculty–administration committee from twelve to eighteen with more student members than originally assigned. He also agreed to have the eight suspended students examined before an ad hoc committee of faculty selected by the faculty itself.

This proved to be insufficient. Dissatisfied with the way the joint committee's deliberations on student political activity were going, FSM leaders announced on November 9 that they would lift their "self-imposed moratorium" on demonstrations. The administration responded by disbanding the combined committee. The next day students set up political tables once more. For the first time graduate students, hitherto relatively inactive, joined FSM as a group. Campus police took the names of seventy-five table-manning participants.

On November 17 the ad hoc faculty discipline committee made its report, recommending that six of the suspended students be reinstated with the record of their suspension expunged. In the case of Mario Savio and Arthur Goldberg, however, a suspension of six weeks would be noted on official records. FSM responded with a petition to the Regents demanding that the courts alone be allowed to order the suspension of students accused of violating campus rules. The Regents intervened to resolve the disagreement by ordering all eight students reinstated but with their earlier suspension noted on their records. In addition, Savio and Goldberg would be placed on probation for the rest of the semester. Savio, Arthur Goldberg, Jackie Goldberg, and Brian Tumen were to be summoned before the Regents to answer charges of violence against the police during the October demonstrations.

FSM called the Regents' action a case of "shocking insensitivity." In a statement expressing an increasingly popular student radical view, it declared that the university consisted solely of faculty and students, and administrators and Regents were there only to serve them. When, as in this case, administrators and Regents became a hindrance to the students and faculty, they should be pushed aside. The Regents had cut off all channels of communication, and FSM would take appropriate action to secure students' rights.

On December 2 several thousand students gathered for a noon rally at Sproul Plaza. Savio, a veteran of Freedom Summer, addressed them, delivering a denunciation of the great university machine that resounded with all the earnest and impassioned rhetoric of the civil rights movement. "There's a time," he announced,

> when the operation of the machine becomes so odious, makes you so sick at heart, that you can't take part, you can't even tacitly take part. And you've got to put your bodies upon the gears, and upon

the wheels, upon the levers, upon all the apparatus, and you've got
to make it stop. And you've got to indicate to the people that run it,
the people who own it, that unless you're free, the machine will be
prevented from working at all.[13]

Soon after, about a thousand students marched into Sproul
Hall and pledged to stay until the administration capitulated or
they were arrested. The students occupied the first four floors of
the building, being careful not to obstruct hallways or office entrances. With them was Joan Baez, the folk singer, who had driven
up from Carmel and who led them in singing the civil rights hymn
"We Shall Overcome," as they filed into the building.

At 6:45 that evening university police told the students that
if they did not vacate the building in fifteen minutes, they would
be arrested. At 7:00 the police locked the doors, allowing people
to leave if they wished to, but permitting no one to enter. Hours
then passed without any police action, and the students relaxed by
singing, folk dancing, and watching a Charlie Chaplin film on the
second floor. By 1:00 A.M. hallway lights had been turned off, and
most students had bedded down for the night.

But the authorities had decided to take direct action. At 3:45
A.M. Governor Brown in Sacramento announced that he had ordered
the police to move in. Over six hundred police by now had gathered
around Sproul Hall. Soon after Brown's announcement they entered
the building, and starting at the top, moved down floor by floor,
arresting students and taking them off to waiting buses and police
vans to be booked. Students were given the choice of leaving or
being arrested. Those who refused to leave were given the option
of going on their own steam or being dragged. FSM later claimed
that the police had clubbed, kicked, and generally mistreated many
students. The police insisted that little or no violence had taken
place. In any case 590 students and over 200 nonstudents, university employees and others, were arrested. All were released on a
small bail by December 4.

The "bust" at Sproul created tremendous excitement both on
campus and throughout the state. FSM immediately called for a
strike of students to stop classes and shut down all university activities. The Berkeley faculty hurriedly met on the third, while the

13 Quoted in Hal Draper, *Berkeley: The New Student Revolt* (New York:
Grove Press, 1965), p. 98.

police were still emptying the building, and passed resolutions condemning the use of the police on the campus. It also endorsed liberalized rules regarding student political activity both on- and off-campus.

Elsewhere, however, the response to the students was not as favorable. The California Alumni Council, executive body of the University Alumni Association, condemned their conduct and praised Governor Brown for ordering the police to break up the sit-in. Many of the state's newspapers also attacked the students for their unlawful tactics. Waiting in the wings, anxious to take action, was the rather conservative state legislature, which held the all-important university purse strings.

Meanwhile a special ad hoc group of Berkeley department chairmen had met and proposed a set of resolutions to end the crisis. The chairmen condemned the sit-in tactics and asked for an end to the student strike. At the same time they declared that the university should adopt more liberal rules on student political activity pending a report on the subject by the faculty Senate Committee on Academic Freedom, and should not add to the punishment the local courts might mete out to the arrested students for the sit-in at Sproul. These proposals were publicly accepted by President Kerr at an immense open air meeting at the Greek Theater on December 7. An hour later at Sproul Plaza an informal assemblage of some ten thousand students and spectators shouted down the proposals.

On December 8 the Academic Senate, the official voice of the full-time Berkeley faculty, met to consider what to do. The meeting of December 3 had been an informal, emergency gathering. This new assembly would speak officially for the Berkeley professors. The night before, FSM leaders, wishing to avoid antagonizing the faculty on the eve of the gathering, agreed to call off the strike. At 3:10 P.M. over a thousand faculty members, the largest number ever known to attend a Senate meeting, gathered at Wheeler Hall to express their views on the events of the last few days. Following a tense and dramatic discussion that forced many professors to confront their attitudes toward teaching and students, the faculty once more endorsed the FSM. The resolution, adopted by a vote of 824 to 115, asked that the university not discipline anyone for anything done before December 8, that political activity on campus be regulated only to prevent interference with normal functions

of the university, that neither free speech nor political advocacy be
restricted by the university, and that future disciplinary measures
relating to political activity be determined by a committee of the
Academic Senate. By a vote of 737 to 284 the faculty defeated
Professor Lewis Feuer's conservative amendment that would have
modified the clause concerning freedom to speak and advocate to
read: "provided that it is directed to no immediate act of force or
violence. . . ."

As the faculty debated, some three thousand students and observers waited outside Wheeler listening to the proceedings over
a public address system. When Feuer's amendment was voted down,
a great cheer went up. Final passage of the whole set of pro-FSM
resolutions produced wild enthusiasm among the spectators. When
the weary faculty filed out of the hall, they were greeted by ap-
plause and shouts of approval.

Seemingly Jack Weinberg's slogan "Don't trust anyone over
thirty," [14] coined in the heat of the past weeks, had been refuted.
The faculty had endorsed the crucial point of the Free Speech
Movement—freedom to talk and advocate—and FSM leaders were
jubilant. FSM issued a statement soon after the Senate's action
entitled "Happiness Is an Academic Senate Meeting." Mario Savio,
assuming the faculty might be attacked by the Regents for their
action, declared that "the FSM will now be a defense committee
for eight hundred patriots." FSM members were further overjoyed
when SLATE candidates supporting FSM won all seven of the
ASUC positions that were being contested in the latest student
government election.

The jubilation was unrealistic. The faculty could propose, but
only the Regents and the administration could dispose. Moreover,
the faculty's interests and wishes could not be counted on to coin-
cide with the students' in every case. This fact was recognized by
FSM leader Martin Roysher when, at a rally soon after the Academic Senate meeting, he noted that "there should be no paternal
subordinating relationship between students and the faculty or the
administration." [15]

On December 17 the Regents met at UCLA with a committee

[14] Actually Weinberg had said, "We have a saying in the movement that
you can't trust anybody over thirty."
[15] Lipset and Wolin, *op. cit.*, p. 190.

of the Berkeley Academic Senate to hear formally the proposals that the Senate voted on at the Wheeler Hall session. The following day the Board of Regents rejected the proposals. Instead it reasserted its "constitutional" authority over student discipline, agreed to appoint a committee to consult with all interested parties on the question of student political activities, and reiterated a November 20 Regents' resolution permitting students to plan lawful off-campus social or political action, with the Regents retaining the right to regulate such activities on campus.

Despite attempts by the Berkeley Academic Senate to convince students that the Regents had moved a long way toward accepting a softer attitude toward student political activity, FSM was disappointed. Savio and other FSM leaders denounced the Regents' action, but decided to do nothing until after the imminent Christmas vacation.

On January 2, just as the students began to stream back to classes, the Regents announced the appointment of Professor Martin Meyerson, dean of the College of Environmental Design, as acting chancellor at Berkeley to replace Strong. Meyerson immediately issued rules regarding student rallies and political speakers that represented a considerable relaxation of previous restrictions. On January 4 FSM held its first legal rally on the steps of Sproul Hall. Also for the first time, legal tables were set up nearby to solicit for actions off-campus and to raise money for political and social causes.

The Free Speech Movement was not over at Berkeley. Still unresolved were such thorny issues as the hundreds of students charged with trespassing and obstruction as a result of the December Sproul Hall sit-in. It would be months before their cases were settled. Also remaining were permanent rules regarding on-campus student advocacy of off-campus issues.

But with Meyerson's rules in effect, FSM had won most of its major points, and during the next few weeks, despite Savio's pleas to students to continue their support, it rapidly melted away. Its only remaining function, FSM leaders admitted, was to be a watchdog of the rights of the hundreds of arrested students who as yet had not been tried and sentenced.

As a coherent movement, FSM was virtually over. It had never won a clear majority of the student body wholeheartedly to its side, and many of those who supported it in a general way did so without deep commitment to its principles. As with most insurgent movements, there were many who marched, distributed leaflets, and sat-in for FSM for the excitement or the communal sense of shared dangers. Participants in FSM and other student movements remarked on how they had felt like part of a community for the first time, a feeling so different from the frightening anonymity of normal campus life. "What enlivened the Free Speech Movement," a Berkeley student later wrote,

> was the exhilaration of feeling that you were dealing directly with the things that affect your life, and with each other. You were for once free of the whole sticky cobweb that kept you apart from each other and from the roots of your existence, and you knew that you were alive and what your life was all about . . . . The F.S.M. was a swinging movement. The F.S.M., with its open mass meetings, its guitars and songs, its beards, and its long-haired chicks, made the aloofness and reserve of the administration . . . the formality of the coat and tie world, seem lifeless and dull in comparison.[16]

For whatever reason students were attracted to FSM, it still received its strongest support when the administration seemed most truculent and arbitrary. In the spring semester, when the movement's chief announced goal of ending the university's control of student political activity seemed almost attained, its support declined. Even if FSM had largely run its course, however, the Berkeley uprising was not entirely over. At this point a curious and interesting epilogue took place, an epilogue that reveals the ambiguous relationship between radical politics and cultural dissent that would characterize the New Left to its end.

Berkeley and the Bay Area was not only a refuge for political dissenters of all sizes and descriptions; it was also, we should remember, the incubator of the new bohemia first identified with the beats. In the North Beach area of San Francisco and on the level land to the west of the Berkeley campus, people who sought to break out of American middle class patterns had gathered in large numbers. Already, by the early 1960s a dropout culture of young people, romantically dedicated to finding spontaneity and joy and rejecting rules and conventions, had appeared. In Berkeley many

---

[16] Gerald Rosenfield, "Generational Revolt and the Free Speech Movement," *Liberation*, January, 1966, pp. 18–19.

of these people were loosely attached to the university, some as ex-students or part-time students, some as university employees, and some merely as hangers-on in the university community. Many of these marginal people had been active in the Free Speech Movement, though not officially, and many had been arrested at the December 2 police bust at Sproul Hall.

Generally the hippies, or counter culture people, as they would later be called, were an embarrassment to the FSM leaders. Aside from the fact that their presence gave FSM critics the opportunity to deny that the Free Speech Movement was genuinely representative of the Berkeley student body, their participation seemed to detract from the seriousness of FSM's cause.

Most of the FSM leaders were not members of the new counter culture. Yet, like most other young political dissenters, they shared much of the counter culture's underlying philosophy and some of its style. Beards, sandals, long hair, guitars, and folk singing were always much in evidence at FSM rallies and at Sproul, as Gerald Rosenfield noted. More important, FSM and the counter culture shared a passion for free expression, a contempt for the cultural values of the middle class, and a common disdain for the constituted authorities and established institutions. For the hippies, cultural dissent often spilled over into political insurgency. Writing as far back as 1960, Al Haber noted that in time of student activist irresolution and doubt, the campus beats often took the initiative in striking at the system.

In the Bay Area the merging of cultural and political dissent was more complete than elsewhere. In 1962 a group of young men and women, embodying in themselves a fusion of counter culture and political radicalism, began to publish *Root and Branch* in Berkeley. Distributed by City Lights Bookstore, the San Francisco firm that had first published the beat poets, *Root and Branch* featured poems by Lawrence Ferlinghetti as well as avant-garde artwork. This display of cultural dissent was combined with articles on C. Wright Mills, the emerging New Left, and the failings of the American economy. As the editors noted, it was symbolic of its purpose that the quarterly was produced on the same multilith machine that had seen "its best days several years ago on the SLATE battle lines." [17] *Root and Branch* editors included David

[17] *Root and Branch: A Radical Quarterly,* No. 1, Winter, 1962, p. 8.

Horowitz, Robert Scheer, and Robert Starobin, all of whom were to be active in FSM and in later radical politics or journalism.

Yet *Root and Branch* notwithstanding, even in Berkeley there was a tension between the counter culture people and the political radicals that had never been resolved. Now, abruptly, in the aftermath of the Free Speech Movement, political radicals found themselves confronted with a dilemma brought on by the sudden intrusion of the cultural deviance issue.

On March 3 a young nonstudent, John Thomson, appeared on campus and stationed himself on the steps of the student union. In his hands he held a small sign. It said FUCK. When a student asked him what part of speech he intended, Thomson added an exclamation mark. Soon after, Thomson was arrested by a campus police officer for "outraging the public decency."

From the perspective of the mid-1970s, what followed seems incredible, but we must remember how different public attitudes toward obscenity were a decade ago, and we must recall the badly frayed nerves of everybody at Berkeley in the wake of FSM. At a hasty FSM meeting called to deal with the new crisis, Arthur Goldberg, former SLATE chairman and FSM leader, declared his support not only of Thomson but also of the interesting activity he was advertising. The next day, following a rally on Sproul Hall steps, several students were arrested, one for reading aloud sections of D. H. Lawrence's erotic classic *Lady Chatterley's Lover*.

In the next few days chaos reigned at Berkeley. Most of the faculty, even those who had supported FSM, expressed disgust at the eruption of the "Filthy Speech Movement." Mark Schorer, chairman of the Berkeley English department who had written the introduction to the Grove Press edition of the Lawrence novel, denounced the advocates of the latest cause as childish. The controversy, he said, is in the "panty raid, booze, and sex division of protests." [18]

The student radicals were badly divided by the Filthy Speech incident. On March 10 FSM declared that it had not initiated the controversy and did not consider it a responsible challenge to authority. The next day, however, FSM leader Steve Weissman declared that Thomson and the other students had been made scape-

[18] *Daily Californian*, March 5, 1965.

goats. After the case had been brought before an ad hoc faculty discipline committee, Mario Savio expressed deep concern over whether the accused would be accorded due process protections. He, for one, did not know whether the obscenities were meant only for shock or were a form of legitimate social protest.

The new controversy badly rattled the administration. Whether under increased pressure from Regents' conservatives, as some said, or out of a desire to demonstrate his indispensability, or merely because the Filthy Speech incident seemed the last straw, Kerr, joined by Meyerson, suddenly resigned. A week later, under the urging of most of the faculty and the more liberal Regents, they just as suddenly withdrew their resignations.

The rest of the story of that fateful and dramatic academic year can be told quickly. FSM, still feebly alive, found itself too split over the Filthy Speech issue to act effectively. When Meyerson banned a local counter culture publication, *Spider*, from campus, FSM decided to do nothing. When Arthur Goldberg was expelled from the university and the students arrested for obscenity were suspended, FSM leaders protested to the Regents. The protest was ignored, and an FSM rally to consider another student strike fizzled. In late April Savio resigned from FSM, and on April 29 it was announced that FSM would be replaced by a Free Student Union that, unlike FSM, would be a permanent part of the Berkeley scene and would function much like a loose trade union to deal with student grievances and advance student interests.

In the remaining weeks of the semester, FSM protested against the disciplining of the students involved in the Filthy Speech protest and attacked as too restrictive the new Meyer Report, a document proposing a complete overhaul of the Regents' rules on student discipline. But although FSM talked, the year ended without FSM taking serious action to put its views into effect. With the beginning of the summer vacation, the Berkeley revolution was over. Berkeley would remain an enclave of incipient radicalism, as it still is today, but it would never again enjoy the center of the stage.

FSM was an important milestone in the New Left. Until this point universities had been considered havens for students, places from which they could sally forth to attack social injustices in the surrounding community. Though parietal rules were obnoxious and university administrations were arrogant, most student dissenters did not see the universities as the enemies of progress. The banner proclaiming university complicity in the warfare state, timidly raised by a few members of SDS in 1962–1963, had not yet made much of an impression on American students.[19]

FSM destroyed much of this student trust in the universities. Now it seemed that they were no better than the society that surrounded them. In fact, in the heat of controversy, they would often appear to be worse than the larger society, if only because they combined oppression and coercion with hypocrisy. Even as FSM raged across the Berkeley campus, student groups at other institutions began to look at the enemy in the administration hall and started to plan how to attack the most immediately accessible symbols of the bureaucratic authority that they believed afflicted the nation.

Even more important, FSM seemed to confirm dramatically the view that students were not merely the leaders of the oppressed, they were the oppressed themselves. Larry Spence, writing in *Studies on the Left*, in the winter of 1965, drew this lesson very explicitly.

> These events in Berkeley should be an impetus to American radicals to finally "kick the labor metaphysic" and drop the vulgar-Marxist belief (shared by administration liberals) that men must be hungry or unemployed or discriminated against to participate in radical political action. A survey of successful revolutions and radical action leads to the conclusion that men must be *conscious*, not hungry, to attempt the reconstruction of society. The Berkeley revolt has demonstrated that such a radical consciousness can be created by means of successful acts of social dislocation . . . .[20]

This conclusion had already been foreshadowed by Mills back in 1960 and by a few in SDS more explicitly two years later. As an insight, it had been rejected, however, in favor of the ERAP back-to-the-people program. Student dissenters had not yet gotten over

---

[19] Nor were the FSM people affected by the premature SDS position of 1962–1963. SDS was surprisingly weak at Berkeley and, considering the degree of Berkeley's radicalization in the ensuing years, would always remain so.

[20] Larry Spence, "Berkeley: What It Demonstrates," *Studies on the Left*, V, No. 1, Winter, 1965, pp. 66–67.

the idea that they were a privileged class that could serve only to create a revolution for others. They did not abruptly reconsider their views because of Berkeley. In fact for the remainder of the decade, the student left would vacillate between the poles of "revolution for others" and "revolution for ourselves," but FSM helped to tip the balance toward the policy of self-liberation.

CHAPTER

4

Liberals Become Radicals
1965-1968

I N RETROSPECT, we can see that the Berkeley experience provided a double lesson for the student left. The first was that universities, like other institutions, were coercive places with rules, bureaucracies, and arbitrary responses that could tolerate only a modest amount of dissent. By any New Left standard, then, college students were an oppressed class, and the campus was as valid a battleground for social justice as any urban slum or impoverished Third World countryside. The second lesson was that the campus was a potential nursery for radical dissent and a promising place for recruiting converts to radical activism. Here, in the guise of deans, trustees, and faculty, students would encounter in microcosm all the guile, cupidity, and manipulativeness of the larger society outside, and here they could learn how to confront and defeat these despicable forces.

Yet the true significance of Berkeley became apparent only rather slowly. Berkeley was not immediately followed by a major rash of campus upheavals. Instead, at first the student movement became increasingly oriented toward the question of the burgeoning Vietnam War, and until 1967 the campuses were neglected, except as staging areas for antiwar demonstrations.

The peace movement of the late 1950s had attracted a certain number of student activists. During this period student peace advocates had worked through the student affiliate of SANE and two student groups, the Student Peace Union (SPU), and TOCSIN, a peace group at Harvard. In these years the students had been concerned primarily with Soviet–American rivalry and the dangers of nuclear testing. In February, 1962, at the suggestion of TOCSIN's Todd Gitlin, the three student peace groups organized a march on Washington that brought five thousand young men and women to the capital to demand a nuclear test ban and an end to the Cold War. The students visited members of Congress, spoke to State Department officials, and picketed the White House. Although SPU contained a number of radicals, the planners of the Washington march were careful to avoid any display of anti-Americanism. To show their neutrality in the Cold War, a group of the marchers also picketed the Soviet embassy.

This demonstration was the high-water mark of the early student peace movement. Later in the year students worked for a number of "peace candidates" in Massachusetts, New York, and Chicago, but none of these came close to winning office. During the Cuban missile crisis, just before the 1962 Congressional elections, most students, like most Americans generally, supported Kennedy and endorsed his decision to force the Russians to remove their missiles from Cuba. On a few campuses rallies called to protest the President's ultimatum to the Russians were taken over by pro-Kennedy hecklers, who jeered and threw rocks and eggs at antiwar speakers. Much of the remaining steam went out of the student peace movement when the United States and the Soviet Union concluded a limited nuclear test ban treaty in the summer of 1963. The following year, after a rapid decline in membership, SPU disbanded.

Vietnam jolted the student peace movement into life once more. American involvement in Vietnam predated 1965, but most students took little notice of it. In 1964 two Marxist youth groups, the Trotskyite Young Socialist Alliance and a student offshoot of the Red Chinese-oriented Progressive Labor party, raised the cry against American involvement in Vietnam. Taking the name "May 2nd Movement" from the date of their demonstration, both groups, about a thousand in all, marched in New York City to protest the war.

SDS members had attended the meeting where the march was planned, but SDS took no part in the New York demonstration. Then, in the fall, through its Peace Research and Education Project, SDS began to give serious attention to the growing Vietnam involvement.

SDS saw the expanding Vietnam War as a dangerous new development in American foreign policy. For the first time the United States was openly showing its imperialist hand in the world. It was true that we had few if any direct investments in Vietnam, but Vietnam was a "pilot project" that would test counterinsurgency methods and also demonstrate to the world that the United States would not tolerate any advance for the forces of Third World change. What the United States wanted above all was stability in the poorer nations, even at the cost of repression and inequality, and we would intervene actively to impose it if necessary.[1]

Besides its predictable outrage at the growing interventionism represented by Vietnam, SDS saw in American foreign policy an opportunity to awaken the American public to the need for an activist dissenting movement. The peace movement had achieved little until now, a Peace Research paper noted, because it had failed to link America's aggressive posture in the world with social injustice at home. Of course Americans were worried about the dangers of war and were uneasy at American failure to pursue democratic goals abroad, but this concern was not enough. They must be made to see that American interventionism was also having harmful domestic effects. Most notably, American foreign policy was making it ever more difficult to tackle such problems as continuing poverty and inequality in the United States itself.[2]

At this point the SDS leaders could recommend little more to the students than programs to educate the public to the dangers of intervention and to awaken people's sympathies for Third World peoples. Then, early in 1965 President Johnson handed the student left a perfect issue by ordering American planes to bomb North Vietnam.

The reaction of young dissenters was rapid and spontaneous. On campuses all over the country, protest meetings and rallies were called, sparked by SDS activists, the May 2nd Movement, the Student Peace Union, the Young Socialist Alliance, or various ad hoc

[1] SDS Peace Research and Education Project, "Statement on the Peace Movement" (pamphlet), SDS File, Social Protest Project, Bancroft Library, University of California, Berkeley.

[2] *Ibid.*

groups. In mid-March the teach-ins began. Initiated by a University of Michigan dean to head off a protest strike by a group of liberal faculty members, the idea of a day devoted to discussing and condemning the Vietnam War soon caught on all over the country. Within a few weeks similar meetings were held on more than thirty campuses. The biggest took place, predictably, at Berkeley, where a veteran of FSM, Jerry Rubin, brought together an imposing roster of speakers, including such antiwar celebrities as Norman Mailer, Dr. Benjamin Spock, and Norman Thomas, as well as radical pacifists such as Staughton Lynd and Dave Dellinger, Bob Parris of SNCC, Robert Scheer and Edward Keating of the radical magazine *Ramparts,* and current SDS President Paul Potter. In all some twelve thousand students and faculty members participated in the marathon Berkeley Vietnam Day teach-in.

Although SDS contributed to the teach-ins, it was not the chief force behind them. By 1966, however, SDS and several other New Left organizations had begun to take a major part in the anti-Vietnam campaign.

SDS backed into the role of anti-Vietnam leadership, was never fully comfortable with it, and soon gave it up. On the face of it, this is a puzzling fact. The Vietnam War was to be a searing experience for the American people and would do more to shake the power structure of the nation than any event since the Great Depression. Yet SDS was never completely happy with the war as a focus and generally abdicated a leadership role to other left groups.

Part of the reason for this puzzling course was the sheer competition for leadership. Anti-Vietnam opinion was far more widespread in the country than a strong left perspective on domestic affairs. It encompassed pacifists, liberals, conservative isolationists, and every variety of old radical groups that the nation could exhibit. In the sheer din of would-be leaders, SDS found it difficult to make its voice heard above the others.

Also many SDS members were not certain that Vietnam cut to the heart of what was wrong with the United States. The May 2nd people had no doubt that American imperialism, whether directed against Asiatics or against black people at home, was the appropriate focus of revolutionary effort. Composed of young supporters of Red China who had been expelled from the American Communist party in 1962 and had organized the Progressive Labor party in April, 1965, the May 2nd people were Marxist–Leninists of a very old-fashioned sort. They believed in the revolutionary potential of the working class and claimed that capitalist America only held off the day of reckoning by its imperialist exploitation of subject peoples around the world. They regarded themselves as a vanguard party whose function it was to develop revolutionary consciousness among the working class, and they insisted on "correct" theoretical views from their members. In short, they resembled the American Communist party of the 1920s in their ideology, their bureaucratic structure, and their theoretical rigidity more than they did the post-1960 New Left. The only thing that distinguished them from the American Communist party was that their hearts were in Peking rather than Moscow.

Although Progressive Labor had little doubt that Vietnam got to the heart of the matter, SDS was not so sure. Suppose the United States succeeded in extricating itself from Southeast Asia. Would it thereby become any less sick or unjust? There was a serious danger that if the left was tempted into emphasizing Vietnam, it would be bereft of an issue if and when the war ended. Vietnam could, of course, be used as a tactical device to help radicalize various inert elements of society, but that seemed as far as it was wise to go.

The other left element in the informed anti-Vietnam coalition, besides the various Marxist–Leninist groups, included the radical pacifists close to A. J. Muste, Sidney Lens, and Dave Dellinger of the magazine *Liberation*. Among the younger people of this group, the outstanding figure was Staughton Lynd, a young historian of colonial America, the son of the sociologists Helen and Robert Lynd of *Middletown* fame. Staughton Lynd was a Quaker and a pacifist, who had spent some time in the 1950s in the Macedonia Community established by World War II war resisters. Early in his academic career he taught at a black college in Atlanta, and in 1964 he went to Mississippi to help organize the freedom schools for black children.

To Lynd and the *Liberation* people, the war was above all a moral issue. No doubt it could be used to awaken awareness of other social and political ills, but ending it by any means necessary so long as they were nonviolent was a goal of primary importance in itself. The radical pacifists of course opposed the war from the very outset, but it was a year or two before they evolved the resistance tactics that became their characteristic approach to the Vietnam evil.

Despite their doubts about the Vietnam issue, SDS leaders decided to sponsor an antiwar march on Washington in April, 1965. Although SDS would lead the march, no antiwar element would be excluded, and even such Marxist groups as the Young Socialist Alliance, Progressive Labor, and the Communist party campus affiliate, the DuBois Clubs, would be welcome.

Although SDS was rather dubious and tentative about the rally, it proved a great success. Some twenty thousand people of many political persuasions came to the capital to denounce America's role in Vietnam. The protesters gathered at the base of the Washington monument to hear speeches by the radical journalist I. F. Stone, Senator Ernest Gruening of Alaska, Staughton Lynd, Robert Parris, and SDS President Paul Potter, interspersed with social protest and antiwar songs by Joan Baez, Judy Collins, and Phil Ochs. When the rally broke up, the protesters marched to the Capitol and presented an antiwar petition to a Congressional aide. When some of the marchers attempted to approach the Capitol, contrary to a law forbidding demonstrations within five hundred feet of the building, they were stopped by the SDS leaders, who disapproved of massive civil disobedience tactics.

Despite SDS's gingerly treatment of the April march, the demonstration gave SDS a lot of favorable publicity on the campuses. SDS membership, about fifteen hundred in forty chapters before the march, climbed to over two thousand organized into eighty chapters soon after April. Still SDS leaders could not come to terms with the antiwar movement, and in the next few months they dithered over what role to play in the effort to stop the Vietnam War. Still dear to the heart of Paul Potter were the ERAP type of community-organizing ventures. Potter had been one of the main speakers at the Washington rally, but after April he opposed any further mass demonstrations. Conducting such demonstrations seemed like preaching to the converted. Those who turned out were already anti-Vietnam, and SDS leaders could not see how these large rallies could broaden the base of support for radical change. Besides, as we have seen, SDS leaders feared that an exclusive focus on Vietnam would prevent the larger lesson of American imperialism from coming across. One could even be a liberal and oppose the Vietnam War! This uneasiness with an antiwar emphasis led to a strange course. Instead of endorsing mass antiwar demonstrations at its June, 1965, convention, SDS resolved to go to the ghettos and slums and somehow awaken community awareness of the evil of war in Southeast Asia. An ERAP type of community organizing, in a word, would serve to stop the war as well as solve local community problems.

To many student leftists, these tactics seemed circuitous if not outlandish. The Young Socialist Alliance people called the move an abdication of leadership. By now many younger members of SDS had little use for such efforts among the white poor and favored focusing on students and the use of mass meetings and marches that would hit the public in the eye.

SDS, though scarcely five years old, was already experiencing something of its own generation gap. This was soon exhibited in a major policy shift. Although SDS leaders were far less obsessed with the dangers of Stalinist totalitarianism than older social democrats such as Norman Thomas, Michael Harrington, and Irving Howe, they had continued to condemn Soviet oppression and had continued to be chary of alliances with American Communists. SDS's constitution specifically condemned communism and excluded from membership those who favored "authoritarianism." Now, at its 1965 national convention, SDS dropped the anti-Communist wording in its constitution and opened its membership to all people of the left.

Older socialists and left liberals, who had fought the Communist party in the 1930s, condemned this change. The *New Republic* warned that Communist infiltration had destroyed many liberal and democratic socialist organizations in the past and would do so again if the democratic left was not careful. The new SDS president, Carl Oglesby, pooh-poohed such dangers. SDS was not worried about being taken over. Communist infiltration was a red herring that had been used in the past to destroy radical organizations. Charges of infiltration, he insisted, merely encouraged factionalism, and factionalism was "the reef of the American left." In any case it was necessary for SDS to take the risk. "Democracy is nothing if not dangerous." [3]

[3] See flyer in SDS File, Social Protest Project, Bancroft Library, University of California, Berkeley.

Oglesby's concluding words would be prophetic. In the end the "dangers of democracy" proved real enough. Ultimately they destroyed SDS and badly damaged the New Left as a whole. Yet Oglesby was expressing a fundamental principle of the New Left: faith in the basic decency of people and the indispensability of spontaneous democratic participation.

This romantic Rousseauean commitment to anti-authoritarianism not only extended to membership policy, it also applied to the organization and structure of SDS. Until 1963 SDS conducted its business as most American voluntary organizations did. At the top was a group of elected officials chosen by an annual national convention, which in turn was composed of delegates from local chapters. In addition SDS had a national executive committee with a full-time staff, or secretariat, and a national council made up of the executive committee and representatives from the local chapters. This body made policy decisions between annual conventions.

Although the structure approximated the representative democracy that characterized most American political institutions, it came increasingly to be considered a violation of SDS's own convictions. Despite outward appearances, members said, the organization was hierarchical, bureaucratic, and coercive. This last quality, particularly, disturbed early SDS leaders, who were never able to divorce the practical necessities of organizational efficiency and effectiveness from their personal horror of power and authority.

The first step taken in loosening up the system was to limit the president to one term. In accordance with this policy, Tom Hayden was retired in 1963 and replaced by Todd Gitlin. Gitlin in turn was succeeded by Paul Potter, who in his turn was succeeded by Carl Oglesby, who was followed by Nick Egleson. Each president had to learn his job and perform some useful work in a brief year. Sometimes it was less than a year, since SDS had a way of sweeping out its officers with each change in policy or direction.

The only continuity for the organization was supplied by the national secretary, who was the head of the permanent staff. A succession of these—Lee Webb, Clark Kissinger, Jeff Segal, Paul Booth, and Greg Calvert—ran the organization through most of its existence. In 1967 the offices of president and vice-president were abolished. In 1968 the functions of the national secretary were divided among three secretaries. Finally, at the end the whole

SDS governing structure was converted into a "national collective," apparently selected by the permanent staff. Meanwhile the national council, supposedly consisting of duly elected chapter delegates and executive committee members, became a meeting of anyone who happened to be around Chicago headquarters [4] and wanted to join in. To top off the fecklessness of this structure, the national organization, however constituted, had little power over the chapters which often pursued their own course regardless of what presidents, national secretaries, or the editor of *New Left Notes* wanted.

The irony in all this, as Michael Rothstein later pointed out, was that each move brought not more democracy, but less. Elected officers were increasingly replaced by co-opted bureaucrats. As the national office came to express the views of casual passers-by, it lost touch with the young men and women in the campus chapters.[5] As one disgruntled young woman noted, despite SDS's name, the national office was not especially democratic. "If the movement itself couldn't treat people as human beings," she, personally, failed to see "how it could expect to miraculously transform America." [6]

SDS never did succeed in finding a balance between democracy and continuity. Nor did it ever succeed in maintaining a stable membership or a clear approach or philosophy. SDS Vice-President Carl Davidson's frank report to the members, noted in Chapter 2, makes clear some of the difficulties that the organization had in its middle period. As we saw, Davidson estimated that 80 to 90 percent of the membership in early 1967 was composed of "shock troops," younger members, mostly freshmen and sophomores, who were "rapidly moving into the hippie, Bob Dylan syndrome." These young men and women were ignorant of the intellectual roots of the movement and read little except for what came from the growing underground press. Another 5 to 10 percent of SDS was composed of "superintellectuals," generally graduate students. These knew a great deal about politics and came regularly to meetings,

---

[4] In May, 1965, SDS moved out of New York and established its headquarters in Chicago. The move symbolized both its final rejection of LID tutelage and its desire to get closer to the American heartland.

[5] See Michael Rothstein, "Representative Democracy in SDS," *Liberation*, February, 1972, pp. 10ff. Rothstein was a member of SDS from 1962 to 1967. Though he left it in later years, he remained a radical.

[6] See *SDS Bulletin*, Vol. 4, No. 2 (no date, but probably late 1965), p. 4.

but generally they talked too much and qualified each position they took to excess.

Finally, Davidson noted, there was the small group of organizers. These were the people who held SDS together. Many of them were school dropouts, though they often remained near the campuses. They did the bureaucratic "shitwork" of SDS, reserving rooms, setting up tables, talking to fraternities and dormitory and worker audiences, and recruiting new members. Yet even this group was scarcely a rock of stability for SDS. The organizers alternated "periods of intense organizing with periods of moody mystical soul-searching. Sometimes they [didn't] come back. Their politics [tended] to be erratic, changing whenever they finally [got] a chance to read a new book."

These three groups did not always get along well. The organizers often considered the shock troops frivolous and decadent. The shock troops, in turn, often regarded the organizers as insensitive. The super-intellectuals were even more skeptical of the shock troops, and the shock troops "put the super-intellectuals in the middle-class bag along with their parents and the dean of men." Yet the three groups had respect, as well as contempt and suspicion, for each other. All told, the picture was characterized by friction, confusion, and ambivalence.[7]

Given these structural and intellectual weaknesses, it is easy to see why SDS, in particular, and the student New Left, in general, more often moved with events than moved them. Certainly when it came to deciding on what tactics to use, SDS was often compelled to subordinate theory to the current and momentary reality.

So, despite its misgivings, events forced SDS to take up the Vietnam War as a major concern. As the Johnson administration escalated American involvement in Vietnam, SDS found it more and more difficult to stay aloof. Too many SDS members were students with 2-S, student deferments. The situation was an agonizing personal one for many young activists. White, middle-class students went to classes at nice ivy-covered campuses, while slum dwellers, young working-class youths, blacks, and Chicanos went off to the

[7] Carl Davidson, "National Vice-President's Report," *New Left Notes*, February 3, 1967, pp. 4–5.

jungles of Vietnam. Was it right for young radicals to take advantage of their student status? Was it right to let the poor fight and die, while students, taking advantage of their middle-class privileges, were going scot free? The moral dilemma was made all the worse by the conviction that the student deferment policy was a cynical attempt by the government to anesthetize public outrage against the war. If the children of the powerless and the politically inert fought and died, while the children of the powerful and the politically active remained safe at home, there would be fewer complaints about a stupid and unjust war.

SDS leaders tried to solve this dilemma in late 1965 by sending around a proposal advising students to apply for conscientious objector status and suggesting that they stop their schools from sending the grades on which student deferments were based to the Selective Service. If widely adopted, these moves seemed likely to clog up the Selective Service System.

In making these proposals, SDS leaders tried to avoid advocating illegal actions of the kind that later resulted in the indictment of antiwar leaders like Dr. Spock. At this point in its brief career, SDS was surprisingly timid about bringing the law down on its head. But SDS had miscalculated. Attorney General Nicholas Katzenbach immediately announced that he intended to investigate SDS as well as other draft-resister groups, and another official accused SDS of "treasonous activity." [8]

Nothing came of these threats, and in the end they merely served to give SDS a lot of useful free publicity. In the midst of the furor, SDS leaders held a press conference in Washington to explain that young men would be happy to serve their country in constructive ways, that they were not shirkers, but that SDS would "encourage every member of our generation to object, and file his objection through Form 150 provided by the law for conscientious objection." [9]

Some members of SDS considered this mild statement a cop-out, but it got SDS off the hook with the authorities. Having tasted the delights of notoriety, SDS leaders now were reluctant to abandon their misleading image as leaders of the antiwar movement.

[8] Kirkpatrick Sale, *SDS* (New York: Random House, 1973), p. 230.
[9] *Ibid.*, p. 234.

In November SDS joined SANE and other anti-Vietnam groups, organized as the National Coordinating Committee to End the War, in a march on Washington. Forty thousand people came to the capital over the Thanksgiving holiday for the usual round of speeches, protests, interviews, and petitions. One of the major speakers was SDS President Carl Oglesby, who got a standing ovation when he denounced American "corporate liberalism" for its imperialist policies abroad and its oppression at home, and demanded revolution to overthrow it.

As the intensity of the Vietnam War increased, two new trends began to become apparent in the student left. One was a complete break with liberal and reformist groups and a decided movement to the left; the other was a marked shift of attention from the poor, the black, and the relatively inert to middle-class, white college students and their problems on the campuses. Many forces contributed to these changes, but the most influential, perhaps, was the growing radicalization of the civil rights movement.

Until late 1965 or early 1966 whites continued to play an important but diminishing part in the civil rights movement. In the summer of 1965 SNCC urged Northern students to support its efforts to get Congress to throw out Mississippi's five regularly elected Congressmen and seat those chosen by the Mississippi Freedom Democratic party (MFDP). The MFDP, organized just before Freedom Summer, 1964, had "elected" candidates to various national offices and to the Democratic National Convention. In 1965 a special MFDP shadow election had chosen four black candidates to represent Mississippi in Congress in place of the regularly elected white Democrats. When Congress convened, three of these black candidates challenged the incumbents' right to be seated. SNCC agreed to accept a few white student volunteers for work in the South during the summer of 1965, but it preferred to have whites focus on pressuring Congress in the seating of the MFDP delegation, rather than participate directly in the South, as they had in the recent past.

In the next few months the civil rights movement split between an integrationist group of older people, including Martin Luther King's Southern Christian Leadership Conference, the National Urban League, and the senior National Association for the Advance-

ment of Colored People (NAACP), and the younger militants of
CORE and especially SNCC, who now, increasingly, were waving
the banners of black separatism and black power. It is not necessary to examine closely the reason for the militant evolution of
the civil rights movement. It was related to the wave of ghetto riots
that began in Watts in August, 1965, and spread to a score of large
Northern cities the following summer. It was also related to the
signing of the Voting Rights Act of 1965, which brought to a conclusion the decade-long assault on legal segregation in the South.
Finally it was related to the disillusioning rejection by Congress of
the MFDP candidates. Together, these three developments suggested that the possibility of redress through the legal system was
exhausted and that further substantial white support for black
liberation was neither likely nor necessary. The problems of the
future would be mostly economic and far more intractable than
those in the past. Solutions would threaten white liberals as well
as white bigots. Blacks could now count only on themselves; whites
would not follow the tortuous and dangerous path that must now
be taken.

The change in approach was related to new leadership in both
CORE and SNCC. In the first organization Floyd McKissick succeeded James Farmer; in the second Stokely Carmichael followed
John Lewis. In both organizations the new men represented the
repudiation of white support and nonviolent tactics, and a sharp
turn to self-reliance and black autonomy that the militants labeled
black power.

Black power was a blow to SDS and the white student left.
Some young white radicals saw it as a necessary and inevitable
development in the civil rights movement. After all, for blacks the
participatory democracy that SDS touted clearly meant black self-
determination. As for the anti-white quality of much black power
advocacy, it was no more than white America deserved for its
chronic racism. At times, in fact, white radicals seemed to take
an almost masochistic delight in the growing black militant practice of "putting whitey down." Yet many white dissenters also felt
betrayed by the new turning. Abbie Hoffman an emerging radical
spokesman, in a letter to the *Village Voice* called the black power
people ornery ingrates. Those more discreet than Hoffman kept
their feelings to themselves, but many felt rejected and hurt.

On the official level, the student left endorsed black power. In June, 1966, national SDS passed a resolution underwriting SNCC's position and denying the liberal charge that the black power position was racism in reverse. At Berkeley the local SDS chapter supported Black Power Day and fought the university authorities, who were dismayed by the anti-white tone of the new militancy and were trying to keep the demonstration away from the campus.[10] In all likelihood this liberal dismay was one of the things that recommended black power to the New Left.

But whatever SDS leaders said personally or officially about the growing militancy of SNCC and CORE, it created a number of problems. First, how could SDS match the militancy of black students? Until this point SDS was still committed to working with liberals and the left wing of the Democratic party. In late 1964 and early 1965 two factions of SDS debated about the proper relationship between SDS and the liberal Establishment. One, the coalitionists, led by former Field Secretary Steve Max, hoped to detach "more active and advanced liberals" from the Democratic party and recruit them for left causes. Without such liberals, Max and his supporters held, neither blacks nor the poor could hope to achieve any substantial amount of power. Tom Hayden led a group that believed coalition was pointless. Radicals must go it alone. In the end, both Max and Hayden, as Richard Flacks had proposed, "stepped away" and the issue remained unresolved.[11]

Vietnam and black power brought the issue to a head. When SDS ended its Communist exclusion clause, it was, perhaps unconsciously, creating an opening to the left. Soon after the new policy was adopted, the League for Industrial Democracy severed its connection with SDS on the grounds that it had made a serious error in not excluding Communists. In February, 1966, within a few weeks of LID's repudiation, the Progressive Labor party student group, the May 2nd organization, disbanded and voted to enter SDS. As the May 2nd newspaper explained, the New Left was still ill-defined and not yet clearly committed "in favor of a socialist,

[10] See "Resolution on SNCC" (handbill), SDS File, Social Protest Project, Bancroft Library, University of California, Berkeley. See also handbill in same file by Berkeley SDS.

[11] See Richard Flacks, "Letter," SDS National Conference File, Social Protest Project, Bancroft Library, University of California, Berkeley.

left, or anti-imperialist perspective." People with a Progressive
Labor orientation could help shift the balance in the proper direction.[12]

At first the addition of a goodly number of dedicated revolutionaries to SDS did not have major consequences. SDS remained
in control of a non-Marxist majority composed of dissenters, naysayers, and mavericks, who were alienated from American corporate
liberalism and anxious to destroy the power of the Establishment,
but were still searching for solutions outside the orthodoxies of
Marxist–Leninist ideology.

Not that strategies and tactics developed abroad did not appeal
to the American New Left. Regarding the United States with growing revulsion, the student left inevitably found much to admire in
radical political developments elsewhere. The Soviet Union remained
outside the circle of New Left sympathies, but Third World radicalism was immensely appealing. Mao's China seemed better than
the Soviet Union, not because of Progressive Labor's growing influence, but simply because it appeared less rigid and bureaucratized.
Still better, it seemed in the mid-1960s, was the romantic, spontaneous radicalism of Cuba, the Vietnamese National Liberation
Front, and various Third World radical movements. Castro along
with Kenyatta and Ho Chi Minh became folk heroes to the New
Left, and the writings of Che Guevara and Frantz Fanon became
stylish guides to what was happening or would eventually happen
when the masses stirred in Asia, Africa, and Latin America.

Beginning in 1965 or 1966, in response to black militancy, the
official line of SDS began to take on a more consistently radical
cast. The leftward turn would match the militant shift of the civil
rights movement. SDS resolved not to fall behind SNCC. At the
same time SDS would focus primarily on whites. If, as was now
clear, black militants wanted nothing more to do with white dissenters, whites must turn to their own constituency. To some degree,
ERAP and the "interracial movement of the poor" had been inspired by a similar logic, but there would be a difference between
ERAP and the new approach. The emphasis would no longer be
white, working-class folk, but white students themselves. Rather

[12] Edward J. Bacciocco, "The New Left from 1956–1969: A Study of Community, Reform, and Revolution," doctoral dissertation, Department of Political Science, University of Colorado, 1971, pp. 329–330.

abruptly, in mid-1966 SDS decided the times required that the nation's campuses become the stage for revolutionary activity.

As we have seen, SDS and the student left generally had not followed up the Berkeley Free Speech Movement. Though not an entirely isolated event, Berkeley had not led to a concerted policy of making the university a major activist focus. Still unclear in the minds of many student left leaders was their relationship to the changes in society that they wished to take place. True, the beginning of an answer had been emerging for some time. There was Mills' idea that students, intellectuals, and professionals would lead the movement for change. The Port Huron Statement had suggested that they would also be the major beneficiaries of that change, because they too were an exploited class. Those involved in the FSM at Berkeley had considered the students an oppressed group fighting for its own salvation.

Yet doubt persisted among SDS intellectuals and organizers. Weren't students a minority of the population? Even if one added the white-collar and professional class, wasn't the group still only a fraction of the total population? How could a minority justify making a revolution for its own benefit? And what right did students have to speak for anyone but themselves?

Beginning in 1965–1966 American New Left thinkers began to see a way out of these dilemmas. At about this time they first noticed the work of a group of French neo-Marxists, who were trying to update Marx to make his theories fit the circumstances of the post–World War II industrial West.

These French writers, including André Gorz, Serge Mallet, and Ernest Mandel, noted that not only had the revolutionary potential gone out of the industrial wage earners, they were also fast becoming a minority of the working population. Contrary to orthodox Marxist doctrine, capitalism had succeeded in buying off the industrial proletariat and had neutralized it politically. Now, besides being inert, it was becoming increasingly unimportant relative to new sectors of society that were growing rapidly as the economy became more complex and sophisticated. As the proportion of blue-collar wage earners decreased, the number of salaried technicians, clerks, teachers, professionals, and semiprofessionals increased. In some countries the latter group had already become a majority of the noncapitalist class; in others it was fast approaching that point. And this "new working class" was not a privileged group, as social critics used to believe. The neo-Marxists, borrowing from Mills, viewed the new salaried workers as a new exploited class. Even if their incomes were adequate to keep them from gross physical want, they were without power to control their lives or to control the uses to which their skills were being put. They were, in fact, fine examples of the early Marx's alienated men, isolated from their work and afflicted by impotence.

For the next year or two these neo-Marxist ideas shaped the direction of SDS and the New Left movement. At an important conference held at Princeton in February, 1967, the new-working-class theory from abroad was ratified, refined, and naturalized to the American setting. Sponsored by the newly organized Radical Education Project (REP) of SDS, the conference used the new-working-class scheme to escape some of the theoretical dilemmas that had beset the New Left from the beginning. The work of the neo-Marxists, Greg Calvert, a young instructor of European history explained, provided "a powerful tool for understanding the present structure of advanced industrial capitalism." Until now the myth of the "great American middle class" had "been a major psychological obstacle for most radicals. If white America [was] mostly middle class, and if being middle class [meant] not being oppressed, then there [was] no possibility for finding the resources upon which a radical movement [could] be built in white America." What the New Left had now come to see, fortunately, was that the American middle class was not a middle class at all in the old Marxist sense of a propertied, exploiter class. "The vast majority of those whom we called the middle class must properly be understood as members of the 'new working class': that is, as those workers who fill the jobs created by a new level of technological development within the same exploitative system." These new-working-class people were not poor. In fact they were often prosperous compared to other groups. But this did not deprive them of revolutionary potential. Revolutionary mass movements were "not built out of a drive for the acquisition of more material goods." They were "freedom struggles born out of a perception of the contradictions between human potentiality and oppressive actuality." [13]

[13] Greg Calvert, "White America: Radical Consciousness and Social Change," in Massimo Teodori (ed.), *The New Left: A Documentary History* (Indianapolis: Bobbs-Merrill, 1969), pp. 413, 416–417.

Calvert's perception had already begun to be transformed into SDS policy by the time of the Princeton meeting. When the Radical Education Project was organized in 1966, one of the important functions assigned to it was the creating of a radical consciousness among professionals, academics, and people in the arts. REP would seek out men and women who would contribute their expertise to the furtherance of a radical perspective and would involve these men and women actively in the radical cause. "To build a new left in America," *New Left Notes*, the new SDS paper explained, "requires striking roots in the professions, among university faculties, in the arts, and in many of the mass organizations, such as churches, unions. . . ." [14] SDS had also begun already to talk about establishing a new organization in anticipation of white-collar radicalism, one that would also serve as a postgraduate body for former student leftists.

Besides making these efforts to heighten or preserve dissenting consciousness among those past their student days, SDS, as a result of the new-working-class theory, began to reappraise the direction of the student movement itself. If the nation's scientists, professionals, and white-collar people were being recruited from the campuses, SDS leaders were soon arguing, what better place than the campuses to recruit people for radicalism? Campus confrontation need not be only a way of self-liberation for students or another attack on an Establishment institution, it could also be used to politicize the men and women who would shortly be going out to occupy the technological and professional heights of capitalist society. "If there is a single over-all purpose of the student power movement," Carl Davidson would write in the fall of 1967, "it would be the development of a radical political consciousness among those students who will later hold jobs in the strategic sectors of the political economy." [15] What a fine explosion there would be when the campus activists moved on to the offices, labs, and committee rooms of the Establishment!

Even before the Princeton conference, SDS, at its national convention at Clear Lake, Iowa, had already made the important decision to redirect its efforts toward the campuses. As Davidson

---

[14] *New Left Notes*, August 24, 1966.

[15] Carl Davidson, *The New Radicals in the Multiversity: An Analysis and Strategy for the Student Movement* (SDS: Chicago, 1967), pp. 17–18.

explained to the Clear Lake delegates in August, 1966, the universities were agencies for molding the elite of corporate liberalism. Students were being programmed on campus to become bureaucratic men. This goal was expressed not only in formal courses in business administration, education, and engineering, but in the whole repressive structure of the university system. Dorm rules, dress regulations, and grades were as much a part of the scheme to turn out acquiescent, manipulable people who would go along with the system as the formal training of the "knowledge factories." In the last analysis there was a close connection between dorm rules and Vietnam.

SDS must now end this process of training personnel for the system and help radicalize the campuses. It must do so by avoiding single, minor issues that could be made into nullities by a clever administration's concessions. SDS must insist on student control, not of one small area of students' lives, but of every aspect of their lives. This could be accomplished by organizing, say, a "student syndicalist movement," a kind of student labor union, or perhaps a campus freedom democratic party. Organizations such as these would employ boycotts, sit-ins, teaching assistant strikes, seizures of conservative student newspapers, class disruptions, "all this to be in such a manner as to recruit more and more support." This sort of participatory democracy would be intrinsically valuable, and it would help to "sabotage" the "manipulative, bureaucratic system." Beyond this, it would radicalize students in great numbers and influence the larger society profoundly. "It is my hope," Davidson concluded, "that those exposed to . . . building a movement for student syndicalism will never be the same, especially after they leave the university community." [16]

Speakers at the Clear Lake Convention made it clear that they conceived of the new approach as a decisive move to the left. They were right. The new-working-class theory was Marxist, albeit neo-Marxist, and marked the revival of Marxist thought in the New Left. Moreover, it signaled the end of the liberal noblesse oblige that had characterized the student left from the beginning. As Calvert, the outstanding new-working-class theorist had said much earlier, true radicals considered themselves the victims of the sys-

[16] Carl Davidson, "A Student Syndicalist Movement: University Reform Revisited," *New Left Notes*, September 9, 1966.

tem, not its guilty beneficiaries. Clear Lake so defined the students. From this period onward the student left shrugged off the last vestiges of its liberal past and became a truly radical movement.

Yet the new focus on students and campuses was not universally accepted within SDS. The Progressive Labor wing opposed the policy as a wrongheaded betrayal of the industrial working class. Even Todd Gitlin expressed doubts. The new-working-class idea, he noted, often seemed to consist of "fairly elaborate rationalizations on the part of students who 'accept' their middle class status so deeply they need to feel their privilege is freighted with radical potential." [17] Gitlin had a point. Campus organizing may have been theoretically impeccable and consistent with the New Left's unique spirit, but the eagerness with which radical students took up the new approach grew as much out of the difficulties and frustrations of radicalizing blue-collar whites and the convenience of on-campus agitation as out of any deep intellectual commitment to the new-working-class concept.

For a while, however, the new policy took hold, and the country's campuses soon felt the effects. As we have noted, many things were wrong with American higher education in the mid-1960s. FSM at Berkeley had shone a brilliant spotlight on many of these faults—complicity in the warfare state, indifference to students, arrogance and self-congratulation, impersonality, authoritarianism. These and other flaws deserved attack, but SDS, unlike FSM, was less concerned with these failings in themselves than it was with the possibility that they could be used to raise the revolutionary consciousness of college students. Nick Egleson, SDS president in 1966–1967, made this purpose quite explicit. "Our strategy is . . . simple," he wrote.

> [Take] a small issue and immediately raise the question of student control. Take the draft exam [the examination given by Selective Service to determine who would receive student draft deferments], as at Buffalo or Madison, and ask for a vote and a structure to make future decisions. Take ranking [class ranking, also used to determine deferments], as at Chicago, and ask for a referendum. Take the price of food, as at [San Francisco] State College, and ask for student

[17] Todd Gitlin, "Thesis for the Radical Movement," *Liberation*, May–June, 1967, p. 9.

control of the corporation which runs the lunch room and the book store.

The administration would become nervous and fearful of disruption, and would make mistakes. The battle with the administration would then escalate, and in the course of the resulting upheaval, many students would be radicalized. The campus issues, in a word, would be used for the larger purposes of radicalizing society at large.[18]

This confrontation approach was soon widely adopted by SDS leaders. Jerry Hoffman later recounted how the Princeton SDS chapter used the refusal of a university trustee to speak to SDS about the presence of the war-connected Institute of Defense Analysis on campus as an excuse for a disruptive sit-in. SDS fully expected the Trustees to reject its request for a meeting and knew that the refusal would provide sanction for the escalating of SDS tactics. Hoffman denies that the request was insincere. SDS would have been willing to meet with the Trustees, he says, and in fact would have been pleased if allowed to enter the building where the Trustees were meeting. There is, however, an insincere quality to Hoffman's claim. SDS wanted confrontation, and the Princeton chapter most certainly would have found a way to up the ante until no administration could have gone along with its demands.[19]

This is not to say that SDS was not authentically outraged at what was taking place on campuses. It was, and this outrage was what brought many liberals into the radical fold and drove many radicals on through the danger and the drudgery of campus struggle. Some student radicals sincerely hoped to see a better American university system emerge from the campus struggles. Such a system would be an adversary of the existing society. It would be dedicated to informing radicals in the ways of that society for the purpose of altering it drastically. For a while in 1966–1967 this hope for a better university's replacing the old took the form of efforts to establish free universities. These would be devoted to instruction

[18] See Nick Egleson, "Changes in Our Thinking," SDS Miscellaneous Documents File, Social Protest Project, Bancroft Library, University of California, Berkeley.

[19] See Jerry Hoffman, "Princeton: Radical Organizing and the I.D.A. Campaign," in Julian Foster and Durwood Long (eds.), *Protest! Student Activism in America* (New York: William Morrow, 1970), pp. 310–311.

in radical history, the techniques and theories of revolution, and alternative life-styles and the counter culture. SDS chapters in Berkeley, New York, Chicago, Seattle, San Francisco, and elsewhere supported free university ventures, though national SDS refused to get directly involved. Presumably a truly liberated university would resemble these ad hoc institutions, but would, of course, possess far greater resources.

In a sense the question of cynicism or sincerity is irrelevant. By 1966–1967 SDS national leadership believed that a revolution in middle-class consciousness was essential to overturn the brutal system under which Americans lived, and that the place to inaugurate this alteration was in the universities. Convinced that universities were thinly disguised representatives of all that was worst in America, SDS leaders could justify employing whatever tactics were necessary to force a confrontation. There was nothing inherently evil or wicked in this. It was an inevitable result of the final rejection by SDS leaders of the salvageability of American corporate liberalism.

Yet it took a while for SDS to get things moving along the new track. In the fall of 1966 Egleson, Calvert, and Davidson toured the campuses, organizing new chapters and spreading the seeds of campus revolt. Results followed in short order. Predictably there was turmoil at Berkeley in the months following the Clear Lake Convention. In November, 1966, the Berkeley SDS chapter attempted to block students from getting to naval recruiting tables set up on campus, a move that brought in the police and led to a student campus strike. In Cambridge, Massachusetts, students from the Harvard-Radcliffe SDS surrounded Secretary of Defense Robert McNamara as he left the John F. Kennedy Institute of Politics and forced him to defend the administration's Vietnam policies.

At scores of other campuses during the 1966–1967 academic year, SDS attacked the administration for sending student grades to Selective Service, or allowing the Central Intelligence Agency (CIA) or Dow Chemical Company to recruit on campus. The McNamara occurrence especially caught the public's attention, but none of the campus incidents had the impact SDS had hoped for. Then, in the spring of 1968 SDS led an uprising at Columbia that would become a model of the radicalizing campus confrontation.

Columbia, like Berkeley four years earlier, was an ideal locale for campus upheaval. A large, prestigious institution with a cosmo-

politan student body, it was a member of the Institute for Defense
Analysis (IDA) and seemed even more deeply involved in the mili-
tary-industrial establishment than Berkeley. At Columbia, as at
Berkeley, moreover, the administration was unprepared for the student attack, despite the important lessons of the previous four
years. At Columbia, too, administration ineptness, as well as the
inevitable crudity and truculence of the police, did much to drive
moderates into opposition to the Trustees and the president. There
was a major difference, however, between Columbia and Berkeley.
At Berkeley the Free Speech Movement was largely spontaneous.
At Columbia the radical students, especially the white radical students led by SDS, deliberately provoked a confrontation with
the university administration.

It is necessary at the outset to note how serious the university's
failings were. Through the IDA Columbia had foolishly tied itself
to the Vietnam War. Much of Columbia's faculty, too, had come to
neglect teaching for research and had come to emphasize graduate
over undergraduate instruction. But the university's apparent failings went beyond this. Unlike Berkeley, Columbia, as a private
institution, had to pay a large part of its costs out of its own resources. Contract research and other public sources of support,
though larger than in earlier years, did not pay the enormous expenses of running a major campus. Columbia's way of paying its
expenses was through real estate, and the university received an
unusually large part of its income from such choice land parcels in
New York as Rockefeller Center. But real estate was important
to the university in other ways too. Unlike campus schools located
in small communities, Columbia was physically restricted to a relatively small plot of expensive Manhattan land. In order to provide
for its future growth, it had bought up buildings in its Morningside
Heights neighborhood and retained them for later use. As it grew,
the university evicted the occupants of these buildings without providing them with much help in relocating. These people naturally
resisted being deprived of good, rent-controlled apartments and
forced to seek housing elsewhere at much higher cost. Despite the
common belief, however, few of those affected by Columbia's real
estate practices were black. A number of the buildings in Columbia's orbit were single-room occupancy apartments housing an unstable population of whites, some blacks, and Puerto Ricans, most
of them single, many of them drug addicts, petty criminals, and

prostitutes. But Morningside Heights was not Harlem. Few if any black families suffered directly from any of the real estate ventures of the Columbia Trustees.

Yet Columbia was soon to run into a serious symbolic confrontation with black Harlem over its space problems. The university needed a gym. For decades it had made do with a poor, sawed-off building in the middle of the crowded campus. Hindsight makes it clear that the university should have slowly assembled a substantial parcel of land in the Heights and built when all was ready. Instead it turned to Morningside Park, a strip of almost vertical rock, trees, and grass that bordered the eastern edge of the campus and formed the boundary between Morningside Heights and Harlem below. This area, though designated a park, had been little used by anyone. Its rough topography made it inconvenient, and its dense undergrowth and location made it a perfect hideout for addicts, muggers, and other dangerous types. After dark it was a jungle, where no one who had the slightest sense of self-preservation walked.

Though it was virtually useless to everyone, Columbia should not have tried to build its new gym there. Parks are sacred ground in New York. Open space is scarce, and every patch of green is seen as a blessing. Besides, even if Harlemites seldom went there, it was in some way their turf. The university and Morningside Heights constituted a privileged, white institution in Harlem's eyes, and its interest in the park seemed an encroachment on the black man's neighborhood. Relations between the university and the Harlem community were not especially bad. Though there were few blacks at Columbia, it was no more guilty of conscious discrimination at this time, before the period of active college recruitment of black students, than any other Ivy League university. Inevitably, however, it was a symbol, although as yet only a dimly discerned one, of the white Establishment and hence a potential enemy of the neighboring black community.

Despite the likelihood of trouble, Columbia proceeded to get the city and the state to provide a small portion of the park for a gym at a moderate rental. On the site the university would construct the long overdue facility, which would be used primarily for students and faculty, but would also provide some space for the community. Later, as the gym became a political issue, CORE and a number of black political leaders protested Columbia's incursion, and the university promised to increase the community's share of the gym's facilities.

Whether the gym would have been a boon to Harlem, as some pro-university people later insisted, or whether it was an arrogant steal, Columbia clearly was poking at a hornet's nest. By the opening of the 1967–1968 academic year, the university had a strong Student Afro-American Society (SAS) and a stronger SDS chapter. The black students were naturally interested in an issue that affected the two communities they belonged to, and they were determined to force the university to open its doors further to black students. SDS, with its new emphasis on campus confrontation, was anxious to show up the university as an Establishment bulwark and to radicalize the Columbia student body. The gym issue was the perfect opening for both.

Despite the university's obvious vulnerability on the gym issue, SDS, surprisingly, did not take the issue seriously at first. By the spring of 1968 the Columbia chapter of SDS had been seeking confrontation with the university administration for some time. Founded in February, 1966, SDS had protested the appearance on campus of a CIA and a Marine Corps recruiter as well as the university's cooperation with the Selective Service's class-ranking procedure. Victorious on the class-ranking issue, it was defeated on recruitment, and for a while it was inactive. In the spring of 1967 the campus chapter took up the issue of Columbia's membership in the Institute for Defense Analysis and forced the university to appoint a committee to consider its connection with that agency and other outside agencies sponsoring research.

For a while the IDA issue cooled. Then in March it flared up again. By this time Mark Rudd, a cocky junior at Columbia College, was chairman of Columbia's SDS. The son of a real estate agency operator in Maplewood, New Jersey, Rudd was more radical than his predecessors, and under his leadership SDS staged a disruptive invasion of Low Library, the Columbia's administration building, to push the university on the IDA issue. The administration agreed to break its connection with IDA, though in fact the move it made was formal and did not change the university's relationship with the agency in any important way. The administration also announced early in April that six members of SDS—Rudd, John Jacobs, Ted Gold, Nick Freudenberg, Ed Hyman, and Morris Grossner—had been suspended for leading the disruption at Low, an act that violated the campus rule forbidding demonstrations within university buildings.

On April 23 SDS held a rally at the Sundial on College Walk a few hundred feet from Low Library. The purpose of the rally, SDS announced, was to demand that Columbia honestly end its association with IDA, that the six suspended SDS leaders not be disciplined, and that those accused of the Low disruption be heard by a student–faculty group at public hearings. Nothing, it seems, was to be said about the gym.

But the gym soon became the major issue. SDS speakers at the Sundial confined themselves to the discipline and IDA issues, but the Student Afro-American Society speakers attacked the university's gym construction plans. Soon after this, Rudd led the rally crowd up the steps to Low for the purpose of another break-in. He and his followers were stopped by locked doors, however, and a group of counter-demonstrators gathered on Low's steps to prevent a break-in. At this point someone cried for a march on the gym site, where construction had already begun, and about three hundred protesters marched on to Morningside Park. Rudd and other SDS leaders remained behind, apparently not yet convinced that the gym issue was important. At the site the protesters were blocked by police, and in the ensuing scuffle one of them was arrested.

By this time Rudd had arrived at the gym site, and standing on a dirt pile, he told Dean Colahan, who had arrived to represent the administration, that the protesters' demands regarding IDA and the gym would have to be met in fifteen minutes. When the dean failed to reply, Rudd led the group back to the Sundial, where he proposed that the protesters take a hostage to compensate for the student who was just arrested. The students now marched into Hamilton Hall, seized the building and took captive Acting Dean Henry Coleman of Columbia College and two other administrators, holding them forceably in Dean Coleman's office.

During the rally and demonstration the protesters' footsteps had been dogged by a group of conservative students, who now offered to help the dean escape. Coleman, fearing a fight between the radicals and conservatives, declined their aid. Through the next few days this fear of a battle between the two student groups was to influence the administration's decisions at a number of important junctures.

In the captured building Rudd, Ted Gold, and other SDS

leaders joined with a group of black SAS leaders to form a steering committee. The steering committee then drew up a list of six demands: that the university drop all charges against leaders of the Low demonstration, that the university cease construction on the gym, that Columbia seek the dropping of charges against the student arrested at the gym site, that Columbia disaffiliate itself entirely from IDA, that all future disciplinary action against the students be resolved by hearings before students and faculty, and that the ban on indoor demonstrations be rescinded. Until these demands were met, the demonstrators would refuse to leave Hamilton Hall.

Up to this point Rudd and the other SDS leaders had been uneasy and irresolute. Rudd most certainly wanted no compromise with the administration. The New Jersey junior seems to have accepted completely the new SDS national policy of forcing a showdown with university officials at any cost to drive home the lesson of university iniquity and radicalize the student body. In later months Rudd reputedly admitted that he did not take seriously the issues that SDS had raised at Columbia. In a piece he wrote shortly after the Columbia upheaval, Rudd noted that "liberal solutions, 'restructuring,' partial understandings, compromise [with administrators] are not allowed anymore. The essence of the matter is that we are out for social and political revolution, nothing less." [20] Yet at this point he was obviously uneasy and worried.

Fortunately for SDS, the black students were not. Ray Brown and other black student leaders put SDS on its mettle, threatening to back out of the sit-in unless the white students remained resolute. As an additional contribution to the demonstration, they promised to call in the civil rights organizations such as CORE and SNCC and contact the militant leaders of Harlem. Mention of the Harlem community's support was a tremendous boost to SDS morale. The threat that black militants might attack the university, everyone realized, was a potent weapon on the students' side. The memory of what angry blacks could do to a Watts, a Newark, or a Detroit was enough to send a chill of horror down the back of any university administrator.

[20] See Mark Rudd, "Symbols of the Revolution," in Jerry L. Avorn et al. (eds.), *Up Against the Ivy Wall: A History of the Columbia Crisis* (New York: Atheneum, 1968), p. 290.

Yet the administration's response to the six steering committee demands was a stubborn refusal to discuss anything until Dean Coleman had been released and Hamilton Hall vacated. David Truman, vice-president of the university and throughout the upheaval the most active voice on the administration side, declared "we will discuss anything but we will not act under coercion." The administration, moreover, would not grant amnesty in advance or guarantee a public hearing for accused students.[21]

Meanwhile, at Hamilton the alliance between SDS and SAS was breaking down. The black students, now reinforced by a number of Harlem militants, were rather contemptuous of SDS, and were fast losing their interest in a joint enterprise. The break came when SAS decided to close the building entirely, keeping students from going to classes and faculty from using their offices. SDS felt that this was risky, and SDS leaders were frightened when black leaders told them that there were guns in the building. Why didn't SDS go and get its own building? the SAS people asked. SAS would make its stand in Hamilton.

At 5:30 A.M. the white students, a little dazed by the rejection and by lack of sleep, straggled out of Hamilton. What to do now? Some drifted off to their dorms to get some sleep. Others gathered once again at the Sundial and decided to do what they had been advised: get their own building. In the gray light of early morning, they marched up the Low Library steps, rammed a board through the glass doors, and swept into the university's administration building. Soon they were sipping President Kirk's sherry and smoking his cigars. Shortly after the break-in, Rudd and the other SDS leaders arrived, and all sat down to discuss what would be done now. Whatever Rudd or SDS national leaders such as Davidson and Calvert had concluded theoretically, when confronted by the actual need to act, SDS people were either fearful or confused. The large element of improvisation in SDS behavior during the Battle for Morningside Heights refutes the charge of conspiracy that was leveled at Rudd and the Columbia SDS chapter. It is true that the Columbia student radicals, by and large, accepted the Clear Lake policy of using the university for larger ends. The graffiti scrawled on university walls during the uprising—"create two, three, many

[21] *Ibid.*, p. 59.

Columbias" [22]—expressed the radicals' hope that Columbia might inaugurate a revolutionary wave, but at the outset there was no specific plan to single out Columbia and no blueprint on how to do it.

By now a group of police, summoned by the administration, had arrived in front of Low. Many frightened students quickly left the building, though a number of braver ones simply retreated to the building's upper floors. The students' fears were exaggerated. New York City police officials had told the Columbia administration that they could not clear white-occupied Low without also clearing black-occupied Hamilton. The administration rejected this plan as too risky, and the police simply removed a valuable Rembrandt painting from the president's office and left. Soon after, students poured back into the building.

The Low occupation was an SDS enterprise, but soon other groups of white students joined the sit-in movement. On Wednesday evening, April 24, students of the School of Architecture, defying an administration order to close all university buildings at 6:00 P.M., locked the doors of Avery Hall and barricaded them. The next morning a group of disaffected graduate students similarly took over Fayerweather Hall. Mathematics Hall was occupied later that day.

On Wednesday the administration's attention was still riveted on the dangerous situation in Hamilton, where Dean Coleman was confined and where, supposedly, Harlem black militants had collected guns and were prepared to defend themselves and the black students against the police. The administration, with the aid of a number of prominent New York City black political leaders, sought to negotiate with the SAS leaders in Hamilton, but their offer of terms was refused. Fortunately, despite the impasse, the black student leaders resolved to let Dean Coleman and the other administrator–hostages leave. At 3:30 on Wednesday afternoon Coleman and his colleagues walked out of Hamilton. At about the same time, it was reported, most of the armed militants also left the building. Obviously the SAS leaders had had second thoughts about tripping off a violent confrontation with the authorities.

---

[22] The slogan was a paraphrase of Che Guevara's "Create two, three, many Vietnams," the Latin American revolutionary's formula for destroying American imperialism.

By now the Columbia faculty had entered the picture. Though it had slipped since the great days of Nicholas Murray Butler, Columbia still had a distinguished staff, but it was both a relatively conservative and a relatively passive group. Over the years Columbia professors had been content to let the administration run things, while they devoted themselves to scholarship or government work, or immersed themselves in the exciting intellectual world of New York City.

Yet like the Berkeley faculty four years earlier, they felt a good deal of sympathy for the student militants and were opposed to using harsh tactics against them. On Wednesday and Thursday various faculty groups urged the administration to stop construction of the gymnasium and to turn over all discipline problems arising out of the demonstrations to a tripartite student–faculty–administration committee. An ad hoc faculty group also asked the students to evacuate the buildings and pledged to stand in front of the occupied buildings to prevent the police's entry, should they be called.

The administration was not, however, in a conciliatory mood by this time. Kirk was willing to have the Trustees consider dropping the gym project, but declared that he could not do it himself. By now Truman and Kirk were badly rattled and feared that conservative students would take things into their own hands. These students had organized a Majority Coalition and were demanding university action against the building occupiers. At one point it looked as if the conservatives would clash with a group of Harlem militants, who had gathered at the entrance to the campus and insisted in marching through it. At another point the faculty group barely succeeded in warding off a clash between the Majority Coalition and student radicals outside Fayerweather.

The administration was now determined to call in the police to prevent a battle between the two student factions; but the faculty immediately placed great pressure on the administrators to desist, and they relented. Negotiations now ensued between the faculty and the occupiers. There was no difficulty over the gymnasium. The administration had already received permission from the Trustees to suspend further construction. The student radicals would not yield on the issue of discipline, however. They wanted guarantees of administration amnesty before proceeding further, a point Kirk and Truman would not concede. SDS, in addition, displayed a contemptuous attitude toward the faculty negotiators. On Friday Rudd appeared before the faculty and told it that its proposals were "bullshit." Professor Alan Westin, who had chaired the ad hoc committee, was offended and angrily adjourned the meeting. In the recently seized Mathematics building, Tom Hayden had arrived to fortify the radical occupiers' resolve to keep the Columbia battle from degenerating into just another pointless student–administration squabble.

For several days negotiations dragged on fruitlessly. SDS's immovability was matched by the administration's intransigence, which was underscored by a Trustee statement on Saturday deploring any move to grant amnesty. Among Columbia students in general, there seems to have been a substantial amount of support for the radicals on the IDA and gym issues, but a reluctance to grant automatic amnesty to the building occupiers. Still, the Majority Coalition was active and restless. On Sunday evening a group of conservative students set up a blockade of food to the building occupiers, hoping to starve them out. On Monday evening radical supporters of the building occupiers attempted to break the blockade by charging the Majority Coalition's line. A melee broke out, and several people on both sides were hurt.

At the last minute the faculty tried to resolve the amnesty impasse by proposing that all those implicated in the disturbances be treated equally with no one singled out for special punishment by the contemplated tripartite committee of students, faculty, and administration. If the administration refused to accept this proposal, the faculty would seek to prevent the police from ousting the students from the occupied buildings. If the administration accepted the proposal and the students refused, the faculty would not seek to interpose between the student radicals and the authorities. The administration's response to this convoluted scheme was ambiguous. The student radicals' response was outright rejection and reiteration of their original six points including unconditional amnesty. This was a final stalemate, and negotiations now ceased.

Early in the morning, of Tuesday, April 30, the New York City police moved into the buildings. At Hamilton Hall there was no student resistance. When police entered the building, after giving prior warning, the black students surrendered, believing that nothing was to be gained from bloodshed, and were led off to police vans for booking. At the white-occupied buildings, however, there was considerable violence, though no one seems to have suffered permanent damage.

It is pointless to try to judge who was responsible for the broken bones, contusions, and bloodied heads. The police clearly could have been more restrained. There are many reports of policemen striking and kicking helpless students long after they had stopped resisting arrest. Obviously many of the police, lower middle-class and blue-collar men who had not gone to college, were enraged at the privileged student radicals, who seemed so ungrateful for their opportunities. Many members of SDS were learning a surprising lesson in class resentment that some would take to heart.

On the other hand, there is reason to believe that some students deliberately baited the police by insulting them, their forebears, and their descendants. In the day or so preceding the bust, SDS leaders, planning tactics off-campus, had calmly and deliberately discussed the value of provoking the police. A New York cop, one experienced radical explained to a group, would "blow like a balloon" if told, especially by a girl, that his mother habitually committed vile sexual acts. "And when they blow," he added, "they'll be there naked and the whole country will see the naked face, the naked ass, of fascism." [23]

In all some seven hundred people were arrested, and over a hundred people, including students, faculty, and some police, were treated for injuries.

Predictably the next few days were full of anguish and soul-searching for everyone at Columbia. The steering committee that had coordinated the radicals' efforts called for a strike in protest against the police and the administration. The administration responded by suspending classes, a move that took the wind out of the steering committee's sails. The faculty refused to go along with the student strike, though it was angry at the administration for calling in the police.

For the next few weeks Columbia scarcely functioned as a university. Classes were not held, and no final examinations were given.

[23] Quoted in Roger Kahn, *The Battle for Morningside Heights: Why Students Rebel* (New York: William Morrow, 1970), pp. 195–196. Kahn, it should be noted, is quite sympathetic to SDS and the Columbia student radicals, and his report at this point must, accordingly, be considered accurate.

Meanwhile the campus remained in turmoil. As usual the administration acted foolishly. On May 16 five leading members of SDS—Rudd, Ted Gold, Morris Grossner, Nick Freudenberg, and Ed Hyman—were summoned to appear before the Columbia College dean to answer charges of disruption. They refused to come, and on the date of their scheduled appearance, following the usual Sundial rally, about 350 students entered Hamilton Hall and refused to leave. This time the administration quickly called the police. The New York City Tactical Patrol Force cleared Hamilton without force, but on the campus itself there was unnecessary and indiscriminate violence against students and bystanders that shocked the Cox Commission when it investigated the Columbia upheaval.

There were to be still other episodes in the Columbia chronicle, but in the end, as usual, summer vacation put a period to the turmoil. As the school year ended, the visible consequences of the upheaval were not very great at Morningside Heights. Most of the student protesters were readmitted to school. Criminal charges against the student disrupters were dropped. Despite this clemency, there remained a large pocket of student disaffection, which would cause trouble at Columbia for the next year or two. In late August Kirk announced his retirement as president, and Andrew Cordier, a professor of international relations and a former diplomat, was appointed as his acting successor. The faculty, finally alert to its own powerlessness, succeeded in getting the Trustees to approve a faculty senate. The university permanently stopped the building of the gym.

More important were the effects of Columbia on SDS and the New Left. Columbia convinced many members of SDS that the Clear Lake policy, as elaborated at the Princeton meeting of early 1967, was the correct one for the student left. Soon after the end of the 1967–1968 academic year, Tom Hayden, fresh from his efforts at Mathematics Hall, concluded that the Columbia uprising had demonstrated the worth of campus confrontation. "Many of the students and faculty alike," he noted, "became radicalized by the rebellion." Admittedly, some students and faculty members were driven to the right, but this growing campus polarization was all to the good. Now the "veil was lifted," Hayden wrote, and everyone could see that the university was part of the power structure with special interests of its own that were unrelated to education.

Students could now judge with an unobstructed view whether they supported these interests or opposed them.[24]

Following the events of April and May, 1968, campus revolt spread rapidly across the country. Educational Testing Services estimated that over three thousand campus protests took place in 1968, most of them in the spring following the Battle for Morningside Heights. Many of these revolved around racial issues and were initiated by black students who wanted to force administrations to admit more black students, add black studies curricula, or end various campus discriminatory practices. SDS often cooperated in these, but invariably took a backseat to black organizations. Most of the campus rebellions, however, were concerned ostensibly with either the Vietnam War or campus structural change and involved white students primarily. In many of these white-run confrontations, SDS took a prominent part and supplied much of the experienced leadership. SDS received an enormous amount of free publicity from the wave of campus revolts that followed Columbia and profited commensurately. In the spring of 1968 SDS claimed 350 chapters with 40,000 members. By late fall it claimed 100,000 students in 500 chapters, figures that would never be exceeded.

SDS's income also leaped. Most of the organization's money came from membership dues, sale of REP literature, and a few rich benefactors, including Abby Rockefeller and Anne (Farnsworth) Peretz. It has been charged that SDS received money from either Peking, Havana, or both. Obviously it would have been to the advantage of both Red China and Cuba, and also of the Soviet Union, for SDS to have prospered and grown, but I have no way to check these claims of foreign funds.[25] In any case SDS's budget reached a new high in 1967–1968 of over $114,000 much of which was used to purchase a new press to print *New Left Notes* and other organizational literature.

Finally the Columbia uprising had a particularly profound effect on some of its prominent participants. Whether or not it

[24] Tom Hayden, "Two, Three, Many Columbias," *Ramparts*, June 15, 1968, p. 39.

[25] Kirkpatrick Sale is skeptical of the foreign subsidy charge, but James Michener thinks it is entirely possible. See Sale, *op. cit.*, p. 448; and Michener, *Kent State: What Happened and Why* (New York: Random House, 1971), pp. 96–98.

permanently radicalized many Columbia students is arguable, but it did drive a number of the Columbia SDS leaders over the line into full revolutionary commitment. Within a year Mark Rudd, Ted Gold, and John Jacobs would become identified with extreme guerrilla tactics against the Establishment, which would ultimately take tragic and deadly forms.

CHAPTER

5

The Movement
1967-1968

T HE YEAR of the Columbia uprising, 1968, was the high-water mark of SDS and the student left. In November Carl Davidson exulted over the tremendous growth of SDS during the year. The student left had not only been much smaller in 1967, he wrote, it had also been largely concentrated in the elite schools in the major urban centers. Now SDS was spreading to smaller communities, to smaller campuses, to junior colleges, and even to high schools. On many campuses SDS had entered the student government, and on some SDS actually controlled it.

What Davidson did not call attention to was that the New Left mood had spread out far beyond the student element and had now widened into a national, and even international, radical sensibility that was being referred to increasingly as the Movement.

By 1968 the Movement was a broad phenomenon. At its heart, still, was the student left and particularly SDS, but it had come to include thousands of adults, especially on university faculties, in the arts, in the learned professions, and in the mass media. It was still composed predominantly of males, but increasingly women were beginning to assert their discontent and demand radical change in their relations with men and male-dominated institutions. By now unequivocally radical, the movement had also widened out into a broad stream, on one side touching militant guerrillas, who believed violence was the only way to bring down the system, and on the other side extending to a diffuse radical sensibility that endorsed every "liberation movement" and permeated the cultural and political life of the nation.

At the core of the adult New Left were the younger radicals, who had graduated from the student movement and, as journalists, professors, media people, scientists, and writers, sought to continue and expand their radical affiliations. By 1968 there were thousands of young radical professionals, and they were becoming better organized and more effective.

Some of them belonged to the Movement for a Democratic Society (MDS), the body SDS established in 1967 to nurture New Left radicalism among nonstudents and former students. MDS had ambitious plans and hoped to sweep into its fold as many unaffiliated white-collar radicals as it could corral. According to two MDS organizers, Bob Gottlieb and Marge Piercy, chapters would be formed with professional groups, neighborhoods, or, more abstractly, just general attitudes at their cores. Each of these chapters would tackle problems in the area of its members' competence or interest, and would work to shake up the institutions it was connected with. One group of radical artists in New York, Gottlieb and Piercy noted, was already gathering material for a pamphlet to expose the racist and exploitative labor policies of the Museum of Modern Art. Under MDS such a group might perhaps, also, organize a demonstration to change the name of the famous Picasso picture at the museum from *Guernica* to *Vietnam* or stage a protest around some other symbolic issue. Obviously this sort of sandlot radicalism was a long way from revolution, but it seemed necessary to start somewhere.

MDS never succeeded in gathering up very many of the radical professional organizations formed in the late 1960s. In 1969 it existed largely as a New York group with three chapters composed of teachers, social case workers and computer scientists and technicians. Many radical professional groups were organized in the late 1960s, but most of these were autonomous. If they had any national affiliation at all it was with Radicals in the Professions, a group established in Ann Arbor, Michigan, in July, 1967. Actually radicals in the Professions did not get very far either, though it published a newsletter for a while and sponsored a conference on vocations for radicals in Cambridge, Massachusetts, in early 1968.

A more successful post-student radical group was the New University Conference (NUC) founded in Chicago in March, 1968. This body focused on people affiliated with the universities, primarily faculty and graduate students. Its purpose, as the agenda of the Chicago meeting reported, was to exchange ideas on campus organizing, to publicize university delinquencies, including war research and social manipulation, to find ways to support radical research, and to discuss radical perspectives in the various academic disciplines. SDS alumni Al Haber, Richard Flacks, Staughton Lynd, Tom Hayden, Jesse Lemisch, and others were among the 350 delegates at the organizing conference.

NUC was most successful in carrying out the last of its announced objectives. Under NUC auspices New Left graduate students and younger faculty members in many of the academic disciplines set up radical caucuses. At first these caucuses worked primarily to shift the intellectual emphases of the disciplines in the direction of greater relevance. The Union for Radical Economics, for example, attacked Establishment economists for "genuflecting" before the "twin deities" of marginalism and equilibrium analysis, and for accepting the myth of "value free" social science. The world quite clearly was not in a stable equilibrium, the union's prospectus stated. Modern academic economics, moreover, were scarcely value free. It was actually a weapon of the political Establishment, and academic economists were servants of the prevailing political and economic system. An upheaval was essential in the profession. "Another type of economist is needed—an economist concerned with the important problems of the world in which he lives and works; an economist willing to jettison the irrelevant . . . portions of the received doctrine."[1]

Each of the various radical caucuses had some equivalent set of intellectual bones to pick with the discipline's Establishment. In sociology it was the profession's "incestuous relationship" with government and the "deadening and repressive" teaching of sociology students.[2] In history it was the dominance of a "consensus" and "elite" history, which emphasized the cooperation and agreement between classes in America's past and gave excessive attention to

[1] *Radicals in the Professions Newsletter,* November–December, 1968, p. 18.
[2] These were the words of the radical caucus leader Martin Nicolaus at the American Sociology Association meeting at Boston in August, 1968. See *ibid.,* September, 1968, p. 17.

white male elites, neglecting blacks, women, Indians, and working-class folk. In literature it was the New Criticism, which established aristocratic canons of taste and judgment and rejected social relevance as a measure of literary excellence. In political science it was the "trivial" survey research investigations, like those being done at Michigan and Columbia, which ignored the problems of power and denied the existence of a ruling class.

Besides these intellectual disputes with the professional Establishments, the radical caucuses objected to the way older men conducted the affairs of the various professional associations. The caucuses charged that national organizations were ruled by an old-boy system that excluded dissenters and minority groups from decision-making roles and important committees. They claimed that the associations, in their role as labor exchanges for younger scholars, discriminated against radicals, blacks, women, and Ph.D.s from the less prestigious graduate schools. They held that the associations failed to take stands on public issues important to scholars both as professional men and as citizens. Beginning in 1968 many of the radical caucuses fought to compel the professional associations to take strong positions opposing the American role in Vietnam.

The Establishments did not always take kindly to the dissenters. Each year after 1967 the annual meeting of many professional associations became a battleground between various radical caucus groups and the more traditional members of the disciplines. On one occasion, at the 1968 Modern Language Association annual meeting, strong feelings erupted into actual disorder when the police arrested Professor Louis Kampf, a member of the radical caucus who tried to prevent the Americana Hotel manager from removing some New University Conference posters from the hotel lobby columns. Kampf was quickly released on bail, the money being raised by his colleagues passing the hat at the MLA Conference sessions.

Such intrusions of "real life" into stately academic environs were unusual. The exchanges between the radical caucus members and the associations' senior people were mostly verbal and generally took place at the annual business meetings after the newly elected association president gave his address. The radicals usually lost, but they did win concessions. Few of the major professional associations were willing to support the radicals' positions on public issues, but in almost every case they yielded on intellectual or professional matters. With each annual meeting more of the program was devoted to woman's history, the economics of war and imperialism, the black family, Marxist philosophy, the proletarian novel, or some other subject that the radical caucus people considered more relevant than the usual convention fare. In addition, the associations often went out of their way to open up their offices to women, blacks, and other groups and to make the association's job-finding role fairer.

The radical caucuses were made up predominantly of younger academics. These young men and women were at the beginning of their careers, and their professional work was often more impassioned than convincing. Yet as time passed, their impact on their disciplines grew, and older scholars began to find themselves and their work relegated increasingly to the grim category of "dated," as the scholarly journals and the university presses gradually opened to New Left interpretations and as younger instructors began to make converts among undergraduates and Ph.D. candidates.

One of the more interesting forums for radical thought was the Socialist Scholars Conference, which was held annually between 1964 and 1970. At these meetings hundreds of radical scholars from Europe and America, representing every field and every radical persuasion, gathered to hear papers and participate in forums. These covered a broad range of topics, reflecting the scholarly and intellectual concerns of the reinvigorated left. The participants in the conferences were by and large preaching to the converted, but the meetings were respectfully reported in the press and raised the prestige of radical scholarship among American intellectuals and academics.

The radical mood within the scholarly community was expressed, then, largely in efforts to bypass or supersede the intellectual or bureaucratic Establishments of the disciplines. This was all very well, but was it the best way to contribute to the Movement? Should a radical historian or sociologist remain in the sheltered and privileged environment of the universities and the learned professions? Was it enough to push "radical" history or sociology, or to serve as a radical gadfly at faculty meetings? With injustice and misery everywhere, with the nation and the world reeling under the impact of revolutionary forces, could any intelligent, informed man or woman in good conscience bury himself in the 1870 Paris

Commune or the sociology of the ghetto? Even these subjects seemed pale stuff by the side of what was actually happening in Paris and Harlem.

This existential dilemma was usually resolved by each Movement academic within his own conscience. No doubt temperament and prudence played their part in the final decision that each young radical scholar made. Some simply found the academic environment more congenial than any other they could contemplate. Others could not afford to forgo the financial security of a university appointment. What could a young radical professor with a wife and young children do except stay on and use his energies part time for the Movement?

Though the choices were generally considered in private, they were sometimes argued in full view of the public. One such public soul-searching took place at the 1968 founding convention of the New University Conference. On the side of rejecting academia for activism was Staughton Lynd. The university in America, Lynd declared, more often "corrupts radicals . . . than it destroys them." It accomplished this unhappy effect by making itself the "emotional center" of radicals' lives and keeping them from more than a secondary commitment to the work that they must perform. At the very least a radical intellectual "must have a foot solidly off campus," he concluded, even if this meant surrendering economic security. On the other side of the issue was Jesse Lemisch of Roosevelt University, who, like Lynd, was a young historian of early America. Lemisch defended not only the career investment of radical academics, but also the utility of objective scholarship to the radical mission. "I think," he asserted, "that the idea of finding out how things actually work and have worked is an extremely radical idea. Radical scholars and intellectuals need not apologize for continuing their work on the fundamental workings of society.[3]

Academic people were not the only ones who faced the problem of how to combine professions and radical politics, and not the only ones who organized themselves into radical professional associa-

[3] See Staughton Lynd, "Intellectuals, the University, and the Movement"; and Jesse Lemisch, "Who Will Write a Left History While We Are All Putting Our Balls on the Line?" These two essays were originally printed together in the first issue of the NUC *Newsletter*. I have used a pamphlet version of them generously supplied to me by Professor Lemisch. The Lynd essay was presented orally; the Lemisch one was distributed in written form.

tions. During 1968 and 1969 each issue of *Radicals in the Professions Newsletter* carried news of some new radical professional body. There were radical teachers, radical social workers, radical scientists, radical artists, radical computer programmers, and radical media people.

The media radicals were of two kinds: those who remained within the established newspapers, magazines, publishing houses, or television networks and those who broke entirely with the Establishment outlets and set up alternative radical ones. The first was the larger group, and the growing number of young radicals in the media surely accounts for some of the favorable publicity the New Left received in the 1960s. Many of these young media radicals, working for *Life, The New York Times,* or some major New York publisher, must have faced the same crises of conscience as the radical scholars.

The second group was spared the anguish. As the left grew, it spawned a large and lively litter of media outlets of its own. In 1967 radicals established the Newsreel for radicals interested in film and Radio Free People for radicals in the audio field. These two organizations were dedicated to spreading the radical message through documentaries, tapes, and recordings.

For radical media people there was, in addition, an ever growing radical press, which they could use to express political, philosophical, and artistic commitments. Radical reporters and journalists increasingly found outlets in such older left-wing publications as *The Monthly Review, The Nation,* and *Liberation.* In 1970 a group of New Left journalists tried to take over *The Guardian,* a paper founded in 1948 as an organ of the Henry A. Wallace Progressive party. They did not succeed in ousting the Old Left leaders and had to settle for establishing their own publication, but they did manage to open the older journal to New Left viewpoints and younger radical writers. By 1966 another important national outlet for New Left opinion was *Ramparts,* a slick-papered weekly founded by Edward Keating as a liberal Catholic magazine in the Bay Area. *Ramparts* soon ceased to be Catholic in any sense and, with such pioneer New Left journalists as Robert Scheer and Paul Jacobs on its staff, was brashly at work exposing the nation's errors and deceptions.

Besides its influence on the older publications, the New Left directly inspired its own enormous efflorescence of weeklies, monthlies, quarterlies, and even dailies. Taking advantage of new printing techniques, which allowed small runs of five thousand tabloids to be produced for as little as $250, budding Movement journalists were soon cranking out a hundred different left-oriented publications. Some of these were sober and scholarly journals, such as *Radical America*, founded by the Radical Education Project to advance radical scholarship and theory. Others were counter culture oriented. Many of these hippie publications were frankly pornographic, and although they professed to be for "liberation," they were often little more than cheap exploitation sheets. Still others, including the early *Village Voice* (New York), the *Berkeley Barb*, Paul Krassner's *The Realist*, the *Los Angeles Free Press*, *Old Mole* (Boston), and *Second City* (Chicago), combined radical politics with radical cultural style, especially sexual liberation. In addition, journals devoted to rock music, such as *Crawdaddy* and *Rolling Stone*, to counterculture fashion, such as *Rags*, or to avant-garde literature, such as *Big Table*, occasionally included a warmed-over New Left political article.

This network of "underground" newspapers was joined together by Liberation News Service, an organization founded in 1967 by two radical student editors, Marshall Bloom of Amherst and Ray Mungo of Boston University. Neither of the two founders was a particularly stable individual. As Mungo later admitted, he and Bloom founded Liberation News Service because they "had nothing else to do." Neither one was actually a committed radical. We "didn't really believe in 'the Revolution' to come," Mungo wrote, "or else we acted as if the revolution was then and there; we tried to enjoy life as much as possible, took acid trips, went to the movies, and supported people because they were fun or well-intentioned, or in need." [4] Mungo later dropped out of the Movement, and Bloom committed suicide. Liberation News Service at times was as casual and irresponsible as its managers; yet while it lasted, it served the important purpose of supplying the radical press with news of radical doings and of national and international events that interested radicals.

[4] Quoted in Laurence Leamer, *The Paper Revolutionaries: The Rise of the Underground Press* (New York: Simon and Schuster, 1972), p. 49. There was also an Underground Press Service, which furnished news items primarily to the counter culture press, though at times the services of the two agencies overlapped.

Still another autonomous radical enterprise was radical theater. This was often quite informal, with young actors giving performances in the streets to make a specific political point for some particular demonstration or rally. The casts of these skits were generally as ad hoc as the performances themselves, but there were also a few permanent troupes—the San Francisco Mime Troupe, the Bread and Puppet Theater, and the Living Theater of Julian Beck and Judith Malina, for example—that made political and cultural radicalism the core of their repertories.

At least one radical playwright, Barbara Garson, achieved a great *succès de scandale* in 1967 with a satire on Lyndon Johnson called *MacBird*, which ran for many weeks in Greenwich Village and delighted Johnson's growing army of enemies. A graduate of the Berkeley Free Speech Movement, Mrs. Garson pictured the President as a gross and repellent latter-day Macbeth with the blood of John Kennedy on his hands. In retrospect the play seems a puerile and witless spoof. In 1967, however, it suited the mood of many liberals and radicals, who were appalled by the administration's Vietnam policies, and it was fulsomely praised and widely patronized.

Bloom and Mungo notwithstanding, most of the New Left professionals must be admired for their dedication and their courage. Many of them sincerely believed they were risking their professional necks for the cause of oppressed humanity. In retrospect we can see that they exaggerated both the power of the professional Establishments and the media organizations and the desire of these groups to penalize them for their views. In the end few were denied the jobs or perquisites that their talents entitled them to. In fact some of them were probably rewarded beyond their true desserts by the public or by the professions. Louis Kampf, for one, though only an associate professor, was elected vice-president of the MLA in 1969 and soon after became one of the youngest presidents of this large and prestigious academic association. This, however, is hindsight. As far as the dissenters could tell, they could expect sharp retaliation for their disruptive tactics and for their defiance of the rules of the game, and it took considerable courage for them to take on the professional Establishments.

Less admirable, I think, were many of the older intellectuals who climbed aboard the New Left bandwagon when it had built up a full head of steam. These people were drawn to the New Left by a combination of guilt, craving for novelty, self-hatred, and fear of being left out. In the past many of these literary and academic men and women had gone through strange and inconsistent political and intellectual gyrations. In the 1930s they had been either Stalinists, Trotskyites, or unaffiliated radicals. In the 1940s and 1950s they had sometimes been new conservatives. Now, when the New Left was beginning to move, they were anxious to join their names with the radical juggernaut. Standing in the chic upper middle-class world of successful professional people, they enthusiastically cheered on those who had the courage and commitment to risk their futures in the battle for radical change.

At the upper reaches of this group were the New York intellectuals associated with the *New York Review of Books*. This was a journal founded in 1963 as an outlet for serious book reviewing when *The New York Times* temporarily ceased publication during a printers' strike. Never a very rigorous critical force, the *Times'* *Book Review* had nevertheless filled a need and its suspension created an intellectual vacuum. At first the *New York Review of Books* confined itself largely to literary criticism, drawing on established authorities and experts of a wide range of aesthetic and political persuasions. Gradually, under the impact of the Vietnam War, the journal shifted to politics and to the left. By the late 1960s, under the editorship of Robert Silver and Barbara Epstein (and in the wings, Jason Epstein of Random House), it became the house organ of a special version of New Leftism that the journalist Tom Wolfe labeled radical chic.

Radical chic was radicalism turned into an exciting "groovy" fashion that seemed as much concerned with conferring status, attracting attention, or providing its practitioners with a sense of living dangerously, as with advancing social justice. It was epitomized by the notorious 1969 meeting, or party, arranged by Leonard Bernstein, conductor of the New York Philharmonic, for the defendants in the New York Black Panther conspiracy trial. Held in Bernstein's lavish Park Avenue apartment, the gathering brought together a number of the Black Panthers and some of the most elegant and glamorous of New York's New Society, people in the arts and the entertainment industry, predominantly. The meeting was billed as an effort to raise money for the Panther legal defense fund, but to many people who read about it the next day in *The*

New York Times or some weeks later in Wolfe's satiric articles, it
seemed to be another case of thrill seeking by the jaded "beautiful
people." The public noted Mrs. Peter Duchin's ecstatic "I've never
met a Panther—this is a first for me!" and refused to accept Bernstein's protest that he and his rich and famous guests merely wished
to help the Panthers get a fair trial in Judge Murtagh's court.

The radical chic phenomenon of the 1960s was not unique. It
goes back at least as far as the early part of the century when
socialism became a popular parlor sport among the rich and well-
placed. Mr. Dooley, Peter Finley Dunne's loquacious Irish saloon-
keeper, caught its ludicrous flavor when he noted how dramatically attitudes toward socialism had changed since the years of his
youth.

> 'Tis far different now. No cellars f'r th' Brotherhood iv Man, but
> Mrs. Vanderhankerbilt gives a musical soree f'r th' ladies iv th'
> Female Billyonaires Arbeiter Verein at her iligant Fifth Avnoo man-
> sion yisterdah afthernoon. Th' futmen were dhressed in th' costume
> iv th' Fr-rinch Rivolution, an' tea was served in imitation bombs.
> Th' meetin' was addhressed be th' well-known Socialist leader, J. Clar-
> ence Lumley, heir to th' Lumley millyons. This well-known proly-
> teriat said he had become a Socialist through studyin' his father. He
> cud not believe that a system was right which allowed such a man to
> accumylate three hundherd millyon dollars.[5]

In the 1960s radical chic went beyond the beautiful people of
the Bernstein set. It was very prevalent among college faculty; for
a time in some academic communities, parties, cake sales, folk con-
certs, and rallies for the Panthers, Cesar Chavez's grape pickers,
or some other dissenting cause or group became major social activities. By the late 1960s one especially popular cause among stylishly
radical academic folk was ecology, which combined the irreproach-
able love of mother nature with just enough defiance of technology
and capitalism to make it interesting.

Among the urban intelligentsia the radical chic phenomenon
was complex. Its triggering mechanism was probably the Vietnam
War, which badly damaged the moral authority of the United
States in the eyes of so many Americans. In a portion of the intellectual Establishment, this released an intense anti-Americanism.

[5] Quoted in Mark Sullivan, *Our Times: The United States, 1900–1925*
(New York: Charles Scribner's Sons, 1930), III, 429.

In the writings of Jason Epstein, Edgar Z. Friedenberg, Murray
Kempton, Nat Hentoff, Susan Sontag, Mary McCarthy, and Noam
Chomsky, we often encounter an undisguised contempt for America,
which was scarcely unknown among the student left but seems less
attractive in adult intellectuals. Perhaps the most extreme version
of this was Susan Sontag's notorious anti-American diatribe in a
1967 *Partisan Review* symposium which declared solemnly that the
United States was founded on genocide, the cruelest system of
slavery in the civilized world, and the vulgarity of transplanted
European peasants, and concluded with the statement that "the
white race *is* the cancer of human history." [6]

The older radical chic intellectuals, as Susan Sontag's patroniz-
ing remark about immigrant vulgarity suggests, were also often
elitists. Drawn to the underclass of blacks, Chicanos, and American
Indians, by what they considered their authenticity or their primitive naturalness, they could scarcely conceal their contempt for the
white ethnic groups and blue-collar folk who made up "Middle
America." Tom Wolfe, the journalist, called this attitude *nostalgie
de la boue* (yearning for mud); but whatever it was called, it
betrayed how seriously the radical chic intellectuals had been alienated from their own roots and values.

Many of the *New York Review* intellectuals were Jews, as were
many of the student New Left. This is a sensitive fact. Jews are
still not so secure, even in the Western democratic countries, that
they can be complacent about accusations of elitism and lack of
patriotism. Anti-Semitic movements in France, Germany, and the
Soviet Union have been constructed out of just such materials, and
even in the United States Jews have been accused of cliquishness
and doubtful commitment to their native land.

Yet it is necessary to acknowledge that the New Left was disproportionately Jewish. This was a sociological, not a religious or
ethnic phenomenon, of course. Jews made up a substantial portion
of those groups most susceptible to the New Left appeal. By the
1960s Jewish students accounted for a large part of the enrollments
in elite colleges. In addition, they were concentrated in the humanities and the social sciences. Finally they often came from successful
professional families with self-made fathers who had liberal or radi-

[6] See Symposium, "What's Happening to America," *Partisan Review,*
Winter, 1967, p. 58.

cal antecedents. There were non-Jews of similar backgrounds, of course—Tom Hayden, Al Haber, and Staughton Lynd, for example —but it was either the good fortune or bad luck, depending on one's point of view, of many young Jews to belong to the group of the decidedly left-prone.

At times the number of Jewish members embarrassed SDS. Members of SDS were wary about mentioning the subject, but it sometimes came out obliquely. A memo from Richard Rothstein, discussing the location of the SDS national conference in 1965, declared that the Midwest was the logical choice, though there were many who favored New York. "The midwest," Rothstein coyly noted, "is . . . the only place where a more sociologically representative (you know what that means) and geographically representative conference can take place." [7]

A particularly sensitive problem, for both the student left and the *New York Review* group, growing out of this state of affairs was the question of what to do about Israel. To many people on the left, it seemed undeniable that Israel was an advanced base of Western, and especially American, neo-imperialism within the Third World. New Left radicals found it easier to identify with Arab nationalists and Al Fatah, the Palestinian liberation group, than with Israel's old-fashioned social democracy. Jewish New Leftists twisted and turned to avoid the charge of anti-Semitism and insisted that they were only anti-Zionist, not anti-Jewish; but to older Jewish liberals with strong emotional ties to Israel, there seemed little to distinguish between the two attitudes.

Still another perplexity was the growing anti-Jewish responses of some black militants. If the Jewish New Left, especially of the *New York Review* sort, had little use for white ethnic groups, they tended to idolize blacks. They excused the rhetorical and activist excesses of militant blacks and assumed the blacks knew what was best for themselves, though they often denied white ethnic groups the same latitude. So long as Jews and blacks were allies in the fight for racial justice, this response was unambiguous. In the early 1960s blacks began to assert their independence of white philanthropists, many of them Jewish, and some tension developed be-

[7] See mimeographed letter dated SDS regional office, San Francisco, in SDS File, Social Protest Project, Bancroft Library, University of California, Berkeley. The phrase in parenthesis is as in Rothstein's original.

tween the two groups. But this was still relatively minor. Then, in 1967–1968 far more serious problems erupted.

This is not the place to go into Jewish-black relations in detail. Even in the 1950s a certain amount of antagonism between the two groups existed, though it was muted. Many Jews were as bigoted as their white, gentile fellow Americans. Many blacks, in turn, resented the Jewish businessmen, employers, and landlords they dealt with in the ghettos. Yet these attitudes were seldom displayed publicly. As a black sense of identification with Africa and the Third World began to grow, and especially after the cult of things Islamic began to flourish, militant blacks came to the defense of the Arab cause in the Mideast, much like other radicals. Jews who were deeply committed to Israel were disturbed by these anti-Zionist attacks. More important was the 1968 clash between predominantly Jewish school teachers of the New York City Teachers' Union and militant black leaders and black parents over community influence in the New York City schools. This confrontation made many New York Jews uneasy. Lower middle-class Jews from the boroughs of Brooklyn and Queens could not afford to send their children to private schools and feared that in many areas "community control" really meant black control. Also many were part of the New York City bureaucracy—social workers, school teachers, city clerks, civil service accountants—and the clash between the black leaders and the Teachers' Union raised fears that blacks wanted to push them and their kind out of their jobs. Though the collision took place within the special New York context, it helped drive a wedge between the Jewish community and black militants, and forced some Jewish radicals to reconsider their positions.

Yet the defection was not uniform. The intrusion of these issues split the American Jewish community along class and intellectual lines. On one side were the New Left college students, the younger professionals nurtured in the earlier student movement, the radical intellectuals of the *New York Review* sort, and the more modish and with-it of New York's cultural elite. On the other side were the middle-class Jews with small businesses and in the lesser professions, and the civil service.

Actually the division is not quite this neat. The question of Israel and black–Jewish antagonism deeply divided even the student left. It is my impression that after about 1968 not as many Jewish college students were attracted to the New Left as before. Those who were already part of the Movement generally remained, but fewer new Jewish recruits, I suspect, entered it.

Israel in particular divided the Jewish intelligentsia. Opposed to the *New York Review* and the radical chic group was a contingent of Jewish intellectuals whose ethnic and cultural commitment remained strong. Many of these were associated with the American Jewish Committee and its prestigious publication, *Commentary*. In the 1950s *Commentary* published Paul Goodman and other dissenters from the decade's self-congratulatory mood. In the early 1960s it was sympathetic to the growing student left and to black liberation. By 1965 its editor, Norman Podhoretz, and many of its contributors—including Lewis Feuer, Robert Nesbit, Dennis Wrong, Nathan Glazer—began to write skeptically of the new radicalism. By 1967 or 1968 *Commentary* had become one of the most effective critics of the New Left within the American intellectual community.

The spread of the Movement to young professionals and the literati reveals once more the tangled interconnection of cultural and political dissent. How many people were in the Movement not because they had deep political commitments, but because they were bored or, to put it more sympathetically, because they wished to find more interesting ways to live their lives? It is hard to respect the sensation seeking of the *New York Review* literati. Ray Mungo's confession about Liberation News Service borders on an admission of moral bankruptcy. Not all Movement people were dilettantes, however. Modern urban life in America had truly serious drawbacks. Many sincere and earnest young radicals hoped to find, through the Movement, personal life-styles that would be more satisfying than the world of conventional professional striving. At the same time they sought to make the Movement a self-contained world, detached from, and independent of, the world of modern America. Movement people must work out "alternative ways of living in the society, alternative ways of bringing up and educating children," asserted Bob Gottlieb and Marge Piercy in the prospectus for the Movement for a Democratic Society. "We need counterforms of recreation and enjoyment and communication to replace the cultural manipulations, the addiction to consumption, the passivity of packaged entertainment, the subtle conditioning and gross lies of the media." [8]

This double concern for abstract social justice and for personal fulfillment was present in the New Left from the very beginning of course. Yet there was always a severe tension between the two facets of the Movement. Some people resolved it by choosing the cultural, life-style side; others by choosing the political half. Many, clearly, sought to combine the two in varying proportions.

One of the more colorful attempts to fuse cultural and political radicalism was made by the Yippies, or the Youth International party, founded in late 1967 by Abbie Hoffman, Jerry Rubin, Ed Sanders of the rock group called The Fugs, and Paul Krassner, editor of *The Realist*. As their name indicates, the Yippies sought to capitalize on the hippie phenomenon that had abruptly surfaced. By 1967 hippiedom had become an important cultural force among the youth of the United States. A highly complicated movement, one of its roots was the beat generation of the 1950s, with its disdain for conventional bourgeois forms and materialism and its respect for the subterranean culture of black musicians and drug takers. The hippies added some new elements to this mixture. Youth was one. Unlike the beats, the hippies were almost all adolescents and were more often dropouts from school than from the adult workaday world. Another was LSD, or acid. The beats had had cheap wine, pot, and occasionally heroin. The hippies dropped the alcohol and added lysergic acid diethylamide.

LSD made an important difference. Psychedelic drugs fully arrived on the scene in 1964 or 1965, although they had been used previously, in the form of mescaline, by Latin American Indians and a few Western scientists and curious intellectuals. During the late 1950s psychologists became interested in LSD as a consciousness-altering substance that produced hallucinating effects that seemed to resemble schizophrenia. During this period scientists and medical people experimented with it, hoping to learn something about mental illness and how the mind worked. Among the experimenters were two young psychology professors at Harvard, Timothy Leary and Richard Alpert. Leary and Alpert as well as a number

[8] Robert Gottlieb and Marge Piercy, "Beginning to Begin to Begin: Movement for a Democratic Society," *Radicals in the Professions Newsletter*, March, 1968, p. 21.

of student volunteers took dozens of exploratory "trips" during which they experienced powerful and vivid hallucinations. These experiences altered their perceptions of themselves and the objective world, not only for the period of the trip, but at least in the case of the two professors, permanently. Leary and Alpert soon lost their scientific interest in LSD and founded a quasi-religious cult of extreme personal subjectivity, which, like a number of traditional Eastern religions, rejected the external physical world for an inner world of self-awareness. This inner world, the two insisted, represented a superior reality, and once helped to perceive it by psychedelic means, the LSD users could readily return to it again and again.

Both Leary and Alpert were eventually fired from Harvard. Leary later became an active propagandist for LSD and in 1963 established a Psychedelic Training Center in Mexico. When this was closed by the authorities, he founded the League for Spiritual Discovery at Millbrook, New York. In 1966 the United States government forbade the sale of LSD, driving it underground and undoubtedly adding to its appeal to cultural dissenters.

By this time LSD, given a tremendous boost by novelist Ken Kesey and his wild, careering "Merry Pranksters," had become an important part, if not the defining element, of the hippie culture. This culture took root in varying degrees in many urban centers and college communities, but predictably its twin capitals were San Francisco and New York. In the first, the run-down area adjacent to Golden Gate Park, Haight-Ashbury (Hashberry), with its cheap housing and relaxed inhabitants, became the headquarters of thousands of long-haired, sandal-wearing flower children from all over the country. Here they tripped on pot and LSD, rapped with the other "heads," and lived by begging, selling drugs, cashing checks from home, or getting handouts from the Diggers, a group of senior hippies who ran a store where the broke and the broken could get free food and clothing. In 1967 the word went out to the youth culture that Haight-Ashbury was "where it was," and thousands of would-be flower children descended on San Francisco to join in the fun. In New York a similar community developed in the East Village, a run-down ethnic neighborhood just to the east of Greenwich Village. Here, along Saint Marks Place and near Tompkins Park, there appeared the same young people wearing love beads, Indian headbands, and junk-store castoffs, the same run-down, cold-water pads, the same "head shops" sporting psychedelic signs and selling rock records, junk fashions, incense, and, occasionally, some interesting sculpture or painting.

For every bona fide hippie who truly believed in the hippie-psychedelic message of love, gentleness, feeling, and reverence for human beings and "all living things," there were dozens of synthetic ones who were attracted by the outward trappings and style of the authentic flower children. Some of these mouthed the words of "love, not war" and feigned the contempt for inhibitions and technology that characterized the cultural naysayers. Others merely adopted the dress, hair style, and patois of hippiedom. Whether deep or shallow, however, the hippies became an influential part of the youth culture.

As the hippie phenomenon ballooned, the New Left was forced to confront the question of the hippies' political potential. Many young radicals believed that they meant something important for the Movement. However callow or misguided the hippies might seem to be at times, their way of life betokened a major disenchantment with middle-class American life. Obviously thousands of young Americans were accepting Leary's advice to "tune in, turn off, drop out." True, this solution was evasive. Drugs were not an adequate substitute for revolution, and "doing your own thing" was fine in its way, but some people's thing was clearly harmful to other people's. Surely the youth culture's rejection of conventional society could be used for better ends than mere personal escape.

Radicals who believed this often disagreed about how the hippie phenomenon would change the system. Some believed the hippie way of life would spread spontaneously to the larger society and come to permeate and in the end dramatically transform the consciousness of Western man. The revolution would not need organizations or parties, manifestoes and conventions; it would be accomplished by the accelerating change in consciousness, which would slowly undermine the established institutions and inexorably replace them with better ones that would be more attuned to the new way of regarding the world and human existence. This comfortable thesis would be fully developed in Charles Reich's *The Greening of America* in 1970, but it was already being announced earlier in a psychedelic version by Leary. "It will be an LSD country in fifteen years," Leary told an interviewer from the British Broadcasting Corporation in 1967. "Our Supreme Court will be smoking marijuana within fifteen years. . . . There'll be less interest in warfare, in power politics." [9]

As the left encountered ever greater political obstacles in the early 1970s, many radicals took refuge in this hope of spontaneous revolution through the impact of the counter culture on consciousness. In the late 1960s, however, it was a view accepted only by those who, like Leary and Alpert, had made the psychedelic experience into a religion. The Yippies were less passive. According to the Yippie version, the counter culture was a weapon against the Establishment and could be actively wielded to break the Establishment down. Like Leary, Abbie Hoffman urged everyone to turn on and make the revolution within his own head, but he also wanted to laugh the Establishment to death. Hoffman and Jerry Rubin were superb clowns, each with an acute sense of the ridiculous and a mad, antic streak. Like every clown, they were born exhibitionists who desperately needed an audience and knew how to attract attention. At one point in the Yippie phase of his career, when called to testify before HUAC, Rubin turned up at the committee room wearing the uniform of a Revolutionary War soldier. Two years later he came before the same committee wearing a Black Panther beret, Viet Cong pajamas, bells, a bandolier of bullets, and a toy rifle, his face covered with war paint. Even more inventive, Hoffman went with some friends to the New York Stock Exchange in 1967 and tossed money from the visitors' gallery to the cheering brokers on the trading floor. On another occasion Hoffman called for a midnight party in New York's Grand Central Station, and collected eight thousand hippies for a frantic saturnalia that brought the police running.

Efforts to fuse the hippie movement with radical political activism go back at least to mid-1967. Rubin, Ed Sanders and the Fugs, and hundreds of flower children joined the October, 1967, march on the Pentagon to protest the Vietnam War. Their chief contribution to the proceedings was a wild exorcism ceremony to levitate the Pentagon off its foundations to "end the fire, and war . . . [to] end the plague of death." [10] These antics, and the placing of flowers in

[9] Quoted in Theodore Roszak, *The Making of a Counterculture: Reflections on the Technocratic Society and Its Youthful Opposition* (New York: Doubleday, 1969), p. 168.

[10] Norman Mailer, *The Armies of the Night* (New York: New American Library, 1968), p. 142.

the upright barrels of the military police's rifles, delighted the media and both amused and outraged the public.

Early in 1968 the formation of the Yippies brought the hippie movement and the New Left together in a more deliberate way. The occasion for the alliance was the impending presidential election and its preliminaries. Nineteen sixty-eight promised to be a particularly important presidential year. Since President Johnson had entered on his first full term, New Deal liberalism had been pushed to its culmination in the shape of the Great Society. Congress had enacted a health insurance scheme for older people that rounded out the social welfare system. It had funded large programs for retraining the poor and attacking the roots of poverty. It had passed new civil rights legislation that dismantled legal segregation and restored the vote to blacks in the South. It had established national endowments in the arts and in the humanities to help support projects and organizations in the creative arts and humanistic scholarship and to subsidize promising artists and scholars. Under Johnson, welfare state liberalism had been carried to its logical conclusion.

Little of this impressed the New Left. Radicals regarded the Great Society and the welfare state with a mixture of contempt and fear. Liberal "palliatives" were only Band-Aids applied to deep social wounds. They could not solve the fundamental problems of capitalism. If, however, liberalism somehow succeeded, what need would there be for radical change and for radicals? At the very best radicals would be absorbed by the liberal Establishment. Liberalism, in fact, was the enemy. Compared to liberals, the far right seemed almost benign. Operating under the old Russian nihilist principle that the political "worse is the better," radicals usually rejected liberal candidates for major office, even when the liberals' opponents were men of the extreme right fringe.

An example of this often infuriating attitude was the response of the Berkeley chapter of SDS to the 1966 Pat Brown–Ronald Reagan gubernatorial campaign in California. In an SDS working paper entitled "Vote No for Governor!" Ed Moritz conceded that Reagan might be a neofascist and Brown a well-intentioned liberal, but, Moritz said, SDS people should not accept the argument that the left must support the lesser of two evils. For one thing, Reagan could not do the damage that the liberals said he could, but even if the liberals were right, a Reagan administration in Sacramento

would benefit the left not hurt it. It "would probably radicalize at
least the poor and Negroes and maybe Mexican-Americans and
other minority communities as well as labor." As for the university,
a Reagan purge of liberals and radicals would push students and
faculty further left than ever.

The real danger to the left, Moritz explained, was not repression, but "co-option."

> It is when the society makes outcasts of some of its members, that
> revolutionary organizations flourish . . . . [The] main reason there
> has never been a viable left in the 20th century is that the center
> (Democrats and Republicans) has constantly co-opted both the ideas
> and the manpower of the left, over and over again, leaving it with few
> true believers and no power.[11]

However valid the "worse is the better" principle, Moritz was
probably right about the co-option problem. American radicals had
in fact often been absorbed and submerged by the major parties.
Yet the New Left found it difficult to resist the schemes of a left–
liberal coalition that would give radicals an influential voice in
national affairs and enable them to enjoy a modicum of power. It
was not always easy for leftists to stand perpetually on the street
with their noses pressed against the candy store window.

In 1967 their natural yearning to get some of the candy too
was translated into the New Politics Convention of left liberals and
radicals held at the Palmer House in Chicago. Unfortunately the
meeting was a disaster for those who hoped to forge a black–white
left, liberal–radical coalition, and a new left-of-center party. People
with almost every shade of left-liberal opinion came to Chicago in
response to the call for a new third party issued by the National
Conference for New Politics, a group formed in 1965 by Arthur
Waskow and a number of other older Movement people. Many antiwar liberals came, as did many Old Leftists and a few members of
SDS. Also present were the most militant of the black nationalist
groups. The most prominent of these was the Black Panthers, a
group organized in Oakland in the mid-1960s as a protective shield
for ghetto residents. In their first months the Panthers had allotted
much of their time to shadowing the Oakland police to see that

[11] Ed Moritz, "Vote No for Governor!" SDS File, Social Protest Project,
Bancroft Library, University of California, Berkeley, p. 3.

they did not oppress blacks. The Panthers soon became involved in a shoot-out with the authorities in which a policeman was killed and Huey Newton was arrested for murder. By 1967, under Newton, Eldridge Cleaver, and Bobby Seale, the Panthers had expanded beyond their original base, and as the Black Panther party aspired to become the leading voice of black nationalism.

The majority of the delegates at the Palmer House were white, but they were a cacophonous crowd without leadership or a unified point of view. Quick to take advantage of this situation, the 150 or so blacks organized a black caucus and announced that unless it was given a voice equal to all the other delegates, it would boycott the convention. Many of the white delegates, both liberals and radicals, were appalled by this undemocratic and arrogant demand, but either out of guilt or conviction, they acquiesced. This was clearly a mistake. Voting as a block, the black caucus forced the convention to accept its thirteen-point program, including blanket endorsement of the recent Newark Black Power Conference resolutions, some of which were still secret, and a condemnation of "the imperialistic Zionist war." A resolution to form a third party was defeated, but another to organize locally to support radical candidates in 1968 was approved.

Almost everyone considered the convention a fiasco. Black militants came away with contempt for the whites. Roy Innis of CORE concluded that the white radicals and left liberals were not worth negotiating with. They had nothing to deliver, and he preferred to deal with the power structure itself than with people who had so little to bestow. A few white liberals and radicals with a masochistic streak seemed pleased with the results. Bertram Garskoff of the Ann Arbor Citizens for Peace concluded that the whites were "just a little tail on the end of a very powerful black panther" and that he for one wanted "to be on that tail—if they'll let me." [12] But other white delegates and observers were disgusted. Arthur Waskow, one of the organizers of the conference and a member of the radical research foundation the Institute for Policy Studies, said that the meeting had been castrating for whites. John Maher of SDS noted that the "public spectacle" at Palmer House did "not deserve to be taken seriously by anyone, least of all by those who

[12] Quoted in Richard Blumenthal, "New Politics at Chicago," *Nation*, September 25, 1967, p. 274.

have committed themselves to the building of a new political force in this country." [13]

Though in some rhetorical ways the most militant of all black revolutionaries, the Panthers recognized that whites were essential to blacks seeking liberation, and despite the discouraging outcome at Chicago, they decided to form a national party and run a presidential candidate in 1968. In March the Panthers, with white radical supporters, held a convention in the Bay Area and founded the Peace and Freedom party, with a ten-point program emphasizing the necessity for black self-determination. Acting in fact as the tail to the Panther, a white radical caucus at the meeting appended a statement expressing the hope that the Peace and Freedom party would eventually recruit thousands of white and Mexican-American workers for a truly mass political organization. This would take time, the statement acknowledged, but meanwhile the party would help to build "an organizational base" and involve "people in a broader spectrum of issues." [14] The convention also endorsed a resolution to free the imprisoned Huey Newton, a resolution that would shortly become a maddening refrain among the Panthers and their white allies.

In August the new party held its first presidential nominating convention and chose Eldridge Cleaver as its candidate. Cleaver favored Jerry Rubin as his running mate, but the delegates turned him down. In the end it was decided that each of the state Peace and Freedom parties would choose its own vice-presidential candidate, though all agreed to accept the party platform emphasizing community control of public services and a socialist economy.

The Peace and Freedom party would later become a moderately useful rallying point for those with New Left political aspirations, but it counted for little in 1968. Far more important still was the Democratic party, now badly split by the Vietnam War into pro-administration hawks and anti-administration doves. Not all radicals had as yet given up on the Democrats. No matter how far they had moved politically, it was difficult for young men

[13] See "Symposium: Chicago's Black Caucus," *Ramparts*, November, 1967, p. 108.

[14] "Summary of the Minutes of the Peace and Freedom Movement Founding Convention . . . at Richmond, California," Peace and Freedom File, Social Protest Project, Bancroft Library, University of California, Berkeley.

and women whose parents had voted for Roosevelt and who, as children, had absorbed the values of the New Deal, not to be at least ambivalent toward the party of the Great Society.

The groups most seriously concerned with the Democratic party's fate were those who, while still not radicals, were part of the reservoir from which the New Left hoped to draw future strength. In 1968 these left–liberals were disgusted by American intervention in Vietnam and were seeking alternatives to Johnson as the party's candidate.

At first it seemed as if Robert Kennedy, who wore the still-glamorous mantle of his late brother, might challenge Johnson. Kennedy was an acknowledged dove, and his hostility to the President was notorious. Besides, despite his millionaire origins, he was a rough-hewn scrapper who appealed to blacks, Hispanic-Americans, and other ethnic groups. Unfortunately Kennedy, having concluded that there was no way to deny an incumbent president renomination, refused at first to be drawn into a campaign against Johnson. Far braver, or perhaps more quixotic, was the junior Senator from Minnesota Eugene McCarthy. In December, 1967, McCarthy, deeply convinced of the stupidity and immorality of the Vietnam War, announced his intention to contest the renomination of Johnson.

Immediately the little-known senator became the focus of the left–liberal antiwar forces. On every college campus students lined up to sign petitions and raise money for the McCarthy campaign. In the Northeast hundreds of students shaved off their beards, cut their hair, and changed from dungarees and sandals to tweeds and loafers, and went off to campaign for "Gene" in the crucial New Hampshire Democratic primary. The improbable "children's crusade" proved a startling success. McCarthy came within a few hundred votes of Johnson, a remarkable performance against an incumbent president in a state primary.

At this point Kennedy saw the light and announced that he had reconsidered his position on the presidential race. Soon the two Democratic doves were battling to see who would become Johnson's challenger. Then the contest changed abruptly, when, on March 31, the President announced that he had stopped the bombing of North Vietnam, had opened negotiations with the National Liberation Front and North Vietnam, and would not seek renomination at the Chicago convention.

The New Left deplored the Kennedy–McCarthy campaign, but feared it as posing a classic threat of co-option of radicals by the Establishment. Soon after the New Hampshire primary, SDS leaders complained bitterly about campus defections by erstwhile radicals, who now saw some hope in the system. Moreover, things might get worse, they noted. If either of the two Democratic doves actually won the nomination, thousands of radicals or near radicals would undoubtedly vote for the victor in November. President McCarthy or President Kennedy might well end the Vietnam War, but what would that do for the radical cause? Neither man was a radical. At best they represented the more progressive elements of the corporate liberal Establishment that now recognized that Vietnam was becoming too expensive to tolerate.

When, after winning the California primary, Robert Kennedy was assassinated in Los Angeles by an Arab nationalist, a few New Leftists grieved. Tom Hayden, who admired Kennedy, apparently wept beside the coffin when it rested in state at Saint Patrick's Cathedral. Generally, however, the young members of SDS were unmoved by the tragedy or professed to see it as another sign of America's rapid decay.

As the time for the Chicago convention approached, however, many radicals found it difficult to remain indifferent to the outcome. The segment of the New Left most deeply concerned included the groups in the direct line of descent from the radical pacifists of the Fellowship of Reconciliation and the Committee for Non-Violent Revolution. In April, 1967, a little group of West Coast student radicals, including David Harris, former president of the Stanford University student body, established the Resistance, an organization dedicated to defying the Selective Service and any agency or activity connected with the war. The California students were probably influenced by an earlier group from New Haven, which in the summer of 1966 had fanned out across the country carrying the germ of the Resistance idea to campuses across the nation. Resisters would refuse to accept student deferments and would go to jail rather than cooperate with the war machine. To dramatize the Resistance mood, several hundred young men in New York and the Bay Area publicly burned their draft cards in the spring of 1967.

The young men were soon seconded by their elders. By the end of 1967 many sensitive men and women, revolted by the bombings and the atrocities, took up the Resistance strategy. In October over a hundred professors, intellectuals, journalists, authors, and clergymen organized Resist, an antiwar organization, and issued a statement attacking the war as unconstitutional and suggesting that students resist the draft and servicemen disobey illegal or immoral orders in Vietnam. Among the signers of "A Call to Resist Illegitimate Authority" were the Reverends Philip Berrigan, S. J., Robert McAfee Brown, and William Sloan Coffin, along with Allen Ginsberg, Paul Goodman, Noam Chomsky, Dwight MacDonald, Herbert Marcuse, Sidney Lens, Linus Pauling, Susan Sontag, Carl Oglesby, Dr. Benjamin Spock, and Howard Zinn. The successful October march on the Pentagon, sponsored by the National Mobilization Committee to End the War in Vietnam (Mobe), was an outgrowth of the new, defiant Resistance mood.[15]

The Resistance, as a revival of the moral witness and mass disobedience principles that had characterized radical pacifism, was particularly congenial to men like Dave McReynolds, Dave Dellinger of *Liberation,* and Staughton Lynd, men whose radicalism derived as much from Jesus as from Marx or Marcuse. SDS, however, was uncertain how to take the Resistance. On the one hand, SDS detested the war, but it did not approve of having radicals dragged off to prison by the authorities and lost to the Movement. Besides, SDS had already had its brush with the law over the draft and did not welcome a repeat performance. The Progressive Labor wing of SDS was particularly skeptical, dismissing the Resistance strategy contemptuously as "just another version of the pacifist, moral witness concept." [16] Although SDS went along with the October Pentagon march and Tom Hayden and Rennie Davis became active in Mobe, the SDS national office remained a reluctant participant in Resistance activities.

As the summer of 1968 approached, the various antiwar forces began to focus on Chicago, where the Democrats would meet. At the Pentagon demonstration the previous October, Jerry Rubin

[15] The Mobe was organized in September, 1966. It was composed of both avowed radicals and liberals and was held together by the respect that both groups felt for A. J. Muste and Dave Dellinger, men who were prime instigators of the new organization.

[16] Quoted in Immanuel Wallerstein and Paul Starr (eds.), *The University Crisis Reader* (New York: Random House, 1971), Vol. 2, p. 140.

had announced that the next target for the antiwar people would be the Chicago convention, but for a while it was not clear what form the action would take. The Mobe people wanted to march, distribute leaflets, and orate, as they had at the Pentagon. The Yippies, pessimistic about the convention's outcome, wanted a gigantic "festival of life" to contrast with the "festival of death" of the convention itself. For the delectation of the national audience, they would present lights, theater, magic, free music, and, it turned out, their own original Democratic candidate in the person of Mr. Pigasus, a mannerly and dignified boar. Actually, Hoffman later explained, the purpose of the festival, besides the fun of it, was to "make some statement, especially in revolutionary-action terms, about LBJ, the Democratic Party, electoral politics, and the state of the nation." [17]

The National Mobilization Committee, representing the older pacifist groups and Resistance people, was dubious about going to Chicago to demonstrate as allies of the mad collection of political hippies under Rubin and Hoffman. Many of the Mobe people remained highly skeptical of the drug culture, believing that drugs were "basically a diversion, a distraction, an irrelevance, an impertinence, a conceit, a siphoning off of energies desperately needed elsewhere, a way of opting out that is heartlessly unfair to those who are left, a way of saying to those others, 'My pleasure is more important than your misery.'" [18] After debating for some time whether to join the Yippies at Chicago, the older radicals of Mobe finally decided to go. SDS had similar qualms. Tom Hayden later declared that the "SDS national office fought against the action all the way, in any form it was put forward." [19] In the end, however, SDS voted to send "organizers" to Chicago, not so much because it had faith in the reformist approach to ending the war as to "get the McCarthy kids out of their bag and into SDS chapters in the fall." [20] Neither Mobe nor SDS wished to be associated with the

[17] Abbie Hoffman, *Revolution for the Hell of It!* (New York: Dial Press, 1968), p. 102.

[18] Henry Anderson, "The Case Against the Drug Culture," *Liberation*, April, 1967, p. 36.

[19] See Tim Findley, "Tom Hayden: *Rolling Stone* Interview, Part 1," *Rolling Stone*, October 21, 1972, p. 50.

[20] Quoted in Kirkpatrick Sale, *SDS* (New York: Random House, 1973), p. 474.

childish antics promised by the "crazies" and the "freaks" that Hoffman and Rubin were bringing to the convention.

It is hard to decide whether Chicago was a festival of life or a festival of death after all. Unlike New York or San Francisco, the city was a mid-American community both in the geographic and the cultural sense. Though it had its small bohemia and its cosmopolitans, it was at heart an aggregation of working-class, ethnic enclaves, and politically it reflected these cultural characteristics. Mayor Richard Daley was the last of the old-fashioned power-broker bosses, and he ran the city by ensuring law and order and by respecting the values and prejudices of his constituents.

Daley was also a Hubert Humphrey Democrat, and he had little sympathy for McCarthy or for Senator George McGovern, who, now that Robert Kennedy was out of the race, had become another dove candidate. In good part, the Democrats had chosen Chicago for the convention for security reasons, and Mayor Daley was determined that nothing would happen to disgrace his party and his city.

The mayor had not reckoned on Hoffman, Rubin, and the Yippies. Days before the convention opened, hundreds of protesters poured into Chicago. Many of them represented the Mobe under Dave Dellinger and Rennie Davis; hundreds more came at the call of the Youth International party; still others were antiwar radicals affiliated with SDS or the Panthers, or not affiliated at all. Both the Yippies and Mobe had applied for permission to parade and to use city parks for rallies and for sleeping out overnight. Shortly before the convention began, a local judge denied the demonstrators the right to remain in the parks after 11:00 P.M. The Mobe was denied the right to march to the convention hall.

On Friday, August 23, the Yippies staged the opening act of the festival. Gathered at the new civic center, a group of Yippies nominated Mr. Pigasus for president to the delight of assembled reporters and television camera crews. Also to the delight of the media people, the Chicago police arrested Jerry Rubin and folk singer Phil Ochs and took Mr. Pigasus off to the Humane Society. Meanwhile other Yippies were gathered in Lincoln Park, training marshals for the march that the courts had forbidden. Before long the police moved in and arrested a number of them.

This was just the beginning. It seems clear that neither the Mobe people nor the Yippies planned violence. This charge later became the basis for the long, drawn-out court trial at which Rubin, Hoffman, Tom Hayden, Bobby Seale of the Panthers as well as Dellinger, Davis, and other Mobe people were tried by the federal government for conspiracy. Mobe leaders wanted to march to the convention amphitheater to demand that the Democrats select a peace candidate and write a peace platform. They thought the police might attack them, but they did not plan to break up the convention or to commit violence. Nor did the Yippies. Both Rubin and Hoffman were peaceful people—in a violent sort of way. They wanted to ridicule, not beat, the Establishment to death. They favored disruption, indeed, but disruption by the same tactics that they had used at the Stock Exchange—confusing their opponents and keeping them off balance. As Hoffman himself later pointed out, the Chicago authorities could have neutralized the Yippies by going along with the joke. The previous spring the Yippies had staged a massive Yip-in in New York's Central Park, and thanks to Mayor John Lindsay's order to the police to keep their hands off, no one was hurt. Hoffman and Rubin, though warned otherwise, fully expected the Chicago police to be equally shrewd.

They were not. On Sunday evening after the 11:00 curfew, the police drove the Yippies out of Lincoln Park, beating many in the process. The next day Mobe led an illegal march from Lincoln Park to police headquarters to protest the arrest of Tom Hayden, who, the police charged, had been letting air out of police car tires. When the marchers reached Grant Park, opposite the Hilton Hotel, they broke ranks and made their way to the statue of General John Logan perched on top of a small hill. A number of the demonstrators climbed the statue with the idea of attracting attention. The police moved in and roughly dragged the demonstrators off the statue.

The big confrontation came once more in Lincoln Park that evening as the convention formally opened at the amphitheater several miles away. As the curfew hour approached, police gathered at the park. The demonstrators also assembled and watched curiously while Allen Ginsberg and a straggle of followers marched up and down chanting "Om, Om, Om," supposedly the Hindu word for the fundamental sound of the universe. Other, more occidental, chants broke out from the demonstrators, who were now crowded behind a flimsy barricade: "Hell, no, we won't go!" "Parks belong to the people!" "Dump the Hump!"

When a police car slowly pushed through the barricade, demonstrators began to throw stones, in reaction, it is said, to the near injury of a girl demonstrator. The car withdrew, its windows wrecked and its occupants badly shaken. Soon after canisters of tear gas began landing near the demonstrators, followed by charging police in gas masks brandishing shotguns and rifles. Before the park was cleared, many people, spectators and reporters as well as demonstrators, were beaten or gassed.

The remaining days of the convention were full of similar disorder, much of it caught by the television cameras or by the news photographers. During the days of the convention, the doings and misdoings on the streets of Chicago attracted almost as much attention as those at the amphitheater or in the delegates' hotel rooms. Besides the ebb and flow of marchers, police, tear gas, and bird shot, the antics of literary celebrities—Jean Genet, William Burroughs, Ginsberg, Norman Mailer—were added to the festivities.

The spectacle was appalling to most Americans. The public reaction was generally unsympathetic to the demonstrators and to the pro-left celebrities. The McCarthy people, although they forbade demonstrations by their own supporters, were angered by the police's truculence. Many of the networks and press people were also outraged by the tactics of the Daley officials. By and large, however, the viewing public concluded that the crazy students were up to their old, disgraceful tricks, and that the others, the writers and poets, were naturally only irresponsible bohemians and Communists. Humphrey, who of course won the nomination, was not blamed for the performance, but the Democrats certainly lost votes in November because of what took place in the streets of Chicago ten weeks earlier.

On April 9, 1969, eight participants in the Chicago protest—Dellinger, Rubin, Hoffman, Davis, John Froines, Tom Hayden, Lee Weiner, and Bobby Seale—were arraigned before a federal judge in Chicago to answer charges of conspiracy to commit a riot. The trial of the Chicago Eight before Judge Julius Hoffman went on for five months and amid raucous confusion and disorder. During the course of the long disorderly proceedings, the defendants acted on the premise—probably correct—that the government was intent on making an object lesson of dissent and determined to discourage the growing opposition to the Vietnam War. Their response to the attack had a double objective: to disprove the charge of conspiring to commit disorder and to demonstrate the repressive intent of the government's case.

The tactics they used included adopting some of the Yippie cultural defiance—introducing songs into evidence, defiantly wearing long hair, placing pictures of Che Guevara on the defense table, and displaying a National Liberation Front flag in the courtroom. Hayden later admitted that Rubin and Hoffman particularly "wanted to create the *image* of a courtroom shambles." [21] They also tried unsuccessfully to bring their views of the country's "war, racism, and cultural decadence" into the trial and to read into the record statements made before the convention detailing their innocent intentions for Chicago. When Judge Hoffman would not wait for Bobby Seale's lawyer to recuperate from an illness, Seale, the only black defendant, refused to cooperate and was ordered brought to the courtroom gagged and chained. Before the jury came in, Judge Hoffman, a touchy man obviously hostile to the defense, cited the defendants and their lawyers for contempt 175 times, mostly for showing disrespect for the court.

In the end the jury brought in verdicts of guilty on the count of individual intent to incite riot against five of the defendants, though it dismissed the conspiracy charge, and Judge Hoffman sentenced the five to terms of up to two and a half years. By this time Seale's case had been severed from that of the other seven defendants, and he was tried separately. Judge Hoffman also sentenced the seven defendants and two of their lawyers to various prison terms on the contempt charges.[22]

All of the defendants, except Seale, were allowed free movement during the course of the trial so they were able to attend meetings and rallies and make public appearances for their cause.

[21] Tom Hayden, *Trial* (New York: Holt, Rinehart, and Winston, 1970), p. 69.

[22] The sentences were appealed, and in November, 1972, the appeals court overturned the verdicts on the grounds that Judge Hoffman had been antagonistic and had committed legal errors. The case on the contempt charges could, the appeal judges said, be reopened, however. Under this latter ruling, in December, 1973, the government brought seven original defendants, plus two of their lawyers, to trial for contempt of court. On December 4, 1973, Judge Edward Gignoux convicted four of the nine of contempt, but decided not to impose any further sentences, noting that they had already spent time in jail and this should be sufficient punishment.

Under the auspices of an organization called The Conspiracy, the footloose crew charged around the country between appearances in court, speaking to student groups, radical clubs, and pacifist organizations, generally for fees that were used to help defray the cost of the trial.

One of the highlights of the early trial period, Hayden later reported, was a visit to Lincoln Park that Hoffman, John Froines, and he made to watch a group of SDSers, who called themselves the Weathermen, provoke the overt violence that the government had accused the Chicago Eight of planning. Hayden did not know it at the time, but as he watched the Lincoln Park goings-on, he was witnessing the end of the New Left organization he had helped to create almost a decade before.

CHAPTER

6

The Collapse of SDS
1968-1969

MEN AND MOVEMENTS are propelled by both internal and external imperatives. SDS was no exception. In the year following the Chicago Democratic Convention and Columbia, the organization that had become the center of the New Left was torn to pieces both by forces that came from within itself and by forces that were generated by world and national events.

Much that took place in 1968 and 1969 in the external world of the American New Left was disruptive. In November, 1968, Richard Nixon was elected President, and soon after his inauguration he began the process of Vietnamization, which slowly reduced American involvement in Southeast Asia. At the same time Nixon and his Attorney General, John Mitchell, began a major attack on the antiwar movement and on student radicals. Incapable, apparently, of granting even to Democratic opponents the status of legitimate adversaries, the Nixon administration considered the left dangerous and a fair target for harsh and sometimes illegal repressive measures.

Nixon's damaging impact on the New Left was also indirect. The President was as frustrating a target for the left as he was for liberals. The man would not stay put. He talked about reducing the American commitment in Vietnam, and gradually he brought the troops home and reduced draft calls. In 1971 he would achieve a détente with Red China, something the Democrats had been reluctant or unable to do for over twenty years. At the same time, however, he stepped up the Vietnam bombing, and in the spring of 1970 he outraged both the left and the Democratic doves by sending American troops into Cambodia in what seemed like a gratuitous escalation of the fighting.

Nixon's inconsistency confused the left. In addition, as an avowed conservative, he was really a less appealing villain than his predecessor. In hating Nixon, the New Left found itself on the same side as the liberals, an uncomfortable position for young men and women whose self-definition had always depended so much on setting themselves off from liberalism.

By this time the New Left had also experienced the abrupt rise and the equally abrupt collapse of the 1968 revolutionary upheaval in France. France, the mother of modern revolutions, had also had its New Left. In fact so did almost all of the rich capitalist nations. In Holland the revolutionaries were called Provos. In West Germany, the European country with the largest New Left student group, they belonged to the Sozialistischer Deutscher Studentbund, abbreviated coincidentally, SDS. In Japan there was the Zengakuren, a multifaceted radical student body. France had its National Union of French Students and its Union of Higher Education. Italy, Sweden, even sedate Britain, had student organizations that expressed the radicalism of the young and their disenchantment with both the Moscow-oriented Communist party and the traditional Social Democratic parties.

These groups differed from the American student left primarily in their greater theoretical sophistication. In most other respects they strongly resembled their American counterparts. They too were anti-imperialist; they too were concerned with personal liberation and life-style issues; they too were strongly influenced by Marcuse and the neo-Marxists; they too detested bourgeois values and institutions; they too were contemptuous of the bureaucratic Old Left.

The resemblance is not surprising. Everywhere in the advanced industrial nations, social conditions were approximately the same. All were affluent compared to their own pasts and compared to other nations; all had produced large groups of middle-class students who were relieved of the goad of necessity and afflicted by

guilt and self-disgust over their own good luck; all were marked
by an extreme generational chasm explainable in terms of the Great
Depression and World War II. Aside from the racial question, the
one important difference between the United States and Western
Europe and Japan was the Vietnam War. Even here, however, the
distinction can be exaggerated. If Germany, Japan, and France
were no longer embroiled in overseas adventures in the 1960s, their
own aggressive and imperialist pasts and their postwar cooperation
with the United States were enough to arouse shame and anger
among their younger citizens.

The revolt of the students at Nanterre University outside of
Paris in May, 1968, and the resulting political upheaval in France
electrified the American New Left. For a few weeks during the late
spring, it looked as if students really could be a revolutionary force
in the capitalist countries. Everything that Mills and Marcuse had
preached seemed to be confirmed by the existential slogans and
pronouncements of the French student leaders and by their success
in provoking French industrial workers into making demands for
worker control of factories.

Even after the defection of the Communist-controlled National
Confederation of Labor and the collapse of the French general
strike, the American New Left remained exhilarated. The events
in France would be a beginning. A battle had been lost by a narrow
margin; the next one would be won. As Staughton Lynd noted
in July, "the momentous implication of the near-revolution in
France is that revolutionary social change in a mature capitalist
society is possible." [1]

Yet the French example was confusing and divisive. If some
members of SDS saw the May revolt as confirming new-working-
class ideas, others, especially the Progressive Labor element, were
convinced that it proved the central role of the industrial workers
in the revolutionary process. According to the Progressive Labor
people, students might be a vanguard, but although they could
start the fight, "the working class must finish it." [2]

Another confusing experience for SDS was the New York
teachers' strike in the fall of 1968. If any group in society epito-

[1] Staughton Lynd, "A Good Society," *Guardian*, July 13, 1968.
[2] *New Left Notes*, June 24, 1968.

mized the new working class it was the teachers. Well-educated, presumably, but poorly paid, they looked like the perfect candidates for radicalization. Yet the New York teachers' behavior during the long strike seemed to radicals indistinguishable from the most reactionary racism of the blue-collar workers. When faced with black demands for community self-determination in educational matters, the United Federation of Teachers acted no better than the corrupt conservative Teamsters or the building-trades unions. As the *Guardian* observed, the teachers were victims of "benighted union leadership," and "racism undoubtedly [was] a significant factor" in teacher opposition to community control of the schools.[3]

It is difficult to estimate how important these developments were for the New Left. On the face of it, the reason for their being taken so seriously is not clear. Surely no one on the left had any reason to doubt Nixon's shiftiness or disrespect for constitutional safeguards. At best the lesson of France only confirmed SDS factions in their previous prejudices. The teachers' strike was localized in New York City and was no real test of the new-working-class theory.

Yet these events were disturbing to the New Left and to SDS in particular. The young left, we must remember, was volatile. Many members of SDS were unstable young men and women, who had profound insights with every new book they read and with every new headline in *The New York Times*. SDS was constantly spinning off new theories and programs in response to events that seemed obscure and irrelevant shortly after they had taken place. If this changeability was true of the leaders, it was even truer of the rank and file. Thousands of new recruits joined SDS during 1968 in the wake of Columbia and Chicago. Many of them were merely curious and rebellious and given to easy enthusiasms as well as easy discouragement. Such a mass could be, and probably was, swayed by the day-to-day changes that the nation was experiencing. Yet in all fairness, we must say that the volatile and apocalyptic mood of the late 1960s was not confined to young people alone. Many adult Americans read portents in the daily news and were convinced in these years that abrupt, cataclysmic change was imminent.

[3] "Guardian Viewpoint," *Guardian*, September 14, 1968.

But in the end it was the pressures within the Movement itself that determined the fate of SDS and the New Left. As SDS struggled to make sense of the violent and confusing events in Paris, Chicago, New York, and elsewhere, it found itself facing a new set of challenges from within the Movement. SDS—and the New Left in general—was without question male-dominated. In theory women were equal members of SDS, but their role generally was a subordinate one. Women were supportive; they were auxiliaries. Bettina Aptheker and Suzanne Goldberg were leading participants in the Free Speech Movement at Berkeley, and for a short while, in 1966, Jane Adams was SDS national secretary. But generally the Movement women made the coffee, rolled the bandages, and served as sexual partners for campus radicals. Many Movement women, in fact, were little more than camp followers of the sort that always tag along after men engaged in a dangerous or glamorous calling. If this is a somewhat overdrawn picture, it is the one that many women radicals eventually came to accept as true.

By 1967 or 1968 the women's liberation movement began to challenge this situation dramatically. Given the new sensibility of the 1960s, women's liberation was probably inevitable. The decade was a period when virtually every group that felt itself despised or victimized by the power of others developed a defiant response. Blacks, of course, were the first, but their protean struggle for liberation soon galvanized others. By the end of the decade Puerto Ricans, Mexican-Americans, American Indians, and homosexuals had all created their own liberation movements. Each of these groups wanted in some way to throw "the Man" off their backs. To some women, by the middle of the decade, the desire was literal as well as figurative.

It is impossible to assign a precise date to the beginning of the women's liberation movement. Betty Friedan's 1963 best seller, *The Feminine Mystique,* however, was an important bench mark. Friedan claimed that since the hopeful beginning of female emancipation seventy-five years before, women had retrogressed. The women aviators, scholars, politicians, artists, and entrepreneurs of an earlier day had become rarer in the post–World War II era. A smothering domesticity had taken over, and women were being told, and many had come to believe, that fulfillment for any normal woman meant a life limited to home, husband, and family.

The Feminine Mystique touched a responsive chord among middle-class women all over the country. The back-to-the-kitchen movement that had swept over American women in 1945 now seemed confining and stultifying to thousands of well-educated young women. Friedan's book gave voice to their frustrations and resentments, and in June, 1966, the National Organization of Women (NOW) was formed with Friedan as the first president.

Oriented primarily toward issues that concerned women college graduates, NOW devoted its energies to ending job discrimination, liberalizing abortion and birth control laws, and providing child care centers for working mothers. Most of NOW's demands concerned middle-class, liberal women, and NOW was soon attacked as the NAACP of the revived women's movement.

Meanwhile radical women began to get restless and resentful. At an SDS conference in December, 1965, a discussion of the woman issue produced hoots and catcalls from the male delegates. The women did not let go, however, and the issue was brought up the following year at SDS's Clear Lake meeting and again at Ann Arbor in June, 1967, where workshops were held on the role of women in America. These workshops, it seems, led a group of Chicago women, including Naomi Weisstein, Heather Booth, and Sue Munaker, to form an independent radical women's organization in August, 1967.

By 1967 SDS was giving radical women a more respectful hearing, but SDS leadership was wary of the new movement. It is undoubtedly true that male members of SDS were chauvinists. Raised, like most Americans, according to a set of male-defined standards, they were not above putting assertive Movement women in their place by calling them aggressive and unfeminine. Besides their ingrained prejudice, however, SDS leaders feared another fragmentation of the Movement, equivalent to that caused by black liberation. This was becoming a growing possibility as "consciousness raising" among radical women brought to the surface fierce resentments against men and a desire for an autonomous women's liberation movement.

To keep radical women in the organization, SDS made concessions. *New Left Notes* began to feature articles by radical feminists attacking not only the sexist Establishment of America, but also the male chauvinism that permeated all American institutions and values, including those of the left. A radical women's perspective, these articles insisted, demanded not only that women be given the same economic and educational opportunities as men, but that the fundamental relationships between men and women be sharply altered. This meant that marriage must be drastically changed or even abolished outright. Child-rearing practices must no longer presuppose the woman as the nurturing parent. Women must no longer be counted on to stay home and do the dishes. Radical men continued to find many of these demands disturbing, and when proposals endorsing the more radical demands of women's liberation came before SDS groups, male delegates continued to hoot them down.

In December, 1968, at the Ann Arbor national council meeting, a debate on the women's role in the Movement produced a double split. One was between the National Office group, as it was coming to be called, which held that women were indeed oppressed as women, and the Progressive Labor faction, which asserted that women's oppression was just another version of class oppression and would be ended with the overthrow of capitalism. Within the National Office a further division existed—between those who wanted women radicals to remain within mixed organizations and those who acquiesced in the desire of women radicals to go it alone.

At Ann Arbor the more conservative version of the National Office view was adopted, but in the end the SDS male leaders' fears of separatism proved justified. The autonomous position proved appealing to many radical women and resulted in the formation in late 1968 of WITCH and then Redstockings. Both of these organizations, through spokesmen such as Shulamith Firestone, Robin Morgan, and Roxanne Dunbar, denounced radical men as chauvinists. They insisted that only women could liberate themselves. All males, not just capitalist ones, oppressed women, and even the socialist revolution, which was supposed to free all people from oppression, would probably leave women where they were before. Sexism, like racism, predated capitalism and would postdate it, unless women, like blacks, fought for themselves.

Radical women were not alone in demanding autonomy in the

fight against "Amerikan"[4] oppression. By the late 1960s various "native American" groups composed of American Indians had begun to insist on sharing in the restitution that white America was beginning to grant to blacks. And if black and red liberation, why not brown liberation too? Puerto Ricans, through the Young Lords, and Mexican-Americans, through Reies Tijerina's organization, Alianza, in New Mexico, now began to demand a larger share of government largess and better treatment by white America. Third World liberation soon became a major radical force on campuses, already punchy from the attacks of SDS and black militants. At San Francisco State, Third World students' demands for privileged admission and special ethnic programs kept the college in turmoil for months during the winter and early spring of 1969. Over seven hundred people were arrested during the course of the disorders, and scores were injured when police battled striking blacks, Chicano and Oriental students, and their SDS allies.

One of the more interesting liberation groups was organized by homosexuals, who no longer cared to disguise their difference from the majority of Americans. Homosexuals of both sexes had long been active in the New Left, where their sexual preferences were usually known. Among the cultural radicals, particularly, heterosexual taboos seemed irrelevant and confining, but even among the *political* left, the treatment of homosexuals by the police and the "straights" seemed brutal. Though many New Left people found it difficult to shake off the sexual prejudices of the majority, they generally agreed that strict role definitions of masculinity and femininity in American society were of a piece with the other rigidities and repressions of American society. These diminished the range of human experience and probably even contributed to the American need to bully the rest of the world.

Gays began to "come out of the closet" toward the end of the decade and began to proclaim, often aggressively, that they would no longer stand for the contempt and discrimination they had always suffered. Within the Movement itself homosexuals began to chide the left for its own prejudices. Among women radicals the issue of homosexuality raised a furor when it became clear that a

---

[4] By spelling the word "Amerikan," using the German "k" rather than the English "c," radicals intended to suggest the resemblance between the United States of the 1960s and Nazi Germany.

number of the most militant liberationists were lesbians, whose jaundiced attitudes toward men could be blamed on their sexual preferences. Generally the major New Left organizations refused to take a clear stand on homosexuality, but the issues troubled them and would cause difficulties later.

Each of these liberation groups, though important in the Movement, took a backseat to black liberation, the first and strongest of them all. Within the black liberation movement, the most powerful voice continued to be that of the Panthers, who by 1969 had evolved from a local black defense organization into a politically sophisticated Marxist group that recognized the value of white cooperation to achieve its dual goal of black political autonomy and socialist revolution.

The Panthers were at this point a highly charismatic group. In their semi-military dress, black berets, and proud, erect, "macho" bearing, they personified courageous resistance to racist America. Besides, their treatment by authorities aroused enormous sympathy, even among liberals. The Panther swagger and violent rhetoric had infuriated the police, and in Chicago, Oakland, New York, Los Angeles, New Haven, and elsewhere, Panthers had been shot, beaten, arrested, and prosecuted by local police and courts. Perhaps some of the persecution had been called down on their heads by their provocative actions and words, but to many people on the left, they epitomized romantic revolutionary courage in the face of harsh and brutal repression.

The new radical energies unleashed by the various liberation movements toward the end of the decade did not strengthen the New Left. Rather they were profoundly enfeebling. With so many voices clamoring to be heard, would any one of them be heeded or, alternately, could all this unfocused passion be brought to bear on the weak spots in American society? SDS in particular was nonplussed by the fragmenting of the Movement. It had never adapted successfully to black militancy, but now that women, Hispanic-Americans, homosexuals, and American Indians were all insisting on going it alone, what—or who—was left for SDS? The obvious answer was white male students and the white new working class as in the past, but here a new challenge had arisen in the shape of an increasingly militant Progressive Labor party drive to take over control of the organization.

For a while following the merger of the May 2nd Movement
with SDS in February, 1966, the Progressive Labor people avoided
a head-on collision with the mainstream leadership of SDS—the
National Office, or National Collective, group. But this situation
could not last. The split between Progressive Labor and the SDS
leadership finally became visible at the SDS national convention
at Michigan State in early June, 1968, just as the French uprising
was beginning to lose steam. Progressive Labor proposed at this
meeting that SDS adopt a new program, which Progressive Labor
labeled the Student Labor Action Project (SLAP). The experience
of France, the Progressive Labor preamble declared, showed that
"the industrial working class is the key force on the people's side
in the advanced capitalist countries." [5]

Progressive Labor believed that SLAP would establish a close
relationship between students and industrial workers. Students
would support campus workers in their demands against the universities; they would aid strikers by picketing, distributing leaflets,
and boycotting; they would work in factories during summers to
learn about labor conditions and to help heighten the political
awareness of wage earners; they would help expose as frauds capitalist claims to an inherent harmony between labor and capital.

The SLAP proposal, signed by four Boston-area student members of the Progressive Labor party, was not an ad hoc response
to the events in France, though Progressive Labor tried to use the
French experience to support its position. Rather it was an expression of Progressive Labor's fixed Marxist-Leninist ideological position: classes were defined by their relation to the means of production, and the two classes into which every capitalist society was
divided—the capitalists and the industrial proletariat—were locked
in a mortal combat that labor would inevitably win. Progressive
Labor's position allowed for no other factors. "Objectively speaking" there were no other groups between the capitalists and the
workers; there were no other significant elements in the relations
between the capitalists and the masses besides the drive for higher
profits.

The reaction of the National Office people to Progressive Labor
and SLAP was complex. They feared that SDS would be over-
whelmed by Progressive Labor. It was one thing to allow young

[5] *New Left Notes,* June 24, 1968.

PLers free voice in the organization; but SDS was not a hard-line Marxist-Leninist organization, and the National Office group did not want it to become one. The National Office people were beginning to backtrack on the new-working-class theory. Engineers and school teachers seemed to be a very long way from revolution, and blacks and slum youth seemed to be on the edge of violent reaction. Still, SDS found it hard to give up its theory. From the beginning SDS and, indeed, the New Left had been distinguished by its focus on personal liberation. The new-working-class theory meant that revolution for oneself was also revolution for the fastest-growing element in the Western world. It also conveniently allowed SDS to express covertly its fear and disdain of the hard hats and the Middle American philistinism that radical students saw around them. Orthodox Marxism, moreover, seemed peculiarly abstract and irrelevant to many young radicals. They were interested largely in their own lives and their own condition. Leaders of local SDS chapters, confronting interminable debates with Progressive Labor people over the role of industrial workers, noted that rank-and-file members, especially the newer ones, soon grew bored and impatient. The incessant arguments with PL were turning off the students who formed the backbone of the organization.

At the June East Lansing convention the National Office people turned back Progressive Labor's attempt to get SDS to adopt SLAP, but the argument was not resolved. Hour after hour the debate rolled on, and in the end little, if anything, was accomplished at the meetings.

In the following weeks the quarrel continued in the pages of *New Left Notes*. By this time Progressive Labor had organized the Worker Student Alliance (WSA), composed of members of Progressive Labor as well as a large group of what can best be described as naïfs who accepted PL's position without recognizing its source. Worker Student Alliance groups were particularly strong at San Francisco State College, in New York, and in the Boston area, but they also appeared as informal caucuses within many other SDS chapters.

Progressive Labor and WSA continued their agitation for SLAP into the fall. At the national council meeting in Boulder, Colorado, the issue of a worker-student alliance was debated with passion. Obviously it was not merely a question of the merits of SLAP, but also of the control of SDS. When the SLAP proposal

was defeated by a two-to-one vote, one National Office leader was
seen jumping up and down shouting "We won; we smashed the PL
bastards!" [6]

Meanwhile other cracks were beginning to appear within SDS.
Chicago, Columbia, and Nanterre had all been violent confrontations. SDS members had been prominent in only one of them—the
Columbia upheaval—and here they had not distinguished themselves for physical courage. But each of these violent student revolts had attracted world attention, and that was heady stuff to
young radicals. Besides, the Panthers, with their macho pose and
their violent rhetoric and occasional violent action, had begun to
arouse tremendous admiration among radicals. Once the public had
identified the New Left with street fighting and violence, it was
hard to turn back, and a cult of violence soon appeared within
SDS, a cult that paraded under the name of action politics.

One source of the new trend within SDS was the Ohio-Michigan regional SDS and especially the large SDS chapter at the University of Michigan in Ann Arbor. The Michigan SDS had descended from VOICE, one of the earliest campus radical organizations and the seedbed of the revived SDS in 1960–1961. By 1968 the
Michigan campus chapter had become stodgy and conservative in
the eyes of such new activists as Bill Ayers, Jim Mellen, and Terry
Robbins, who headed a faction calling itself the Jesse James Gang.
The activists soon demanded that the campus SDS commit itself
to building seizures and other irrevocable acts, because only these
were truly revolutionary. Students, they argued, could, by violent
tactics, align themselves with the Third World struggles as they
were expressed here in the "mother country." In October, 1968,
under pressure from this group, the VOICE old guard resigned as
a body from SDS, leaving the campus chapter in the hands of its
opponents.

Another action-oriented group was the inelegantly named Up
Against the Wall, Motherfuckers.[7] The New York-based Motherfuckers had been active in the Columbia uprising and represented

---

[6] See the remarks of Progressive Labor member Jim Prickett, "SLAP
Generates Controversy," *New Left Notes*, December 4, 1968.

[7] The name came from a poem by LeRoi Jones (Imamu Baraka) and
echoed a phrase the police supposedly used when they stopped and searched
hippies and blacks on suspicion of committing a crime.

an undisciplined combination of dropouts, delinquents, and hippies committed to trashing stores, fighting the police, and in general raising hell in the name of revolution. A similar group, under the label White Panthers, appeared in Berkeley in the wake of a violent confrontation between "street people" and radicals and the University of California administration and police. Organized into "affinity groups," or communes of a few mutually supportive friends, the White Panthers demanded a "total assault" on the culture that would include rock, dope, and "fucking in the streets," along with violent reprisals against the university and the Berkeley city authorities. As one of these groups, the Berkeley Commune, speculated: "is it time to admit that Hate as well as Love redeems the world?/there is no outside without inside/no revolution without blood." [8]

These local developments soon began to make an impression on the National Office. Fred Gordon, SDS internal education secretary, noted approvingly in September, 1968, that the Motherfuckers represented "a new life style, a Reichian mind-body unity that expresses its alienation spontaneously and organically through violence against the symbols of authority . . . and agents and agencies of the ruling class." [9] A month later Mike Klonsky, SDS national secretary, praised the growth of action programs in SDS chapters.

With startling alacrity, the SDS National Office responded to the combined pressure of the action groups and the burgeoning liberation movements by abandoning the central credo that had marked the student New Left since its birth: that students and young intellectuals, by fighting against the psychological and cultural repressions of industrial society, would create the revolution both for themselves and for mankind as a whole.

During the crucial year that began in June, 1968, the National Office leadership included Mike Klonsky of Los Angeles, formerly a West Coast regional office leader; Bernardine Dohrn of the radi-

---

[8] The poem is entitled "An Open Letter to the Prophets and Their Apostles." In Berkeley Commune File, Social Protest Project, Bancroft Library, University of California, Berkeley. See also White Panther File, *ibid.*

[9] See Fred Gordon, "Politics of Violence," *New Left Notes,* September 23, 1968. The phrase "Reichian" alludes to Wilhelm Reich, sexual revolutionary and inventor of the orgone box. Reich was something of a minor New Left hero, in part because of his persecution by federal authorities for what the government considered medical quackery.

cal National Lawyers' Guild, who was elected the new inter-organizational secretary in 1968; and Fred Gordon, a University of California (San Diego) graduate student, elected internal education secretary. Other important National Office people, though they did not hold formal SDS office, were Mark Rudd, leader of SDS at Columbia, Steve Halliwell of New York, and Eric Mann of the Boston SDS region. Soon to become prominent National Office leaders were Jim Mellen, Terry Robbins, and Bill Ayers of the activist Ohio-Michigan regional office.

Though all through 1968 the National Office people succeeded in beating off Progressive Labor and its front group, the Worker Student Alliance, the struggle pushed the national organization further to the left. Already, at Michigan State in June, 1968, Bernardine Dohrn had declared herself "a revolutionary Communist." Six months later Mike Klonsky published the document "Toward a Revolutionary Youth Movement," which represented an important turning for SDS. SDS, Klonsky admitted, had exaggerated the revolutionary potential of students and had neglected workers, especially young workers. Young workers were not a class, but they were oppressed anyway—by the schools, the courts, and the police. Though these young workers would not by themselves be able to overthrow the capitalist system, they could help transmit radical ideas to the mass of the working class and could activate them to revolutionary struggle.

This part of the "Revolutionary Youth Movement" (RYM) statement represented a compromise between the early SDS and Progressive Labor. Students were no longer to be considered the chief agents of revolution, but neither was Progressive Labor's traditional industrial proletariat. Students and youth, according to the RYM statement, still had an important place in the revolutionary scheme of things.

So did black people. If youth was a distinct revolutionary entity, so were the blacks. In contrast to Progressive Labor's classic Marxist position that blacks were primarily part of the working class and that racism at bottom was a device to oppress all workers economically, Klonsky insisted that the blacks' status was defined by race and that racism was primarily cultural. The black liberation struggle, accordingly, was not identical with the struggle of white workers and included, legitimately, the right of blacks to racial—or national—self-determination.

At the SDS national council meeting in Ann Arbor in December, the National Office and Progressive Labor slugged it out to a draw. Klonsky's RYM statement was passed by the delegates as official SDS doctrine, and so was a Progressive Labor–sponsored resolution declaring that racism was economic in origin—the creation of the bosses to divide the working class in order to increase profits.

This contradictory result came from the confusion that reigned at Ann Arbor. Many of the two thousand delegates had little idea of what was at stake in the debates that the SDS faction leaders conducted. The Progressive Labor core was disciplined and well-informed, but many of the other delegates, like most members of SDS from the very beginning, were innocents without strong ideological commitments. The Progressive Labor resolution was sponsored by a group from San Francisco State, where blacks, Third World militants, and white radicals had been fighting bitterly against the tough administration of President S. I. Hayakawa. The people from the San Francisco State chapter were heroes to many rank-and-file delegates, and these delegates voted out of enthusiasm for the SFStaters without much regard for consistency.

Consistency returned at the SDS national council meeting in Austin, Texas, in late March, 1969. By this time the national organization had established close ties with the Black Panthers. The price of Panther cooperation, however, was SDS endorsement of black nationalist demands. This had already been foreshadowed by the RYM statement, and now, at Austin, the National Office-led majority repealed the Progressive Labor statement on racism and replaced it with a declaration that accepted the Panther position. In the debate that raged around the racism issue, the National Office insisted that racism was not purely an economic phenomenon that could be cured by destroying capitalism. Nor were blacks merely one sector of the proletariat. Racism was an independent malevolent force that could ultimately be obliterated only if blacks were recognized as an "internal colony" of the United States and were granted self-determination. As for blacks trudging alongside the proletariat toward the revolution, blacks in fact would lead the revolution. Militant blacks generally, and the Panthers specifically, were the vanguard of the American revolution, just as Third World peoples were the vanguard of world revolution.

Progressive Labor suffered a setback at Austin, but it did not surrender. In the succeeding months both sides prepared for a showdown at the scheduled June national convention in Chicago. Meanwhile, as older New Leftists such as Staughton Lynd deplored the growing factionalism, the National Office group itself split in two. On one side was Klonsky, joined by Noel Ignatin, Les Coleman, and others, who stood with the RYM statement as passed at Ann Arbor and confirmed at Austin. This group would soon be identified as RYM II. On the other side was a group led by Dohrn, Rudd, Jim Mellen, Bill Ayers, John Jacobs, Howie Machtinger, and Terry Robbins. Mellen, Robbins, and Ayers, of course, belonged to the Midwestern action faction that had endorsed aggressive tactics against Establishment institutions, and they now prepared to make this a central point of the SDS program.

The convention took place in the Chicago Coliseum, a large, badly lit barn of a place, where some fifteen hundred to two thousand assorted delegates assembled on June 18. Progressive Labor came to Chicago hoping to avoid expulsion from SDS. It probably did not want to seize the organization so much as dominate and control it from behind the scenes. RYM and the action group, still allied as the National Office, or National Collective, came prepared to keep Progressive Labor from using SDS as a Maoist front.

The National Office people's tactic was to convince the substantial number of unaffiliated and often uninformed delegates that Progressive Labor was both racist and hostile to the Vietnamese National Liberation Front. The grounds for these charges were Progressive Labor's refusal to support black nationalism and its announced claim that the National Liberation Front–North Vietnamese negotiations with the United States in Paris represented a betrayal of world revolution.

As the convention began, the National Office people passed out two position papers. One, signed by Klonsky and Les Coleman, was a brief revised statement of Klonsky's earlier RYM manifesto, and is usually referred to as RYM II. The other, signed by eleven action people—Mark Rudd, Bernardine Dohrn, John Jacobs, Bill Ayers, Jim Mellen, Terry Robbins, Howie Machtinger, Karen Ashley, Jeff Jones, Gerry Long, and Steve Tappis—was eccentrically called "You Don't Need a Weatherman to Know Which Way the Wind Blows," after a Bob Dylan song popular with the youth culture. This was a murky sixteen thousand–word document detailing the position of the group that was soon to be called the Weatherman organization.

The Weatherman document differed from the RYM II statement in denying any important role to the white working class in the approaching revolution. America, the mother country of imperialism, had succeeded in buying off and totally corrupting the white working class. From its "world-wide plunder" the United States "doled out to the enslaved masses within its borders" the "crumbs" of its imperialist gains. These admittedly provided "for material existence very much above the conditions of the masses of the people of the world."

> The US empire, as a world-wide system, channels wealth, based upon the labor and resources of the rest of the world, into the United States [the signers lectured their fellow Americans]. The relative affluence existing in the United States is directly dependent upon the labor and natural resources of the Vietnamese, the Angolans, the Bolivians and the rest of the peoples of the Third World. All of the United Airlines Astrojets, all of the Holiday Inns, all of Hertz's automobiles, your television set, car and wardrobe, already belong, to a large degree, to the people of the rest of the world.

Not all Americans, of course, shared equally in this abundance, the document went on, but white working people got a goodly portion. Since the white working class was thus the beneficiary of "white skin privilege," it could not be counted on. Instead, the struggle against American imperialism would be undertaken by Third World peoples in Vietnam, Angola, Puerto Rico, and other colonies or near colonies. In the United States itself it would be led by black people, who "are an internal colony within the confines of the oppressor nation."

Would whites have a part in any of this great liberation struggle? Adult white workers would not, at least at first, but white youth would. The young of all races, the document asserted, were alienated from American society. They were often unemployed. The schools bored and processed them. The government drafted them and made them fight for causes they despised. Their parents, their teachers, and the "pigs," nagged, badgered, and busted them for their habits, their hair styles, and their interests. At the bottom particularly, among the sons and daughters of the white poor, there was a deep pool of discontent that could be tapped for revolutionary purposes.

How could it be tapped? In Aesopian language, probably intended to fend off legal prosecution, the Weatherman statement
suggested a set of tactics that were based ultimately on violence:
Let underground cadres be formed to engage in various actions
that would appeal to the alienated youth of the working class.
Close down the schools; attack the pigs; mount city-wide action
demonstrations. Ultimately the willingness of radicals to put their
lives on the line would win the admiration of the kids, as well as
demonstrate that some whites could risk as much as Third World
revolutionaries.

Even white youth would have to recognize that their role was
secondary, however. They could help, but in the final analysis the
battle against imperialism was the essential one, and here non-
whites, both in America and abroad, would lead the attack.[10]

The Weatherman statement is a curious document. On its
surface, it seems to be a repudiation of all that the New Left had
stood for. Instead of students creating the revolution for themselves and by themselves, they would support a revolution *for* the
non-white peoples of the world and the United States, and primarily *by* these peoples, with whites serving merely as auxiliaries.
The statement also sounded a new note of violence. On the whole
the New Left had eschewed violence. At the beginning it had
closely imitated the early civil rights movement and had also
drawn on the radical pacifist tradition. Even when blacks abandoned passive resistance, student radicals continued to avoid physical violence. Despite the vehement rhetoric of many campus radicals, they visited remarkably little destruction of property or
physical injury on their opponents before 1968. Generally, in fact,
in the matter of physical force, radicals were more sinned against
than sinning, but even the violence inflicted on them was relatively
minor. If the student left was dismayed by police brutality at
Berkeley or Columbia, it was primarily because physical violence
still shocked them. As "good" middle-class boys and girls, they
had learned to express anger in words, not acts, and as young radicals they continued to be dismayed by beatings, physical attacks,
and property destruction. With the Weathermen, apparently, all
this had changed.

[10] The most convenient source of the Weatherman statement is Harold
Jacobs (ed.), *Weatherman* (n.p.: Ramparts Press, 1970), pp. 51-90.

Yet the turnabout concerning both violence and who should make the revolution is not as great as it seems at first. Weatherman, as Tom Hayden later declared, was in many ways "the natural final generation of SDS, the true inheritors of everything that had happened from 1960 on!"[11] Like the earlier New Left, the Weathermen accepted the near impossibility of radicalizing the white working class. Though Weathermen considered themselves Marxists or even Communists, they were scarcely orthodox ones. Throughout the Weatherman document, as several critics would point out, there is a barely concealed contempt for the attitudes and life-styles of adult blue-collar America. The white industrial workers seemed as hopeless and worthless to the Weathermen as to C. Wright Mills or Herbert Marcuse.

Also linking the Weathermen to the earlier New Left was their cult of youth and at least a moderately sympathetic response to the counter culture. This would emerge more clearly as Weatherman ideology and practice evolved, but it was present at the very beginning in the implied support for the youth culture that was ascribed to white slum kids. It is suggestive that pictures of the National Office people and Weathermen show them with long hair and the dungarees and open shirts of working-class youth. Progressive Laborites, more anxious to identify with the fathers than the sons, wore their hair cropped and their clothes neat.

As for the violence, it was there in the Weatherman document as the dubious contribution of the Ohio-Michigan action group and, perhaps, of Mark Rudd and Ted Gold, two Columbia leaders determined to redeem themselves after the timid performance of Columbia SDS the year before. And the personal element was reinforced by important tactical imperatives. To make contact with tough, white, working-class youth, radicals would have to show how tough they were themselves. The Panthers too had to be convinced that white radicals meant business. This violent action and violent rhetoric would indeed set Weatherman off from the earlier New Left. Yet, as we shall see, violence did not come easy even to the Weathermen, and all told it did not amount to very much. In the end, once again, the young radicals would be more often victims than successful practitioners of violence.

[11] Quoted in Tim Findley, "Tom Hayden: Rolling Stone Interview Part 2," *Rolling Stone*, November 9, 1972, p. 29.

The Weatherman and RYM II documents were never formally debated.; nor was Progressive Labor's position ever explicitly discussed. Instead, on the first day the factional battle in the Coliseum coalesced around such things as the agenda, the number of workshops, whether to allow the capitalist press to be present, whether to permit an American who had returned after participating in the Chinese Red Guard movement to speak, and similar minor matters. Despite the triviality of the issues, the delegates were disorderly and combative and waved Chairman Mao's little red book in each other's faces. On Thursday, the second day of the convention, delegations from a Chicano group called the Brown Berets, the militant Puerto Rican Young Lords, and the Panthers appeared and addressed the delegates. Progressive Labor later charged, probably correctly, that the National Office was cynically using the Panthers to defeat them. At first, however, it seemed that the appearance of the Panthers would backfire. In the course of his remarks, Rufus "Chaka" Walls, minister of information for the Illinois Black Panthers, declared "we believe in the freedom of love, in pussy power." Shock waves went over the audience, and Progressive Labor started to chant "Fight male chauvinism!" The next Black Panther speaker, Jewel Cook, only made things worse when he told the delegates that Walls "was only trying to say you sisters have a strategic position for the revolution . . . prone." Pandemonium followed Cook's crude witticism. Someone proposed a full discussion of the Panthers' sexism, but National Office–supporter Naomi Jaffe jumped to her feet and shouted that women would refuse to have women's liberation used as a political football.

The final crisis began the next day. As debate on a Progressive Labor motion on racism began, Cook once more came to the podium to present a Panther statement on the internal politics of SDS. After long study, he declared, the Panthers had concluded that Progressive Labor had deviated from Marxist–Leninist ideology on the question of national self-determination. If Progressive Labor continued its revisionist attitudes, its followers would "be considered . . . counterrevolutionary traitors" and would "be dealt with as such." Members of SDS as a whole would "be judged by the company they keep and the efficiency and effectiveness with which they deal with the bourgeois factions in their organization." [12]

<hr>

[12] *New Left Notes*, June 25, 1969.

There was no question about what this meant. The Panthers were presenting an ultimatum to SDS. Either the National Office expelled the Progressive Labor party, or the Panthers would repudiate SDS. Where the ultimatum came from is not clear. Was it an independent Panther tactic, or was it concocted by the National Office group in collaboration with the Panthers? [13]

Progressive Labor, of course, assumed it was the National Office's doing. As soon as Cook finished, Progressive Labor floor leader Jeff Gordon jumped to the platform and denounced the National Office people for opportunism. At this point Mark Rudd asked for a recess, but he was shouted down. Bernardine Dohrn then took the microphone and asked whether SDS could continue to tolerate the "racist" Progressive Labor party within its ranks. Anyone who wanted to discuss the question, she said, should join her in the next room. At this the National Office supporters, about a thousand delegates, many of them apparently taken by surprise, moved out of the main hall of the Coliseum to the adjacent sports arena.

There the National Office people discussed what should be done about the apparently unbridgeable gap between the National Office people and Progressive Labor. None of the accounts extant tells us what took place in either hall, except that the debate was earnest and prolonged. At midnight the National Office group adjourned to resume the discussion the next day. Finally, close to midnight on Saturday, the National Office group marched back into the main hall, and amid shouts of "shame" and "smash racism," Dohrn read Progressive Labor out of SDS with a statement accusing it of racism and anticommunism. Then, as if to emphasize the peculiarity of the whole expulsion process, the National Office people, rather than the "expelled" Progressive Labor, marched out of the hall with their fists raised, leaving the field of battle to their opponents.

The next day the National Office group met again at the First Congregational Church near SDS's Chicago headquarters, and elected Mark Rudd national secretary, Jeff Jones inter-organizational secretary, and Bill Ayers education secretary. In addition, it chose an eight-man national interim committee composed of both

[13] Kirkpatrick Sale concludes that it was probably the second of these. See Sale, *SDS* (New York: Random House, 1973), p. 569.

RYM II people and Weathermen—Mike Klonsky, Howie Machtinger, Bernardine Dohrn, Linda Evans, Bob Avakian, Corky
Benedict, Barbara Reilly, and Noel Ignatin—and charged the committee with planning a series of national actions for the fall. Meanwhile at the Coliseum Progressive Labor, declaring itself the real
SDS and the National Office group a mere splinter, elected its own
officers and resolved to establish its claim as the true remnant of
SDS.

During the next few months SDS split further, as RYM II
and the Weathermen came to a falling out over future SDS tactics. In the weeks following the Chicago schism the National Office
people planned a major street confrontation in Chicago for October. Along the way smaller actions were initiated to "bring the
war home" to the United States.

The first of these was a raid on a local junior college by an
all-woman Weatherman group in Detroit calling itself the Motor
City SDS. In August, during summer session, nine "Weatherwomen" invaded McComb Community College in a Detroit white,
working-class suburb. The women entered a classroom where students were writing their final exams, locked and barricaded the
doors, and "rapped" with the students about racism, imperialism,
and how the capitalists were processing them into cheap and pli-
able labor. The startled students, rather than becoming instant revolutionaries, called the police, who arrested the disrupters. Early
in September some seventy-five Weatherwomen, organized into a
"Women's Militia," raided a Pittsburgh high school. They ran
through the halls shouting "jailbreak!" and then held a rally outside the school. The police came and tried to stop the women from
talking to the students, and when the women fought back, the
"pigs" moved in and arrested twenty-six of them on charges of riot
and inciting to riot.

Provocative actions of this sort angered the RYM II people.
At the end of August Mike Klonsky, who until then had served
as a member of the national action steering committee along with
Dohrn, Terry Robbins, and Kathy Boudin, resigned with a blast
against the Weathermen. The McComb Community College attack
indicated the arrogance of the Weathermen, he declared. The
schools of course were imperfect, but through the schools, working-
class young people were able to prepare for the jobs they needed

to live in this country. For Weathermen to think that they could win working-class support by threatening the future livelihood of blue-collar youth showed how little they understood or cared about the real problems of the working classes. Klonsky's departure was followed by the defection of Noel Ignatin, Les Coleman, and other RYM II people, many of whom were connected with the Radical Education Project of national SDS. The RYM II group's complaint, like Klonsky's, was that the Weathermen were at heart against the white working class.

This defection and sharp criticism from such prominent Movement people as Staughton Lynd, Todd Gitlin, and Greg Calvert had little effect on the Weathermen. At a conference in Cleveland in late August, the Weathermen made plans for the Chicago national action. There would be, they decided, a four-day series of rallies, high school "jailbreaks," a women's action, a rock concert, and a demonstration in front of the federal courthouse where Judge Hoffman was conducting the marathon conspiracy trial of the Chicago Eight. Also at Cleveland, it seems, the Weather Bureau, the small, tight-knit leadership cadre of Weatherman, consolidated its control over the remaining rump of SDS. The disciplined central control of SDS had been growing ever since the appearance of RYM. Now, the formation of the Weather Bureau represented the end of the road for the loose, almost anarchistic, diffusion of power that had characterized the original SDS.

Finally the Cleveland meeting raised in an acute way the question of women's role in Weatherman. Until this point Weatherman had exhibited as many male chauvinist characteristics as other New Left organizations. In June at the Coliseum the National Office group had been more friendly to separatist women's liberation views than Progressive Labor had been. Unlike PL, the National Office did not insist that the end of female oppression depended on the advent of socialism. Yet the Weathermen remained ambivalent on the question of an independent women's movement and skeptical of women's assertiveness within the Movement.

In the next few months women forced Weatherman to give them a greater role in the organization, and formed the Women's Militia that carried out the September Pittsburgh high school raid. In Cleveland the Weatherwomen openly challenged monogamy on the grounds that it relegated women to a dependent relationship with men. The defiant mood of radical women also affected local Weatherman chapters, where it produced serious internal stress. In the New York Weatherman collective, for example, the female assault on monogamy led the members to experiment with complete sexual freedom, including homosexual relationships. This apparently proved an easier course for the women than the men, who found it difficult to shake off heterosexual preferences. It is hard not to conclude that the challenge of the sexual revolutionaries contributed to the disaster that was shortly to overtake what was left of SDS.

Meanwhile Weatherman moved ahead on the Chicago action. At one point the Weatherman leaders tried to bring Mobe into the demonstration; but the Mobe people wanted some reassurance that violence would be controlled, and when they could not get that assurance, they rejected the overture. In the weeks after the Cleveland meeting, Weathermen went through preposterous gyrations preparing for what would become known as the Days of Rage. For the first time young American radicals deliberately prepared for violent confrontation with the police, and they agonized over it at lugubrious length. Was violence tolerable? Did radicals really want to hurt people? Would they get hurt themselves? There was endless self-examination to see if cowardice or expediency was overcoming resolution. Often the young men, and especially the young women, found they were more afraid of hitting than of being hit.

In the practice runs that preceded Chicago, the Weathermen's deeds were often grossly disproportionate to Weatherman rhetoric. The New York collective, for example, planned seven actions for the period before Chicago. They carried out only two. The scheme to take over a rock concert at Flushing Meadows was frustrated when the concert sound engineer turned up the speakers and drowned out the disrupters after they had seized the stage. The second action consisted of attacking a Queens high school and marching around it making speeches. As two anonymous New York Weathermen admitted, "the action seemed almost too easy. . . ." [14] During the weeks before the national action, the New Yorkers also practiced self-defense tactics, "rapped with the kids" in city parks, and performed guerrilla skits. One of the more exciting actions, apparently, was spray-painting "Off the Pig," "Join the Red Army,"

[14] See anonymous, "Weatherman: The Long and Winding Road to the Underground," *Defiance, No. 2: A Radical Review*, March, 1971, p. 9.

and similar slogans on Washington Square Arch, the New York Public Library, and other public structures. Like children repudiating early toilet-training taboos, the New York Weathermen found this juvenile vandalism exhilarating.

The Days of Rage, when they finally came, proved a fiasco. For weeks Weatherman had circulated warnings that the Chicago action would be "very heavy." The Weathermen did not want a massacre, and when stories began to spread that Weathermen would bring guns to Chicago, the Weather Bureau denied it and insisted that the rumors were the doings of the police, who wanted an excuse for mayhem.

In the end only five to eight hundred young radicals turned out for the Chicago action on October 8. The New York group had expected to bring a thousand young people to Chicago and ended up with only thirty! Similar disappointing showings from other communities kept the national action contingent down to a point where some volunteers arriving in Chicago were tempted to abandon the whole demonstration.

In the end Weatherman went through with the action, though it was not able to complete its schedule of demonstrations. The action actually began a few days before October 8, when some unknown parties blew up the statue of a Chicago policeman at Haymarket Square. The statue was a memorial to the police who had been killed by a bomb thrown while they were attempting to break up an anarchist meeting in 1886, and its destruction enraged the police. On Tuesday, October 7, Weathermen and Weatherwomen began gathering at three centers in different parts of the city, wearing crash helmets, combat boots, and heavy jackets. On Wednesday evening about 250 of them assembled in Lincoln Park in one of the city's fine neighborhoods for the announced purpose of commemorating Nguyen Van Troi, a dead Vietnamese revolutionary, and Che Guevara, the Argentine-born guerrilla leader recently killed in Bolivia. At 10:50 a Weather Bureau leader announced that the demonstrators were going to march on the Drake Hotel, where Judge Hoffman was staying, and "get him." With a shout the crowd trudged out of the park and along Clark Street, watched from a short distance away by the Chicago police.

Suddenly someone threw a rock through the plate glass window of the North Federal Savings and Loan Association. At this sign the crowd started to run, breaking windows on either side of the street and smashing in the glass of parked cars. The runners soon turned east on Goethe Street, while continuing to throw bricks and rocks through the windows of banks, businesses, and a few private homes. At one point the mob came upon a parked Rolls Royce and took particular pleasure in thoroughly demolishing it.

At State and Division streets the Weathermen encountered a line of police. A few in front broke through, swinging clubs and chains, while the police fought back. The police then fired a smoke bomb, and the Weathermen broke ranks to reassemble again. Once more they ran along, smashing "pig" property. The police tried again to block them, and savage scuffles broke out. Finally the police drew guns and fired, hitting several of the demonstrators. By about 11:15 the crowd had scattered, leaving behind their wounded, great patches of broken glass, and twenty-one injured policemen. Seventy demonstrators were in the hands of the police.

The whole action lasted less than an hour. Miraculously, no one was killed on either side, and the amount of property destroyed was minimal. Yet Weathermen, surprised and elated by their audacity, considered the action a great victory.

Other radicals were not so sure. Fred Hampton of the Panthers called the Weathermen "adventuristic, opportunistic and custeristic," the latter an allusion, of course, to General Custer's suicidal last stand. Mike Klonsky of RYM II told a group that "the key [to success] was reaching out to the masses of the people, not running in the streets by ourselves." [15] The Panthers, along with the Young Lords, staged their own demonstrations in the city's black and Puerto Rican neighborhoods, and RYM II held a nonviolent rally to protest the trial of the Chicago Eight.

The Weathermen were obviously isolating themselves from the rest of the New Left. Yet they were not deterred. The next day Weatherman's Women's Militia, sixty-five strong, gathered in Grant Park under the leadership of the ferocious Bernardine Dohrn for the purpose of attacking the Chicago army induction center. The women were nervous and frightened, and Dohrn tried to bolster their courage. "A few buckshot wounds, a few pellets, mean we're doing the right thing here," she told the armed and helmeted Weatherwomen. The fear that they felt must be contrasted with

[15] Quoted in *Dock of the Bay* (San Francisco), October 21, 1969.

the fear, death, and suffering that black, brown, and yellow people experienced all over the world, she claimed.

When the women finally began to advance out of the park, they were met by a line of police. As they neared the line, Deputy Chief of Patrol James Riordan ordered them to stop. Ten or twelve women, led by Dohrn, pushed against the police line, but they were quickly subdued by mace and clubs. The remainder, at police insistence, took off their helmets and dropped their weapons. The whole incident lasted about four minutes and resulted in twelve women being arrested, five policemen being slightly injured, and Chicago Assistant Corporation Counsel Stephen Zucker being bitten in the hand!

These two fiascos almost aborted the national action. Weatherman canceled both the high school "jailbreak" scheduled for Thursday and a "Wargasm," as the rock concert was labeled, scheduled for Thursday night. Also abandoned was the plan to disrupt Judge Hoffman's courtroom.

By now Governor Richard Ogilvie of Illinois had alerted some twenty-five hundred national guardsmen, giving them orders to back up the police if necessary. Given the unimpressive results of Wednesday night's action and the failure in Grant Park, the Weathermen decided it was stupid to provoke the fire of armed troops. The "pig" was obviously capable of hitting back harder than expected. But rank-and-file Weathermen also blamed the Weather Bureau leaders for the limited results of the last two days. They had turned up late at both actions, and they had not provided the bold, aggressive examples that others needed to follow.

In truth, the results were scarcely spectacular. Yet, as they discussed the events of the first two days at Gerrett Theological Seminary in Evanston, Weathermen had a sense of accomplishment. Wednesday's demonstration had been like "unfurling a gigantic Viet Cong flag in the heart of Chicago," one Weatherman noted. One purpose of the action had been to "establish . . . [the Weathermen's] presence in the nation's mind," and this purpose had been accomplished.[16] After all, this was the first time that a revolution had been attempted in the mother country of imperialism, and there

---

[16] Quoted in Tom Thomas, "The Second Battle of Chicago," in Harold Jacobs (ed.), *Weatherman* (Berkeley: Ramparts Press, 1970), p. 212.

were few precedents for it. Even the Women's Militia demonstration, one participant said, had raised the level of struggle and had made it clear that women could fight.

During the next few days the Weathermen in Chicago mostly talked. On Friday the police raided a Weatherman meeting at the Covenant Church and arrested forty young radicals, charging them with participating in the Wednesday rampage. Some of the remaining 150 Weathermen were chagrined by the ease with which the police had taken their fellows into custody and declared they would not join the last demonstration still scheduled for Saturday.

Despite this, a final action was carried off on Saturday at Haymarket Square. Shortly after noon some 20 Weathermen moved into the square. The police also entered the square and started to beat them. The Weathermen fought back, and the whole group, including Mark Rudd, was arrested. Soon after, another 300 Weathermen arrived and marched off followed by police cars. After they had gone a few blocks, a Weather Bureau leader shouted "Break!" and the crowd started to run down Madison Street, battling the police. The scuffle lasted only fifteen minutes, and some 180 demonstrators were arrested. The rest merged with the spectators and got away.

This ended the Days of Rage. The action had been foolish and self-destructive and had succeeded only in offending almost every former SDS political ally. Yet, as Weathermen prepared to depart for home, they claimed a great victory. "In the last four days," declared a Weatherman leader on the eve of departure, "we have learned some important lessons. The most important . . . is that we can fight too. . . . We have shown the pigs that we can fight. We have shown the pigs that they have to overextend themselves on another front. . . . We are going to take the lessons we have learned here in Chicago home with us as we go back; we are going to bring the war home!" [17]

This was empty bravado. The Weatherman achievement had not been impressive, even in Weatherman's terms. No one died; no martyrs were made; the "pig" had scarcely been touched. When the box score was made up, the results were three hundred Weathermen

---

[17] *Ibid.*, p. 225.

arrested, almost all of whom were released after paying a small fine
or serving a few days in jail. A few who received six-month sentences were quickly released following appeals. Twelve leaders were
indicted on conspiracy charges, but they did not appear and became
federal fugitives. The damage to the Establishment was the sort
that could be repaired by the glaziers in a few days. The only real
casualty was Richard Elrod, a Chicago assistant corporation counsel, who smashed his head against a wall and broke his neck when
he tried to tackle a demonstrator.

As for the propaganda impact, it was slight and negative.
Weathermen had not demonstrated to the world or to the white slum
youth, who were their special concern, that radicals were really
tough fighters who deserved support. White slum kids, if they
noticed the Weatherman tactics in Chicago at all, would have considered them amateurish and stupid. Even in the days of the white
gangs, slum youths did not charge a police line, but in any case,
there were no white gangs anymore. There were white delinquents
in plenty, but they were scarcely good raw material for a revolutionary movement.

The Weathermen had completely misjudged white blue-collar
youth. A year after the Days of Rage, Mark Naison, a member of
RYM II, described how disappointing the youth work of the radical
Bronx coalition in an Irish working-class neighborhood in New York
had been. After establishing a storefront headquarters and trying
to reach out to the young in the old ERAP fashion, Naison
reported:

> We observed impatience, an inability to work without immediate
> emotional gratification, and a preoccupation with a mystique of power
> and action which could be mobilized by an advertising campaign or
> a pennant race as well as by the left. We found very little collective
> spirit. The kids related to politics as something that could give them
> a quick thrill in an emotionally barren life. Within the youth of the
> community, politics seemed to play the same role as drugs!

Naison was appalled to learn that the most politically aware people
in the neighborhood were the junkies. The Movement had to provide some alternative to drugs, but the Bronx group had not yet
succeeded in finding such an alternative. The youth culture unfortunately spoiled the young for left politics, teaching them that

pleasure *now* was the end. For this purpose heroin was clearly hard to beat, since, Naison concluded, it made "you feel a lot better than a demonstration or a good fuck." [18]

If the Days of Rage achieved anything at all, they hastened the dissolution of the New Left. As we shall see, the Movement did not die abruptly, nor did even Weatherman suddenly disappear. But the Chicago action did destroy much of the moral authority of the left and put the entire Movement on the defensive. Left journals such as the *Nation, Guardian,* and *Liberation* could not contain their anger and chagrin at the foolish behavior of the Weathermen. Liberation News Service and the radical underground press concluded that the Weathermen were insane. James Weinstein, a New Left intellectual associated with the early *New Left Review,* admitted that the Days of Rage had forced people to take sides, but both the people and the Movement had taken sides against Weatherman. Chicago, he wrote, demonstrated Weatherman "fury but little else." [19] Michael Lerner, a former Berkeley FSM leader, now a radical University of Washington professor, said of Weatherman tactics that "nothing could have served the interests of the ruling classes more." [20] Progressive Labor, predictably, was livid and denounced the Weathermen as "police-agents and hate-the-people lunatics." [21]

As for SDS, to all intents and purposes, it died at the end of the year. For a while after the June split, two organizations, both calling themselves SDS, existed. Progressive Labor, with its headquarters in Boston, held on to the old name and even began to publish a new version of *New Left Notes,* the official SDS publication. In the early fall Weatherman, which had seized SDS national offices in Chicago and the *New Left Notes* editorial offices immediately after the June split, dropped any pretense of being the old organization. Beginning in September, *New Left Notes* changed its

[18] Mark Naison, "Youth Culture in the Bronx," *Radical America,* September-October, 1970, pp. 70–74. Naison was a member of the New York regional SDS in 1969 and apparently associated with RYM II.

[19] James Weinstein, "Weatherman: A Lot of Thunder but a Short Reign," quoted in Jacobs, *op. cit.,* p. 392.

[20] Michael Lerner, "Weatherman: The Politics of Despair," quoted in *ibid.,* p. 400.

[21] Flyer of SDS National Headquarters (Boston).

name to *The Fire Next Time,* and then at the end of 1969, when Weatherman went underground, ceased to publish. As of this writing, an organization calling itself SDS still exists and still publishes *New Left Notes,* but this is Progressive Labor wearing, like a hermit crab, the empty shell of the dead Students for a Democratic Society.

CHAPTER

7

The End
1969-1972

THE END of 1969 saw the New Left in complete disarray. SDS, dressed in the street-fighting clothes of Weatherman, was now in its final phase, one that was becoming increasingly withdrawn and alienated from the remainder of the Movement.

The August split had puzzled and dismayed many SDSers. In the more isolated chapters especially, members often did not understand what the shouting was all about, and they waited indecisively for further developments. A few chapters eventually got around to joining Progressive Labor. Many disaffiliated from both PL and Weatherman. Some kept the name SDS; others adopted other initials. The RYM II people sought to reestablish a new autonomous youth organization with a white working-class strategy as its center. In November, 1969, they held a convention in Atlanta and formally denoted RYM as a new organization that would replace SDS as the focus for radical white youth. By the spring RYM was dead.

Meanwhile Weatherman was converting itself into a clandestine organization committed to bombing and guerrilla warfare. But first there was one more open convention in which Weatherman revealed its complete loss of contact with the Movement and with its own origins. The convention in Flint, Michigan, at Christmas, was called a National War Council in line with the new ideology. The four hundred or so delegates who attended spent much of their time practicing karate exercises and singing songs about trashing, bomb throwing, and killing pigs. Drunk on sex, pot, and sleeplessness, the Weathermen displayed a rhetorical tone that reached a new peak of irrational violence. Mark Rudd told the delegates that "it's a wonderful feeling to hit a pig." John Jacobs declared, "We're against everything that's 'good and decent,' in honky America. We will burn and loot and destroy." At one point the delegates, in some terrible perversion of scholastic quibbling, discussed whether it would be "correct" to kill white babies! The final touch was Bernardine Dohrn's bloodthirsty glorification of the recent Charles Manson murders in Los Angeles: "Dig it: first they killed those pigs, then they ate dinner in the same room with them, then they even shoved a fork into the victim's stomach. Wild!" [1]

The Flint War Council broke all of Weatherman's remaining ties with the Movement and normal civil life. When it was over, Weatherman, organized into "affinity groups" of a few close, trusted friends, went underground. In February the SDS Chicago office, which had been located on Madison Street since 1966, was closed, and the old SDS files were sold to the Wisconsin Historical Society for a quick $300. Soon after, Weatherman bombs began to go off around the country, set by secret revolutionary cells and affinity groups.

The most active bomb group consisted of seven or eight young men and women operating in New York City. They were a group of unusual young people. Cathlyn Wilkerson, a graduate of Swarthmore, was the daughter of a rich advertising executive and radio station owner. Kathy Boudin, a Bryn Mawr graduate, was the daughter of Louis Boudin, a prominent civil liberties lawyer. Diana Oughton, another Bryn Mawr graduate, was the child of a prosperous Illinois restaurant owner and Dartmouth graduate. Terry Robbins was a dropout from Kenyon, the elite men's college in Ohio. Ted Gold's father was a New York doctor and his mother a professor of education at Teacher's College. At least three other persons are known to have been in the house. Although we do not

[1] Quoted in Kirkpatrick Sale, *SDS* (New York: Random House, 1973), p. 628.

know who they were, those whom we can identify represented an unusual concentration of social and educational privilege.

Early in March these Weathermen moved into a handsome Federal-style town house on Eleventh Street in the best part of Greenwich Village. The $250,000 house belonged to Cathy Wilkerson's father, who was away on vacation in the Caribbean, and it must have seemed a delightful irony to be plotting the demolition of "pig Amerika" amid James Wilkerson's valuable porcelain figurines and antique furniture.

Shortly before arriving at the town house, this Weatherman cell had set off three fire bombs at the home of Judge John Murtagh, who was then presiding at the trial of a group of New York Panthers accused of plotting violence and disruption, and was accounted by the Weathermen a prime enemy of the revolution. On the morning of March 6, the group unloaded a number of heavy boxes from a white station wagon and brought them into the house. The boxes contained dynamite and blasting caps for making high explosive bombs. Later that morning, while Oughton and Robbins were preparing pipe bombs and nail-studded antipersonnel devices, an explosion rocked the building. This was followed by two more blasts, which ignited the gas connections in the basement. The whole interior of the house collapsed, and a giant cloud of black smoke rose high into the early spring air.

Three unidentified people stumbled out of the building's rear and disappeared. Boudin and Wilkerson, dusty, shaken, and cut, were helped out of the front window by passersby. Taken into the house of a neighbor, they quickly put on the clean clothes they were given and escaped, telling the housekeeper that they were going to a nearby drugstore to get some medicine. In the basement of the wrecked house, the police found the mangled bodies of Diana Oughton and Ted Gold. Terry Robbins had been literally blown to pieces, and was only later identified by his fellow Weathermen.

In the next months the Weathermen were heard from again a number of times. In June Weathermen bombed the New York City police headquarters. Later that year there was a rash of bombings in Chicago, northern California, and Long Island as part of a fall offensive by Weatherman "tribes and families." The following year Weathermen blew out part of the Capitol wall in Washington, blasted the California Department of Corrections Office in San Francisco and the New York State Department of

Corrections in Albany, and planted a bomb in the air force section of the Pentagon. One of the more flamboyant of the Weatherman escapades was the rescue of Timothy Leary from the California Men's Colony, a minimum security prison camp where the psychedelic high priest was serving a sentence for the possession of marijuana. Leary, like many indicted radicals of the early 1970s, later turned up in Algeria, where he joined Eldridge Cleaver and other Panthers, who had gathered to help plan the overthrow of American imperialism.

A particularly outrageous act of violence was the bombing in August, 1970, of the Army Mathematics Research Center at the University of Wisconsin. The purpose of the attack, apparently, was to strike a blow directly at the war machine, and in this it succeeded in a small way. But in the wrenching blast that wrecked the building, a mathematics graduate student lost his life. This was the first time that an innocent bystander had been killed in the wave of assaults, and it shocked many radicals, especially radical college faculty, as had few other incidents in the eruption of Weatherman violence.

By now most of the Weatherman leaders were under federal indictment. To Richard Nixon and Attorney General John Mitchell, the Weathermen and student radicals in general were anathema, and they believed that federal force must be used to stop them. Never very strong on civil liberties, Nixon and Mitchell began a campaign of indictments, infiltrations, and buggings that foreshadowed—and also supposedly excused—the later Watergate activities.

The White House and the Justice Department were responsible for most of these attacks, but they cannot be blamed solely for them. The public mood was angry and inflamed. By now most Americans favored doing something drastic about the violence that was erupting across the nation and the waves of disorder that had begun to roll over the nation's campuses.

One of the most disturbing events of all, from the public's point of view, took place in the spring of 1970. To many Americans, if not to liberals and radicals, the May, 1970, blowup at Kent State University in Ohio, even more than the bombings, epitomized the excesses of the student radicals. Kent State University was a large upgraded teacher's college in northeastern Ohio. It was no more implicated in capitalist misdeeds or Vietnam than five hundred other college campuses. But in the late 1960s Kent had a more aggressive and more militant SDS contingent than most, with much of the militancy supplied by the action-oriented Ohio-Michigan regional leaders, Terry Robbins, Diana Oughton, Bill Ayers, and Jim Mellen, all of whom were to become Weathermen. James Michener, in his book on Kent State, notes the frequent arrivals and departures at Kent of Ohio-Michigan SDS travelers as well as the visits of Mark Rudd and Bernardine Dohrn in the year preceding the events of May.[2]

The Kent State SDS became an active campus force following a visit by Rudd in October, 1968. Soon after he left, SDS joined with campus black militants to demand that visiting recruiters for the Oakland, California, police department be kept off campus and that the university's own guards be disarmed. Without waiting for an administration response, the protesters occupied the university placement office. Fortunately the situation eased when the black students left the building after a five-hour stay.

In April of the following year, SDS returned to the attack, this time demanding the end of ROTC and the closing of various Kent State departments and agencies that were supposedly aiding the war effort or cooperating with law enforcement agencies. ROTC by this time was becoming a major target of antiwar radicals all over the country, and the Kent State SDS was not going to be behind the rest. This time SDS got its confrontation. When campus police tried to block the radicals' attempt to break into the administration building, there was the usual scuffle. Six members of SDS were arrested, and the four who were students were suspended from school.

For the rest of the school year, SDS and the university authorities were at war. There is little point in recounting the details of this battle. There was the usual succession of building occupations, followed by police busts, followed by squabbling over disciplinary procedures, all accompanied by the angry name calling, accusations of bad faith, and all the other charges and countercharges that characterized a hundred campus upheavals of these years. In the end SDS was banned from campus, but in the meantime a portion of the student body was successfully radicalized.

[2] See also Terry Robbins, "War at Kent State," *New Left Notes,* July 23, 1969.

Despite this, Kent State remained relatively quiet during the 1969–1970 academic year. Then, on April 30, President Nixon sent American troops into Cambodia in a move that seemed to escalate still further the hideous Vietnam War. An outraged student outcry immediately went up all over the country. On dozens of campuses liberals and radicals joined to protest the President's move. On May 3 a group at Yale called for a national student strike.

At Kent the student response was especially militant. On Friday evening, May 1, street trashing, possibly initiated by several visiting Weathermen, began in town along North Water Street in the city's small honky-tonk district. The following day a mob of students, some of whom were certainly strangers to the Kent community, set the ROTC building on campus afire. When firemen tried to stop the blaze, several demonstrators attacked them with clubs. Later someone tried to burn down the university library; but the job was botched, and the fire sputtered out. The pattern on the first two days was reminiscent of Weatherman violence and nihilism, though there is no proof that the Weatherman underground was actually involved.

By this time the mayor of the city of Kent had called in the Ohio National Guard, and the guard soon restored temporary order on campus. At first the students fraternized with the guardsmen; but then resentments grew, and angry taunts and insults were soon flying back and forth between the two groups. On Sunday afternoon and evening students pelted guardsmen, who were trying to enforce a campus curfew, with bricks, rocks, bottles, and chunks of concrete. The guardsmen fired some canisters of sneezing powder and started jabbing at students with rifle butts.

By Monday guardsmen and students had become enemies, each suspecting the other of viciousness and bad intentions. This poisonous hostility permeated the air when at noon students gathered at the Victory Bell, a central campus rally area located close to the paths used by students going to and from classes. The meeting was not authorized by the university and directly violated Governor Rhodes' recent verbal order forbidding demonstrations during the emergency at Kent. Few students had heard of the order or knew that the meeting was unauthorized, though some who did chose to ignore the fact. As students collected on the commons near the bell, a campus police officer, perched on a slowly moving jeep, ordered them to disperse several times. Many students did not hear him; others shouted curses, and a few started to pelt him with stones.

At this point the guard commander, seeing that the campus police were getting no results, ordered his men to prepare "to move out and disperse" the crowd. As the guardsmen moved forward, they fired a number of tear gas canisters toward the students. Several students picked up the canisters and hurled them back at the advancing guardsmen. Soon they also began to throw rocks, pieces of wood studded with nails, and chunks of concrete, while shouting obscenities.

Then the fatal act took place. The advancing guardsmen, finding themselves in a cul-de-sac, wheeled around and began to return in the direction they had come from. As they trudged forward, they looked apprehensively at the massed students on their right flank. Suddenly, apparently without receiving orders from their officers, a group of guardsmen stopped, turned almost completely around, and started to fire at the students behind them and to their right. Fifty-five shots were fired in a ragged volley. Some guardsmen fired into the air; others directly into the students. When the fusillade stopped, four students were dead and nine lay wounded.

The massacre should never have taken place. No one at this point was endangering life or property. To have equipped the guardsmen with loaded rifles was a stupid and tragic error. In few states other than Ohio were guardsmen on riot control duty allowed to load with live ammunition. The system in Ohio reflected that conservative state's harder line toward disorder, and there is good reason to see the killings as an ugly instance of official repressiveness in America. On the other hand, it seems equally clear that a portion of the Kent State students were spoiling for a fight and wanted to precipitate something like what in fact took place. The greater wrong, obviously, lies with the guardsmen and their officers for the unnecessary use of lethal weapons, but some students and nonstudent outsiders were callously and outrageously eager for trouble and were also culpable. The fact that innocent young men and women, who did not share their cataclysmic purposes, were the ones who paid is a measure of their puerile irresponsibility.

Weatherman never acknowledged a role in Kent State, though it was quick to boast of various bombings. Of course, if Weatherman had claimed a role in the confrontation, the moral capital accruing to student protest from the Kent State events would have immediately drained away. This surely does not prove that the Weatherman underground played a role at Kent, but neither does it refute it.

At the nation's colleges the reaction to the news of Kent was thunderous. Students at some 350 schools, already furious over Cambodia, went formally on strike. At hundreds more, classes simply ceased. At still more, there were major demonstrations. Most of these were peaceful, but an unusually large number were marked by the bombing of ROTC facilities, window smashing, and building occupations.

Had SDS been intact, it might have seized leadership of the campus revolt and used the almost universal student outrage for radical purposes. But by now SDS was underground and was only interested in middle-class, college youths as potential cadres for a clandestine revolutionary movement. As it was, radicals and liberals furiously battled on many campuses for control of the demonstrations, but in the absence of a strong student radical organization, the moderates generally won out. On most campuses, in the end, the strong emotions of May resulted in conventional liberal campaigns of letter writing, doorbell ringing for dove Congressmen, and sending antiwar petitions to Congress and the President. Some campuses also adopted the Princeton plan giving students release time at the beginning of the fall semester to campaign for an antiwar Congress.

It is easy enough to dismiss these activities as ineffectual. The President did not suddenly withdraw the troops from Cambodia, nor did he end the Vietnam War. The Congress elected in November, 1970, differed little from its predecessor. As for winning over more of the general public to a dovish position on the war, the results were at best mixed. By this time the American public was very unhappy about the war. Hardly anyone believed that we should have gotten into it to begin with, and many believed that we could not win it. A sizable minority, moreover, was now certain that we ought to get out under any circumstances. Many Americans, however, resented the campus disturbances, which violated their sense of the respect due to established institutions and authorities. It was difficult for anyone who was connected with academic life in May, 1970, to view the events at Kent State as anything other than a brutal, criminally stupid overreaction by the government. Even in my own moderately conservative university, no one

I met during the agitated days before the spring semester ended
seemed to doubt that the authorities deserved total execration. Yet
the public as a whole disagreed with this view. Liberal national
organs of opinion supported the students. But lower middle-class
America most decidedly did not. In many places the students were
attacked as anarchists, nihilists, degenerates, dirty hippies, and
dangerous revolutionaries. Students demonstrating in lower Manhattan in the wake of Cambodia and Kent State were attacked
and beaten by hard-hat workers from neighboring construction
sites. In the city of Kent itself, the explosion of fury against the
students blotted out all compassion for the killed and maimed.

Here in a nutshell was the fatal flaw in student radicalism. It
had left the rest of America so far behind that it had lost all contact with the national reality. Rather than winning the public to its
vision of the good life and the just society, it had merely helped
confirm the great social heartland in its allegiance to traditional
decorum and deference and the sacred rights of property. When the
New Left began to look back to see where the rest of America was,
as it was forced to do in the first years of the new decade, it was
appalled to see what an enormous gap had opened between itself
and the great mass of the American people.

In the wake of the student spring protests and the growing
public disquiet, Nixon stepped up his campaign for law and order.
It is now possible to see this for what it was: a typical Nixon
effort to capitalize politically on public fear and anger. The President had first gained prominence during the McCarthy era, when,
as a young Congressman from California, he had helped send Alger
Hiss to prison for lying about his Communist party activities.
Nixon was not an ideologue or moralist then, nor was he in 1970.
Though he often assumed moral positions, he probably felt little
of the indignation aroused in others by student radicalism and
violence, but the President could not resist using public dismay
for political effect. During the 1970 Congressional campaign, although the President himself generally avoided the low road, Vice-
President Agnew cynically played on public fears of the breakdown
of law and order and harshly attacked the radical students and
their faculty allies as people who belonged in penitentiaries rather
than dormitories.

Simultaneously, the Justice Department, the FBI, Congress,

and local courts cracked down on radicals. Grand jury indictments of the sort issued against the Chicago Eight in 1969 and against Dr. Benjamin Spock and four Resist associates in 1968 descended on such groups as the Seattle Liberation Front and the White Panther party. The Senate internal security subcommittee subpoenaed the records of SDS, Liberation News Service, and the New Left–oriented Institute for Policy Studies presumably for the purpose of uncovering subversive activity. The FBI also placed undercover agents, and possibly *agents provocateurs*, on many campuses, and the Internal Revenue Service summoned the tax files of *Liberation*, the War Resisters' League, and the Unitarian-Universalist Association, the liberal religious body that sponsored the left-oriented Beacon Press. At about this time too, we now know, Nixon tried to establish a frightening White House–controlled domestic spying apparatus to infiltrate and disrupt radical groups. He only abandoned the plan when FBI Director J. Edgar Hoover, ironically one of the left's traditional villains, refused to go along. At Kent itself, a Portage County grand jury exonerated the National Guard, criticized the students and the university administration, and ended by indicting twenty-four students or former students and one radical faculty member.

Left observers believe that these attacks from 1970 onward seriously damaged the Movement. It is true that as 1970 gave way to 1971, student disorders decreased. The Weatherman underground gradually subsided after issuing a number of communiqués denouncing Mitchell, threatening future bombings, claiming credit for Timothy Leary's escape, and endorsing the drug culture of the young. The town house explosion apparently shook up the Weathermen very badly—a few literally, most figuratively. Bernardine Dohrn, writing to the Movement in December, 1970 from her hiding place sounded positively like a flower child. The explosion "forever destroyed our belief that armed struggle is the only real revolutionary struggle." "The hearts of the people are good," she announced, and then launched into a rhapsodic description of the new ways of life that Movement people were creating for themselves.

> They've moved to the country and found ways to bring up free wild children. People have purified themselves with organic food, fought for sexual liberation, grown long hair. People have reached out to

each other and learned that grass and organic consciousness expanding drugs are weapons of the revolution.[3]

With this letter we are almost back to Haight-Ashbury, or perhaps even the holy barbarians of the 1950s!

Obviously the strains of extended clandestine existence had begun to prove too much for many Weathermen. A number of those whose identities have never been known probably returned to the surface soon after the town house tragedy and picked up the pieces of their former lives. Almost none of those who were publicly sought for bombings, conspiracies, or skipping bail were ever caught, but even many of these, it seems, followed Dohrn's lead and softened their attitude toward violence or merely ceased to be revolutionaries.[4] Weatherman probably did not survive beyond 1972.

There was a similar subsidence in other sectors of the Movement. During the post-Cambodia summer the number of students who actually came out to work for peace candidates for the fall Congressional contests proved disappointing. By the fall the outrage and determination of the spring had largely evaporated. During the next year various campuses detonated at news of seeming escalation in Vietnam, but generally campus disruption fell on evil days. At the colleges student activism sharply declined. The few confrontations of 1971–1972 were pale events by the side of their predecessors. Increasingly confrontation came to seem pointless and rapidly dwindled away. In the fall and spring of the 1972–1973

[3] Quoted in Carl Davidson, "Whither the Weatherman," *Guardian*, December 26, 1970.

[4] One interesting example of this came to light in 1973. On May 24, 1973, the *San Francisco Chronicle* contained excerpts from a long letter written by Jane Alpert, who had earlier confessed to bombing New York City office buildings along with her lover Sam Melville. Melville was a Weatherman activist who was convicted of the bombings and sent to Attica state prison, where he died in the grim September, 1971, prison uprising. Jane Alpert jumped bail before being sentenced and went underground. She had not been heard from for three years. Her letter was addressed to her "sisters in the Weather underground," and renounced the violence of the Weathermen and the male chauvinism that prevailed in SDS, and urged her sisters in the "dying left" to devote their "immense courage and unique skills to work for women—for yourselves." See *San Francisco Chronicle*, May 24, 1973. A more complete version of Alpert's letter, in which she recounts some interesting details of life in the radical underground, can be found in *Ms.* magazine, August, 1973, pp. 52–55, 88–94.

school year, for the first time since the Berkeley Free Speech Movement in 1964, American campuses were quiet.

The fact then is clear: by 1972 student radicalism had virtually disappeared. Was this the result of repression? Obviously we must take with a grain of salt the assertion of observers who uncritically share a New Left outlook. The left in America has been particularly wont to blame failure on repression. It was one of the virtues of the activists of the early 1960s that they recognized the left's inadequacies and refused to hide behind the charge of repression to excuse past failures.

Rather than blaming repression, it would be tempting to say bluntly that the student left committed suicide. The inner imperatives of SDS that drove it further and further in a Leninist, and then beyond to an "infantile leftist," direction and that made it forget its need to keep in touch with the hopes and needs of some constituency outside itself was obviously a fundamental cause of its collapse. If SDS leaders had worried more about expanding SDS's support among students and the discontented, and less about refuting and defeating Progressive Labor, winning the useless approval of the Black Panthers, or impressing white street kids, it might have survived and flourished. One can easily imagine an SDS, strong and respected on every American college campus, and an MDS, strong and respected in the liberal professions and among the technocrats of industry, pushing America by slow stages ever further left. The new-working-class departure of 1967–1968, it seems to me, was that most-sought-after left hope—a "correct strategy." It was not abandoned because it was proved false by events. Almost nothing happened in the world outside SDS itself between the first announcement of the strategy and its total abandonment. The war in Vietnam went on, it is true, but that had been a feature of American life for at least five years. And the antiwar movement was achieving results. Each month during 1969–1970 the polls showed ever larger numbers of Americans growing uneasy over the continuing entanglement in Southeast Asia. No doubt there was good reason to be impatient with the continuing slaughter, but SDS turned the natural impatience of the young into a mandate for destroying the student left.

Nor does a growing repression explain the shift to fanaticism and ideological intransigence. The charges of repression have been exaggerated. The Watergate events have confirmed the Nixon administration's persistent contempt for the First Amendment and for the normal rules of political fair play, but even Haldeman, Ehrlichman, Mitchell, and Dean could not create the atmosphere that existed during the days when Joe McCarthy terrorized the intellectual community, Congress, the army, and the President of the United States. At no time, I feel, was the government's assault on the New Left by itself serious enough to cripple the Movement. The trials of Spock, the Panthers, the Chicago Eight, the Berrigans, the Gainesville Eight—although time-consuming, expensive, and distracting—resulted in few convictions and almost no jailings. In almost every instance juries or appeals judges rejected the government's case. Compared to the reactions of other democratic governments faced with similar angry and disruptive dissidents, not to speak of Third World countries or the Soviet bloc, the Nixon administration's crackdown was ultimately ineffective. Any radical movement that was driven to desperation by this moderate and feckless pressure was feeble and unstable indeed.

The same instability and factiousness that destroyed SDS also prostrated other parts of the Movement. In 1970 the Socialist Scholars Conference, a major intellectual forum of the New Left, held its last meeting and disbanded, a victim of ideological and tactical disagreements that could no longer be contained. Left intellectuals, of course, continued to ply their trade. In early 1970 James Weinstein, a historian who had edited the seminal *Studies on the Left* in its early years, founded *Socialist Revolution* in the Bay Area to help keep the pursuit of Marxist theory alive. Weinstein and his associates could not supply the intellectual glue to hold the Movement together, however, though they made a valiant effort.

In early 1971 the Panthers split, when Huey Newton and David Hilliard, leaders of the Panther organization in the United States, expelled Eldridge Cleaver and the "international section" from the organization for attacking the national leadership and for supporting the Weathermen. From exile in Algeria, Cleaver, through his wife, Kathleen, promptly denounced Newton and Hilliard as "right opportunists" more interested in pragmatic alliances with the white working class than with world revolution. Mrs. Cleaver, herself not under indictment in the United States, promised to return to America to organize a new Panther group dedicated to armed sabotage and a military underground. Soon after this the Panthers ceased to be politically important.

The antiwar movement too began to be hampered by serious internal divisions. In the fall of 1969 antiwar demonstrations in Washington and San Francisco brought out almost a million marchers under the leadership of the Vietnam Moratorium Committee (VMC), a left–liberal group organized by former Kennedy–McCarthy student leaders. Cosponsor of the fall demonstrations was the New Mobe, a group to the left of the VMC, headed by Professor Douglas Dowd of Cornell and Arthur Waskow of the Institute for Policy Studies, as well as the old Mobe leaders Dave Dellinger and Rennie Davis.

In April, 1970, the VMC disbanded, claiming that the antiwar movement had lost most of its support as more and more liberals and radicals turned to ecology problems. This left the New Mobe as the chief antiwar organization, but it was soon challenged by a Trotskyite group from the Socialist Workers' party. The Trotskyites disapproved of the New Mobe's New Left type of confrontation tactics and opposed mass civil disobedience demonstrations.

In May, 1970, the Trotskyites joined the Mobe for a march on Washington that fizzled badly. Held in tight check by the Trotskyite marshals, the demonstration was so decorous that it received scarcely any attention, and the demonstrators themselves felt let down. Soon after, the New Left people, organized as the National Coalition Against War, Racism, and Repression, split with the Trotskyites. The Trotskyites along with their youth affiliate, the Young Socialist Alliance, now organized their own National Peace Action group. This organization not only opposed the radical pacifist civil disobedience approach, it also opposed the Mobe idea that the antiwar effort could be used to advance other radical causes.

For the remainder of the year the National Coalition and the Trotskyites argued about how best to attack the continued American involvement in Vietnam. Other antiwar groups, largely students, meanwhile proposed to dramatize the peace drive by sending a delegation, representing various shades of antiwar sentiment, to Vietnam to negotiate a "peace treaty" with the North Vietnamese and the National Liberation Front. This scheme was actually adopted by the National Student Association, now partially radicalized by Nixon's Cambodia invasion. The proposal was also adopted at the National Coalition meeting in Milwaukee, along with a resolution calling for a nonviolent civil disobedience demonstration in Washington on May 1.

In December the Trotskyites met to consider their antiwar position and decided to hold another peace march in Washington on April 24, one week before the National Coalition. The purpose of this, National Coalition sympathizers insisted, was less to help stop the war than to undermine the New Left group's efforts.

Early in 1971 the National Student Association delegation departed for Hanoi, Saigon, and Paris and returned with a People's Peace Treaty "negotiated" primarily with the Vietnamese peace delegation in Paris. This "treaty" was endorsed by a national conference at Ann Arbor and by various groups at some two hundred American colleges. The conference also endorsed the May demonstration.

For the next few weeks various groups squabbled about the spring demonstration. The National Coalition finally decided to ask peace advocates to come to Washington on April 24 and remain through the first days of May. The week of April 26–30 would be reserved as a People's Lobby, during which the peace people would solicit signatures from government workers for the People's Peace Treaty. On May 1 would come the march, and on May 3 a group called the May Day Tribe would initiate a civil disobedience action with the idea that "if the government won't stop the war, we will stop the government." [5]

The Trotskyites, hoping to head off the National Coalition, spread rumors that the May demonstrations had been canceled. Then on April 24, at its own march, the Trotskyite paper, the *Militant,* accused the National Coalition and the May Day Tribe of planning to incite to riot.

The ten days of antiwar activities that began in late April were mismanaged. The march on April 24 was dispirited and seemingly pointless. The meeting with the Senate Foreign Relations Committee was a fiasco. Several of the delegates spoke pointedly about the war and demanded some sort of Congressional action to end the fighting, but other delegates wandered off into all sorts of ir-

[5] See Michael Lerner, "May Day: Anatomy of a Movement," *Ramparts,* July, 1971, p. 41.

relevant corners. One told the senators that the antiwar people
encamped at "Algonquin Peace City" at West Potomac Park had
had various "bad trips" with LSD and had not yet learned to
treat each other as true brothers and sisters. A gay liberation dele-
gate denounced the cult of machismo that he claimed was an important aspect of the war. A woman's liberationist recounted how
gentle, humane, and beautiful the Vietnamese people were. The
senators, many of whom were anti-Vietnam doves, were distracted
and antagonized by these counter culture statements and never
seriously discussed the peace issue. The whole thing seemed to
demonstrate how far removed from practical political sense the
antiwar movement had become.

During the days of the People's Lobby, antiwar workers distributed leaflets among Washington government offices. Some of the
civil disobedience people blocked the entrances to buildings, and
many were arrested. On May 1 there was an antiwar rock concert
at West Potomac Park with seventy thousand people in attendance.
Many of these seemed far out even to Movement people. Soon
after the concert the police closed Algonquin Peace City, claiming
that the residents had violated the rules that the authorities had
laid down when they had agreed to set the park aside as an en-
campment. Many of the campers tried to find shelter at local colleges, but most were turned away.

The next few days were very confused. On May 3 the major
civil disobedience portion of the spring demonstration was initiated.
The plan was to sit down on the bridges crossing the Potomac from
Virginia to block all morning commuter traffic coming into the
District of Columbia. The police, alerted to the demonstrators'
intentions, were ready for them and succeeded, often by using unnecessary force, in rounding them up. The arrested people were
shipped off to local jails, and when these proved too small, the
spillover was sent to JFK stadium, where the authorities had established a detention camp. All told some thirteen thousand people
were arrested. Among those jailed were Rennie Davis and John
Froines, two of the Chicago Eight defendants.

Though the New Left peace people took some comfort from
the May demonstration in Washington and from a somewhat
smaller one in San Francisco, they now acknowledged that the
antiwar movement was badly split. There was the division between

the New Left and the Marxists, most notably the Trotskyites, but there was also the independent and feckless effort of the crazies. The same sort of internal divisions that had destroyed SDS were now shaking apart the antiwar movement.

But besides this growing fragmentation, there was the undeniable fact that the war was winding down. Nixon's Vietnamization policy was indeed bringing the boys back, and as the American presence in Vietnam declined, draft calls began to fall. The draft, or the threat of it, had served to fuel much campus discontent and antiwar activity. Some of its effect had been dissipated when the government replaced the student deferment policy with a lottery for selecting draftees, which eliminated much of the ethnic and class bias of early draft rules. Combined with sharply reduced inductions after 1969, the change now did much to defuse the draft as a source of antiwar and radical activity among the young.

Yet the war dragged on. In Paris American negotiators and representatives of North Vietnam and the National Liberation Front argued interminably over the details of a settlement. The United States wanted some face-saving device for getting out. The Vietnamese wanted some scheme that would guarantee an eventual takeover of South Vietnam. The protracted discussions, the periodic American bombings of North Vietnam, and the blockade of Haiphong Harbor to prod the Communists into making concessions, incited radical rage against the policies of the Nixon administration.

At this point Nixon struck a great blow at the surviving New Left by achieving a spectacular détente with Communist China. All through the 1960s the New Left had idolized one or more of the "socialist" countries. As Todd Gitlin explained, "for generations the American Left has externalized good: we needed to tie our fates to someone, somewhere in the world who was seizing the chances for a humane society." [6]

One of the favorite repositories for such externalized good, Gitlin noted, was Castro's Cuba. North Vietnam, understandably, soon became another. Weatherman singled out North Korea, Communist Albania, and indeed almost all of the Third World, as the

[6] Todd Gitlin, "Cuba and the American Movement," *Liberation*, November, 1968.

specially favored among the world's nations. Through the 1960s scores of New Leftists went on pilgrimages and peace missions to North Vietnam and Cuba in defiance of State Department prohibitions.

But above all Mao's China, America's most implacable enemy, a country that seemed to be particularly proof against the disease that hardened revolutions into bureaucratic rigidity, was the New Left's hero country. When a member of the research staff working for the writer James Michener on his study of the Kent State uprising asked a campus leftist what country commanded the greatest respect of radical students, the answer, emphatically, was "Red China."

In April, 1971, the Peking government startled the world by inviting an American Ping-Pong team to tour China, accompanied by American reporters. Soon after, Henry Kissinger, the President's chief foreign policy adviser, came to Peking for secret talks that led to an invitation for President Nixon to visit China early in 1972. In late February Nixon and his entourage arrived in Peking and held long discussions with Mao and Premier Chou En-lai. In wonder and disbelief the whole world watched the pictures transmitted by communications satellite of Mao, Chou, and Richard Nixon toasting one another and world peace amid the imperial glories of Peking. Soon after, the United States acquiesced in the admission of Red China to the United Nations, a move it had opposed remorselessly for twenty years.

Most citizens in the Western countries cheered the unexpected shift in American policy, but the surviving American left was appalled at the turn of events. David Kolodny, an editor of *Ramparts*, noted how his heart sank as he observed the televised state banquet and heard the insincere, banal phrases mouthed by both the American and the Chinese leaders. It had brought "the Chinese revolution down to earth" for all radicals—Maoists and others alike. The radicals' China was "an illusion," after all, he wrote, "and we allowed that illusion to define for us a model of true revolution barely realizing how deeply we internalized that definition or how much it dominated and distorted all our perceptions of revolutionary tactics." China now had much to answer for, not only for the détente with Nixon, but also for recently supporting the military dictatorship of Pakistan over the oppressed people of Bangladesh in step with the United States. In a word, China, the hope of all oppressed peoples, had sold out world revolution.[7]

Yet, as Kolodny himself noted at one point, not all American radicals condemned China. The group around the *Guardian* chose to regard the détente as a Chinese victory over American imperialism. Other radicals tried to excuse China's new policy as necessary for survival, much as Old Leftists had apologized for the Soviet Union's devious foreign policy shifts in the 1930s. Kolodny, for one, could relish the irony of the New Left's being forced to eat its own sanctimonious words condemning Old Left hypocrisy, but other radicals remained stunned and chagrined.

It is impossible to measure the precise impact of the Chinese-American détente on the American left, but it certainly damaged radical morale. If China could now be added to the Soviet Union as just another opportunistic power seeking its own national goals without regard for the cause of humanity, what reason was there to believe that a disinterested revolution would ever succeed? The burden of proof that a truly liberated society was possible was now on the left. To some thoughtful leftists China's defection was a challenge to consider the differences between the revolutionary potentials of advanced and of underdeveloped, Third World societies. In the months to follow, Movement intellectuals would speculate that only where, as in the West, the basic problems of material need had been solved, could the revolution be kept from turning sour. But to others, the Chinese "sellout" marked the final collapse of the utopian dream.

Still another blow to the surviving left was the economic recession of 1969–1972. During the 1960s conservatives and radicals alike made jokes about how the campus revolution was being financed by daddy's checks. It would be unfair, I suppose, to play too much on this, but it is true that an easy job market, especially for college graduates, and even more, the easy disdain for worldly success that postwar prosperity allowed young people to feel, were important elements in student radicalism. If nothing else, prosperity permitted young radicals, especially the young radicals at elite colleges, to feel that in the end a last-minute change of plans was always possible. Steven Kelman quotes one rich member of SDS

---

[7] See David Kolodny, "Et tu China," *Ramparts,* May, 1972.

during the Harvard University blowup in 1969: "Look, as long as you don't have anything permanent on your record you can change your mind later in life about being a radical." [8]

The bad times, particularly for professionals, that came after Nixon took office ended this comfortable situation for many students. As the economy slipped, jobs, especially in teaching, science, and engineering, became scarcer. Now the campus recruiters did not look so bad. There were fewer of them, and those who came no longer seemed like murderers. As for daddy's checks, they did not come so readily either; and when they did they were accompanied by admonitions and conditions. Nor were there as many part-time jobs to provide ready cash for travel, pot, and records. On many campuses students returned rather abruptly to their books and began to worry about grades and credentials. Hair began to be worn shorter, or at least neater, to accommodate the corporation recruiters' preferences.

None of this is intended to be cynical or sarcastic. To say that a large group of left activist students were subsidized directly from home or indirectly by the burgeoning American economy is to say no more than what many student radicals admitted. Obviously, to every deeply committed revolutionary who despised the consumer society and was willing to live in revolutionary poverty, the Movement attracted two or three who gave up little or nothing except for the limited time that they flirted with confrontation and revolution. When the cheering stopped and the money dwindled, these young men and women simply came to terms with their society.

The final gasp of the New Left was George McGovern's 1972 presidential campaign. McGovern was not the ideal presidential candidate from the left's viewpoint. A man in the tradition of Bryan and the Populists, he favored wealth redistribution, a more equitable welfare system, an improved physical environment, and a quick end to the Vietnam War. But he was not a socialist, nor was he sufficiently outspoken in his attack on the war machine or America's expansionist policies around the world to suit most of the left.

[8] Steven Kelman, *Push Comes to Shove: The Escalation of Student Protest* (Boston: Houghton Mifflin, 1970), p. 148.

Some radicals worked hard to get McGovern nominated, using very effectively the newly liberalized nominating machinery that the Democrats had set up in Chicago in 1968. On the whole, however, it was the left–liberals of the sort who had worked for Eugene McCarthy or Robert Kennedy in 1968 who put together the McGovern-nominating drive that triumphed in Miami. Meanwhile, in the fall of 1971, a group of election-oriented peace radicals established the People's party in Dallas and nominated Dr. Benjamin Spock for President with a black radical, Julius Hobson, as his running mate. Though a few leftists worked for the Spock ticket, it was completely upstaged by the McGovern campaign.

Radical ambivalence about McGovern was more than ideological. There was also the recurring question of how a coalition with liberals would affect the left. Early in the nominating campaign, Staughton Lynd expressed with feeling the left's perennial fear of co-option:

> It is indeed maddening after flights from Southern sheriffs, after prison terms, after losing jobs, rejecting parentally-sponsored careers, making lonely decision after lonely decision in the hope of doing honorable work and serving the general good, after watching innumerable new beginnings collapse, after picking up pieces to try once again, after learning that politics means brickbats from within and from without the movement and becoming hardened to this and still going on; it is maddening after whatever version of this each one of us has experienced to watch some Democratic Party Johnny-come-lately rhetorically espouse the positions we labored to establish and garner the fruits of all our seeding.[9]

Other Movement people must have felt the same chagrin, but many asked their fellow radicals to act dispassionately and pragmatically. The chief danger to the left, wrote David Kolodny, in April, 1972, was not co-option; it was despair. Radicals had become "disillusioned not only with the system but with [themselves]." The Movement was fragmented and disorganized and must rebuild itself. Ultimately this meant that it must encourage loyalty to radical organizations, rather than to the Democrats, but the Democrats could be used for this purpose. The left should support the Democrats now, though in a limited way, extracting con-

[9] Staughton Lynd, "Organizing the New Politics: A Proposal," *Ramparts*, December, 1971, p. 15.

cessions for their help. Meanwhile the young McGovern supporters were a pool from which an independent radical party could draw its future strength.[10]

As the campaign itself got under way, *Ramparts* warned radicals not to reject McGovern. Although he was not a radical, he had promised to end the Vietnam War, and that was important. Besides, in some ways, he was a creation of the New Left and deserved the left's support.

There is a puzzle in this last view of McGovern as an avatar of the New Left. How could a movement so fragmented and enfeebled by 1972 be credited with imposing a presidential candidate on a major national party? The answer seems to lie in an important side effect of the decade-long New Left thrust. McGovern, of course, was not a radical. No real radical could possibly have won the Democratic nomination, even under the most liberal party rules, but to the extent that he reflected some of the late 1960s radical sensibility, his success at Miami was made possible by the pervasive effects on articulate professional people of a decade of New Left advocacy, agitation, and advertisement. Although the New Left failed to establish a strong and stable organizational base of its own, it succeeded in popularizing its critique of American society, and this critique seeped down and powerfully influenced the attitudes of many liberals. It was not the self-announced New Left, then, that won the nomination for McGovern; it was the much larger group of left-liberals, who had earlier fought for McCarthy and Robert Kennedy, that seized the party machinery and rolled on to success at Miami.

Nevertheless, during the weeks after the Miami convention, many radicals worked for McGovern. Even Progressive Labor, in its new ill-fitting SDS guise, gave grudging support to the Democratic presidential candidate, in part because PL, too, hoped to draw on the McGovern supporters as future SDS recruits. Yet, unlike many other Movement people, Progressive Labor preferred to have McGovern lose. His defeat would drive many young McGovern campaigners into the arms of SDS, one SDS member from Houston noted.

Radicals who could not bring themselves to work for McGov-

[10] David Kolodny, "The New Left in Trouble," *Ramparts*, April, 1972, p. 10.

ern, nevertheless, voted for the Democratic candidate, though without enthusiasm. As one Berkeley radical declared:

> Obviously because I'm a sensible human being, I'm going to the polls and vote for him. But I'm very critical. In the short run he would be better for my life as a radical and for the Vietnamese people . . . but in the long run, the liberal co-option of the Left is just another way to perpetuate capitalism.[11]

If history were kind to historians, the overwhelming defeat of McGovern would put a neat period to the story of the New Left. But of course it is not. McGovern's defeat was the end for some on the left. Soon after Nixon's second inauguration, Rennie Davis, a founder of SDS, flew off to India and returned a devoted disciple of a fifteen-year-old guru Maharaj-Ji. Abbie Hoffman, after lashing out at former Movement colleagues for trying to grab some of his money, dropped out of politics. In August, 1973, Hoffman was arrested for supposedly selling three pounds of cocaine to three New York policemen. Other New Left leaders quietly slipped out of sight.[12] The underground press, which had flourished mightily in the 1960s, declined in the Nixon years and was barely alive outside of a few large cities by 1973. In 1972 a subdued and sober Huey Newton told an audience of black businessmen in Los Angeles that the Panthers were no longer interested in destroying the system, but hoped to make it "more relevant and kind."[13]

The final word, perhaps, was actually a picture—a cartoon— in the *New Yorker* soon after McGovern's defeat. It shows two young people, a man and a woman, strolling along a city street.

[11] Nancy Strohl as reported by Larry D. Hatfield, "New Left for McG in Varying Degree," *San Francisco Chronicle,* November 5, 1972.

[12] As this book goes to press the newspapers report some final loose ends of the New Left. These include: (1) the capture by the FBI of Howie Machtinger, one of the twelve indicted Weathermen; (2) the trial of Karleton Lewis Armstrong for setting the University of Wisconsin Army Mathematics Research Center blast; (3) the bombing of International Telephone and Telegraph offices in New York City, by a group claiming descent from the Weathermen, ostensibly for I.T.T.'s supposed part in the coup that overthrew Chile's leftist president Salvador Allende; and, finally (4) the dropping of the Weatherman indictment by the government following a court order demanding that the prosecution disclose whether it had used bugging, burglary, *agents provocateurs,* and other dubious means to secure evidence against the radicals.

[13] *Guardian,* July 19, 1972. In 1973 another Panther, Bobby Seale, ran for Mayor of Oakland and conducted a "responsible" and conventional campaign.

The woman has a bulky Afro haircut and is wearing a long dress; the man has long hair and a handlebar moustache and is wearing a shoulder-strap bag and an Indian headband. Behind them is a square, middle-aged man in a business suit and tie, carrying a briefcase. With a look of manic glee in his eyes, the conservative gentleman shouts at the counter culture couple, "The fun's over, kids!"

But not quite. For a while veterans of the Movement such as Staughton Lynd tried to reconstruct an organized radical movement around the economic slippage under Nixon and the growing inequalities of wealth in American society. In late 1971 a group of "old" New Left leaders—men and women who had dropped out of SDS before the Weatherman denouement—organized the New American Movement. This organization was to be something like SDS before the split. It would emphasize the fight against Nixon's economic policies and American imperialism, and would agitate for the people's control of the economy, as well as for day care centers and improved federal industrial health and safety standards. Unlike the old SDS, however, the organization would reject anarchism and accept the need for strong, stable leadership. It would also avoid overemphasizing Third World problems and romantic short-range views of social processes. In a word, it would be free of the callowness and foolish romanticism of the original student left.

As of this writing, little has been heard from this organization. Apparently it still exists, but it has not become a significant rallying point for the Movement.

In some ways the most durable part of the Movement is the cultural dissent that so many political radicals belittled. Though even hair and dress styles have felt the effects of the recent rightward turning, American men remain committed to longer hair and more facial hair than before, and young women persist in the revolt against skirts and girdles that began in the 1960s. Although no one apparently has made a recent survey of American drinking habits by age groups, I suspect that among those who came to adulthood in the past decade, hard liquor consumption is down, displaced for good, as a turn-on agent, by marijuana.

More interesting than these superficial signs of continuing cultural dissent is the commune movement. As politics turned sour, substantial numbers of radicals dropped out of the larger society and went off to live in communes with a few, or a few dozen, like-minded young people. Cooperative communities, of course, have had a long history in the United States, the country preeminently of democratic expression and even more, perhaps, of possible wilderness isolation. Events of the 1960s revived American communitarianism. In the fall of 1967 hundreds of hippies and drug-culture people fled the streets and crash pads of Haight-Ashbury when hard drugs, gangsterism, and narcotics agents turned the scene bad. Many of them went to Morningstar Ranch, a thirty-acre tract in the Sonoma County hills north of San Francisco, which was placed at their disposal by Lou Gottlieb, a former folk singer and member of the *Limelighters* now turned counter culture philanthropist. Other counter culture people, some seceders from Gottleib's ranch, went to northern New Mexico, near Taos, and established new small-scale communities based on shared property, shared work, and direct democracy. Still other cultural dissenters set up communal living groups in the cheap-rent areas of large cities.

For many political radicals, cooperative living arrangements were initially appealing because they reduced living costs. For the cultural dropouts, on the other hand, the communitarian idea was freighted with ideological or quasi-religious significance. In the commune they could fulfill themselves as human beings; they would be free to experiment with new personal relationships and to find the true meaning of life while insulated from the pressures and the hang-ups of the larger society outside.

The bright hope was seldom realized. Few of the communes became economically self-supporting. Almost none of the rural ones, whether located in the arid Southwest or in the green valleys and hills of New England, were able to provide for their own needs in food and raw materials, and members frequently either had to take outside jobs or had to apply for food stamps to live. In almost all communes sex and experimental family relationships became divisive problems, as members discovered that group marriage or polygamy was not much better than the nuclear family or monogamy as a way of governing the relationships between men and women. Private property also caused problems. Commune members with cars or stereo sets, despite the theory of sharing, often came to resent the way other commune members used or misused their possessions. There were also constant difficulties over who should cook, clean up, take care of the children, and do the other routine jobs that had to be done.

Under the circumstances, it is not surprising that the turnover in communes and commune personnel was enormous. Few communitarian efforts lasted more than a year or two. Those that did seldom had their original members for very long. Yet new people kept moving into existing communes, if only for short stays, and many counter culture people, after leaving one commune quickly moved on to a second, a third, and a fourth. Communes that disbanded were soon replaced by others. Despite the turnover, by one estimate there were about three thousand communes in existence by early 1971.

The communes organized around radical politics or by political radicals in the late 1960s or early 1970s were probably no more immune to these disorders than those established by cultural dissenters. Yet as radical mass politics receded, more and more radicals joined cooperative communities in hope that communes might become the nuclei of a new radical thrust. Among the more ambitious of these radical communitarian efforts was the Seattle Liberation Front, one of the New Left organizations indicted by the Attorney General for conspiring to commit riot during Nixon's first term. Organized into some twenty collectives in 1970, Seattle Liberation Front members continued radical activities in the surrounding community while simultaneously experimenting with cooperative, democratic living. The second half of this program, the front's rationale went, would aid the first. As a spokesman for the Seattle radicals declared:

> Precisely because our task is not only to destroy capitalism, but also to radically remake ourselves, the present historical period calls for organization built around collectives. . . . It is only in collectives that we can develop ourselves as creative political organizers without the stifling atmosphere that the large mass-meeting based organizations like SDS made current.[14]

I doubt that the Seattle group survives as a political organization or, for that matter, that it survives at all. In any case it is clear that radical collectives were generally way stations in radical depoliticalization. The journey out of politics was gradual. First

[14] Quoted in Ron E. Roberts, *The New Communes* (Englewood Cliffs, N.J.: Prentice-Hall, 1971), p. 85.

came collectives as a base for conventional radical political activity. Then came collectives as laboratories where radicals could learn about how people interacted so that the lessons might be used for the revolution. Then, finally, came the commune purely for self-discovery. In the end, it seems, many radicals totally surrendered to the dropout, subjective ethic that they had professed to despise.

Whether the Movement is still alive and in what way it still lives is not as important as the fact that it once flourished. It flourished for some twelve years, from about 1960 to, say, 1972. For the first three or four of those years, it was almost totally a student movement, indistinguishable in its philosophy from many liberal groups at the left end of the Democratic party. How it did differ from existing liberal organizations was in its fervor, its relative freedom from obsessive concern with communism, and its commitment, in imitation of the student civil rights movement, to work with people in their local communities.

Beginning in 1967 the New Left began to widen out and also to intensify. By this time SDS had become the major carrier organization for the New Left, and by this time, too, SDS intellectuals had developed a theory, implicit from the outset, of the role of students and young intellectuals as agents of fundamental change. The new-working-class idea represented a shift left to neo-Marxism and became a rationale for encouraging, intensifying, and enlisting the unrest of students on many college campuses. At the same time the New Left caught on among adults, especially those in the arts, the media, and the universities. These people strongly influenced American intellectual life and did much to change the perceptions of thousands of literate Americans. This effect, perhaps, was the most important achievement of the student left, for soon after, SDS itself, acting not in response to important changes in the objective political climate, but out of the immediate political imperatives within the Movement, took a turning that made it lose touch with America. The Weatherman–Progressive Labor split destroyed SDS and badly damaged the morale of the whole New Left.

Yet the New Left carried on for the next three or four years, primarily as an antiwar movement. Soon many of the divisive pressures that had wrenched SDS apart also attacked the antiwar movement. More important, Richard Nixon wound the war down and eventually, after achieving a long overdue détente with Mao's China, removed all American troops from Vietnam. The war's end, combined with a serious recession that affected college graduates particularly, turned students and young professionals away from dissent and social advocacy to cultivating their own gardens. This was the end. As one New Left leader told Nicholas von Hoffman of the *Washington Post* in 1973, "The revolution is over, baby!".

What was accomplished in these twelve or thirteen momentous years? What hath the New Left wrought?

I think it forced the United States out of Vietnam. It is true that American military defeat at the hands of the Viet Cong and the North Vietnamese was an indispensable element in this result. The tenacity of the National Liberation Front wore out the patience of the American public, which was not prepared to sacrifice as much for as long as the Vietnam conflict required for victory. Equally important, however, was the growing feeling, dramatically underscored by the left, that the war was morally bankrupt. Though many conservative Americans were offended by the tactics of the peace demonstrators, they found it difficult to ignore much of what the radicals were saying about the beastliness and injustice of the conflict. The antiwar left often antagonized conventional Americans, but it also succeeded in pricking their consciences. By 1969 or 1970 it had become virtually impossible for reasonable men and women to deny that the war was an immoral, senseless fiasco.

Did the New Left achieve anything of comparable significance in the country's domestic life? This is a harder question to answer. On the one hand, in the wake of McGovern's overwhelming defeat and Nixon's dismantling of Great Society social programs, it is difficult to detect any permanent political results from more than a decade of radical agitation. Even in Berkeley, the most radicalized community in the country, a coalition of radicals running for city office was defeated in 1973 by a group of moderates.[15] In other communities there has apparently been a decided shift to the right. Clearly the radical sensibility that informed some of the Great Society programs under Johnson has receded almost everywhere. There are few politicians today who would bother or dare to raise the old banners of "Fight poverty," "End discrimination,"

[15] This election, in April, 1973, actually resulted in one, but only one, of four radicals getting enough votes to be elected to the Berkeley City Council.

"community control," or "black power." Even women's liberation, a late flowering of the Movement, seems to be in trouble. The Women's Rights Amendment to the Constitution, after breezing through twenty or more state legislatures, is, at latest report, encountering strong opposition in many remaining states.

This is the visible surface, however—only what is easiest to see at the moment. Is there something beneath it? Probably there is. Todd Gitlin, writing in the summer of 1972, declared:

> The Movement is everywhere; it exists perhaps as a disembodied Idea, a historical ghost come too early or too late. . . . If the Movement exists it exists despite itself, because so many people need to believe in it—a curious and fragile existence indeed.[16]

Many former New Left leaders are biding their time, waiting for a more auspicious moment, when the thousands who were radicalized by the Movement are once more ready for action, or when another cohort of young men and women finds life in affluent America unworthy of respect. These former leaders are asking themselves where they went wrong and trying to develop theories of change for "post-scarcity" societies that will not fall again into the trap of dogmatic Marxism. They talk, these days, a great deal about young workers who are discontent with the boredom and the lifelessness of the assembly line, and they profess to see a radical potential in the restlessness of these workers. More realistically, they hope that another international involvement comparable to Vietnam, a depression that penetrates below the top layers of the labor market, an uncontrolled inflation, or a strong new wave of racial rage—that any of these things, none of them beyond the realm of possibility in current American society, will restore left morale and reactivate the quiescent pool of discontent.

Meanwhile the most visible residues of the radical 1960s are the life-styles and the cultural values of many adults who reached maturity after 1960. It is ironic that what has survived from the latest "Red decade" is the emotional, nonrational part that New Left intellectuals considered the most suspect and the least reliable. But perhaps that is the way of revolutions: they are, to quote John Adams on the American Revolution, primarily events in the mind and hearts of the people.

[16] Todd Gitlin, "Toward a New New Left," *Partisan Review,* Summer, 1972, p. 458.

Index

Glossary of Abbreviations

ADA	Americans for Democratic Action
ASUC	Associated Students of the University of California
CIA	Central Intelligence Agency
CNVR	Committee for Non-Violent Revolution
COFO	Council of Federated Organizations
CORE	Congress of Racial Equality
ERAP	Economic Research and Action Project
FSM	Free Speech Movement
HUAC	House Un-American Activities Committee
IDA	Institute for Defense Analysis
JOIN	Jobs and Income Now
LID	League for Industrial Democracy
MDS	Movement for a Democratic Society
MFDP	Mississippi Freedom Democratic Party
Mobe	National Mobilization Committee to End the War in Vietnam
NAACP	National Association for the Advancement of Colored People
NOW	National Organization of Women
NSA	National Student Association
NUC	New University Conference
REP	Radical Education Project
RYM	"Revolutionary Youth Movement"
SANE	Committee for a Sane Nuclear Policy
SAS	Student Afro-American Society
SDA	Students for Democratic America
SDS	Students for a Democratic Society
SLAP	Student Labor Action Project
SLID	Student League for Industrial Democracy
SNCC	Student Nonviolent Coordinating Committee
SPU	Student Peace Union
VMC	Vietnam Moratorium Committee
WSA	Worker Student Alliance
YPSL	Young People's Socialist League